A Squaddy's Tale

A Squaddy's Tale

Memories of the Forgotten War
On The Hook and Hill 355
Korea 1951-1952

JOHN HATCHARD

The cover picture shows Hill 355, also known as Little Gibraltar and was taken in 2002. There is little difference from how it looked in the spring and summer of 1952. Hill 355 is now firmly within the DMZ and inaccessible for veterans visiting South Korea.

To order additional copies of this book, contact:
Xlibris Corporation
0800-891-366
www.xlibris.co.nz
Orders@Xlibris.co.nz
700173

CONTENTS

DEDICATION

To my mother Anne
who gave me back the letters I had written from Korea
a few months before she passed on.

To Brian Langdown
who gave me his friendship from the first day of our enlistment.

For Alec Ahern,
whose death soon after arrival in Korea caused me the most sorrow.

For everyone who helped me, knowingly or unknowingly,
with the writing of these my memories of the time I spent in Korea.

ORIGINS

In December 1999, while living up in the Darling Ranges of Western Australia, I found myself with a lot of time on my hands. The previous ten years had been taken up with lecturing and administrative work at the Oceanic Institute of Classical Homoeopathy in Perth. This involved re-editing the curriculum for the four years course and much of the lecture material ready for an application for accreditation with the State government. This was granted for a period of five years, the first such course in Australia to achieved this.

Along the way, I developed a deep interest in the history and philosophy of Homoeopathy and thoroughly revised the lecture material to be given in the first semester of the academic year. As the resident expert on the subject, it was my task to present these lectures which I did between 1993 and 1999. Then, while applying for reaccreditation, some faceless bureaucrat decided that I was not qualified to teach at the Institute. I did not possess the correct piece of paper although my three years training and fourteen years teaching in high schools had been recognised by the State education department. I spat the dummy and retired!

Needing something equally constructive to fill my time, I discovered where the letters I had written home while on the way to Korea and while there between 1951 and 1952 had been hidden. My mother had kept every one and gave them back to me a few weeks before she passed away. Reading them again, I realised that perhaps there was material in them worth extracting and offering for publication. They became the starting point for my story.

On the voyage to Korea, I wrote home every day so the description of the voyage is quite detailed. However, once in Korea and living like the proverbial "mole in a hole", my letter writing became very spasmodic. After all, it was a tough, all consuming business adapting to the radically different way of life I was now leading. I knew little of the world and its ways, was very naïve about all sorts of things and so many new situations and events had now to be dealt with. At times it required all my physical and mental energy to cope. Inevitably, the gaps in my letter writing have caused some difficulties when I came to set down these memories. I had no real understanding of so many things witnessed and experienced, things I would otherwise have recorded in greater detail had there been the mental and emotional energy to spare, not merely noted.

If this story had been written within ten years of my returning home, gaps in the narrative would have been quite glaring. Sixty years later, computers and the internet have become available. I gained a moderate degree of computer literacy and was able to research certain events that had occurred, look at maps not available to me while there and seek explanations on the internet for questions that arose in my mind both at the time and since.

My account will thus be of more interest than if it had been written fifty years ago. However, this is still a collaborative work. The naïve nineteen years old national serviceman who wrote the original letters is still present in the telling. The eighty year old he has become has brought experience, judgment, curiosity and certain skills to help him round the story out with perspectives and perceptions that he could not possibly have possessed or articulated at the time.

PROLOGUE

My school days came to a sudden end just before my eighteenth birthday. Somewhat unwisely, I did not sit the final examinations that might have taken me on to university and an altogether quite different life. An adolescent affair of the heart had totally wrecked my capacity for study.

In an attempt to help me through the resulting depression, it was arranged for me to go to a youth farming camp in South Wales west of Carmarthen. This was my first solo trip away from home and the experience proved to be exactly what the doctor had ordered as antidote to my heartache and loss of focus on reality. The meaningful and practical activity suited me well and sparked an abiding love for South Wales, indeed of all Wales.

However, during that time away, things were happening on the other side of the world. After years of mutual provocation, the communist North Korea invaded westernised South Korea. Political leaders around the world felt threatened and made undertakings that would be kept by other people. The news was announced that Britain would make a contribution to the United Nations forces gathering to combat North Korean aggression and that national servicemen would be included in it.

The time was fast approaching for me to be called up for national service and I felt a distinct sense of foreboding, a premonition perhaps, that I might be among them and I said as much in a postcard to my parents. Returning home from the farming camp, a jobbing builder doing some work on my parent's house offered me work. Inevitably my call-up papers arrived. I was to join the army whether I wanted to or not.

On December 7th 1950, I was at the appointed place at the appointed time to start my army life. The next few months were full of the tedious stupidity of army training, where opinions and freethinking had to be suppressed since uniformity and blind obedience were clearly preferred. I made a few friends and particularly enjoyed the friendship of Brian

Langdown who lived a mere five miles away from me in Bournemouth. Somehow we endured and survived the square bashing and physical training regime imposed upon us, learned how to handle rifles, lob grenades and how to fight hand to hand. My size eleven and a half feet caused me grief on more than one occasion, but generally coped well enough on field training exercises one period of which enabled me to renew my love of the Welsh countryside that had begun on that farming camp.

Just before Christmas, we learned that our detachment was destined to go as reinforcements for the Gloucestershire Regiment fighting in Korea. Early in the New Year we were relieved to learn that this had been put back for a few months so that we could have more training.

Finally we were posted to 1 Battalion, the Welch Regiment in Colchester. Brian and I parted company for a month, he to become a company clerk, and me for training as a signaller. As things turned out, this was to be to my great good fortune. I became proficient in laying and maintaining field telephone lines, operating field telephone exchanges and the standard wireless sets in use within infantry companies. I was also taught how to use the larger '61' set a skill that was to be greatly to my advantage.

For some reason the army seemed to think I had potential because twice I was approached about making a career in it but a greater involvement in the army wasn't what I wanted. However, whatever my wishes, the army was still deciding my immediate future and my premonition held true when we learned that the Welch Regiment would relieve the restructured Gloucestershire Regiment in Korea and join 29 Brigade of the Commonwealth Division under United Nations command.

It was fortunate that we would be in Korea during the relatively quiet middle phase between September 1951 and October 1952. But first there were various painful jabs against typhus and cholera to be endured. On 29th October 1951 we were trucked to Cardiff, put on a train to Liverpool where, along with 2,000 other men, we boarded the MV *Georgic*.

I

From Call-up to Embarkation

7th December 1950-29th October 1951

Call-up and basic training

Late in October my call-up papers arrived. Among them was a rail travel warrant and instructions to present myself on Salisbury Station by 14:00 hours on December 7th 1950 at the latest. My parents took me to Poole Station and saw me off on my second solo trip away from home in six months. I was just a few days short of eighteen years and four months old.

There were several other chaps hanging around at Salisbury Station; some had been on the same train. A sergeant came along, stood there for a moment looking us over, ordered us to line up and marched us out of the station. We climbed aboard a truck and were taken to Bulford Camp out on the Salisbury Plain. That first afternoon, after being taken to a barrack room and told to choose our bed, we were again lined up and marched off to the stores. There we were issued with army clothing including underwear and blankets. Other items of uniform kit such as ammunition boots, beret, belt, gaiters, back pack and pouches were piled on top as we passed along the counter together with all the items required to keep it all sparkling clean. Boot polish and Brasso were familiar but blanco definitely was not. Returning heavily laden to the barrack room, we were shown how to make up our beds and then lay out other items of kit at the foot of it ready for inspection. We went for a meal then returned to make up our beds, stow away our few personal possessions and take stock of our new situation.

The bed to the left of mine was taken by a chap named Brian Langdown. His home in Bournemouth was only five miles away from mine in Poole. Although we were as different to look at as chalk and cheese, we were to become great friends. Shorter than me, he had a very good tan and a shock of wiry black hair that he parted in the middle. Had he worn glasses and a moustache he might have looked a little like a young Groucho Marx. On the other hand, I was six feet tall and as fair as he was dark. Moreover, I would never get a suntan as deep as his even if I sunbathed carefully for a million years.

Brian and myself at Buckingham Tofts PTA

What qualities drew us together would remain a mystery. Perhaps it was because our birthdays were only five days apart, Brian being the older or because we were the only two with grammar school educations. Whatever the reason, we were to remain close friends for the next two years.

The first morning in barracks we were rudely awakened by the Reveille bugle and then the sergeant burst in bellowing, "Wakey, Wakey, rise and shine". After washing, shaving and having breakfast, we were then introduced to something that was to remain a major component of our immediate future—"barrack room bullshit". There was a regulation way to make up our beds, a regulation way to fold blankets and sheets and a regulation way to lay out our new kit for inspection. There were required standards for sweeping and dry scrubbing the barrack room floor, for polishing brass buttons and buckles, for blancoing belts and gaiters, for ironing uniforms and for giving the toe caps of our heavy ammunition boots a shine like that on patent leather.

The other caper that took up a lot of time at Bulford was 'square bashing', being drilled to respond in unison with the appropriate movements to certain shouted commands. All these were designed to control and neatly move a body of men from one place to another without them appearing to be a 'shambollick mob,' as our drill sergeant was inclined to call us during those first few days. The term 'square bashing' was an appropriate description of the very emphatic noise our ammunition boots made on the parade ground tarmac. For the first two days we must have looked like some weird and ungainly corps-de-ballet as we tried to obey those commands as quickly and accurately as possible.

Those two weeks of basic training struck me as very strange. From the beginning, I found it difficult to take this entire military thing seriously, something which I never really overcame even in Korea. The two weeks we spent at Bulford passed in the usual capers designed to instill the disciplined behaviour required by the military establishment of new recruits and were clearly designed to make us give up certain aspects of our individuality, presumably for some greater purpose.

Nevertheless, by the end of those two weeks, we knew how to fall in, right dress, stand at ease, stand to attention, right turn, by the right quick march, slow march, right wheel, left wheel, about turn, mark time, halt, stand at ease again and finally, with a sigh of relief, stand easy and dismiss. We learned that there was a regulation way to place our thumbs over our clenched fists and swing our arms high as we marched. When commanded to about turn our leg movements were equally clearly choreographed, to borrow a term from the ballet, of which we quite definitely were not members.

Gradually we got our collective act together sufficiently to relieve the Sergeant from the danger of losing his voice. In the beginning he had hysterically insulted us for being a 'total shower' or a 'bunch of spineless old women' and frequently threatening to take us to the stores to draw a handbag and a broom handle to stick down our backs so that we would stand up straight. All this activity was designed to render us as uniform in our attitudes and behaviour on the parade ground as we tried to look in our khaki uniforms. I felt sure that if there had been any process whereby we could be transformed into robots, the army would have used it. The more like automatons we became in our responses to commands the better.

A premonition is fulfilled

On the 22nd December 1950 at the end of those two weeks basic training, military disciplines were considered sufficiently embedded in our consciousness and we were sent to Plumer Barracks at Crownhill in Plymouth for the second stage of our induction to army life—'continuation training'.

The next morning, formed up on the parade square, the Commanding Officer came out to welcome us. Having given us the usual patter about routines of life in these barracks, he then informed us in a very matter of fact way that we had been "earmarked to go as reinforcements to the Gloucestershire Regiment presently with the Commonwealth Division in Korea". I was probably the least stunned of anyone there by this news.

The Christmas holidays were practically upon us and there was some leave coming. I volunteered to stay in barracks for Christmas Day and Boxing Day to do guard duties and in exchange was given two extra days leave. One of the first things I did on arriving home on 27th December was to give my parents the news about having been 'earmarked' for service in Korea. However, since no date had been given as to when this would happen, we were all left a little up in the air.

In the New Year and back at barracks, sessions of square bashing continued during the day and barrack room bullshit in the evenings. Our training, now even more ruggedly physical, included introduction to basic weapons drill with the Mark 4 Lee Enfield rifle. This was the first time I had ever held anything capable of killing someone from a distance. We were instructed how to use it in hand-to-hand combat and when making bayonet charges. Firing live ammunition would come later we were told. Obstacle course runs, another feature of our weeks at Plumer Barracks, caused me real pain. I already disliked this sort of physical exercise but now I came to hate it with a passion.

Some days later, when formed up for muster parade, the CO again came out to see us. This time it was to say that he had made representations on our behalf to the appropriate authorities at the War Office in London stating that it was his opinion we would need much more training before we could be considered of any use in an active war zone. He then told us that his representations had been accepted and we were not to be sent to Korea in the very near future. There was not one of us who was not extremely relieved to hear this.

This proved to be a really lucky break for us because four months later between 22nd and 25th April 1951, 1 Battalion the Gloucestershire Regiment was wiped out as a fighting unit during a massive Chinese Spring offensive. Roughly forty-four men out of over seven hundred and fifty got away to safety. There was no doubting that we had good reason to bless the CO at Plumer Barracks for interceding on our behalf and delaying our departure to join that unfortunate regiment.

Of running and rifle barrels

Early in February 1951 we were posted for further training to Whittington Barracks. This lay on the road between Lichfield and Tamworth, northeast of Birmingham. It was not a pleasant posting. In winter this part of the Midlands was bleak, grey, cold and wet.

Every Saturday morning everyone in the barracks had to take part in a five mile cross country run. Apart from my intense dislike of such activities, I had a good reason to hate these particular runs. Everyone else had been issued with plimsolls for physical training, 'daps' as we called them. The stores had none to fit my size eleven 'plates of meat' so I had to run those five miles in my heavy ammunition boots. The course was usually set around the edges of several soggy ploughed fields. In consequence, each of my boots picked up another pound or two of tenacious mud on the way and every step involved extra effort to pull them free from the soil. Lagging progressively further and further behind the rest of the garrison, I was invariably the last very exhausted person to enter the PT hall having left behind me a trail of muddy droppings across the parade square. As I staggered through the doorway some sadistic PT instructor would give me a resounding slap on the back with the comment, "Congratulations. You have the honour to be the last man in the barracks to finish." He could say what he liked. I was past caring now the ordeal was over.

Another vivid memory of those days at Whittington Barracks was the surprise when my name appeared on Part 1 Orders to attend Company Orders the next morning. At the time, I hadn't the slightest idea what I had done to be put on a 'fizzer' as it was known. It was also a great nuisance because it meant that I would have to stay behind while everyone else left for a few days leave. One of the company clerks eventually put me wise to what it was about. From the beginning the story went as follows.

One morning some weeks before, we had gone on a trench digging exercise. In groups of three, the sergeant had assigned us places to dig our trench. Much to our bewilderment we were required to dig through what looked like overgrown tarmac. When we took a good look around and saw the rusting remains of metal poles and chain link fencing we realised we were on the surface of a long disused tennis court. The small combat shovels we had been issued with to dig these trenches were making absolutely no impression on this ancient tar. Then I had a brainwave. I fixed my pig sticker bayonet to my rifle and began to prise up some of the tarmac so that we could get started. It worked and we were soon well away with our digging.

Back in the barrack room after dinner that evening, we all sat around polishing brass buttons, badges, belt buckles, boots and cleaning our rifles. The pull-through cord used for cleaning the rifle bore had a thin, three inch weight at one end and a loop at the other end through which a small piece of felt could be slipped. Removing the rifle bolt, I lowered the weight into the breech and waited for it to emerge at the muzzle end. It didn't. I pulled it out, held the rifle up to a light, and squinted down the bore. The shape of the hole at the muzzle end was not round as it should have been but the shape of a rugby ball. Puzzled, I took it over to the Corporal and showed him.

He squinted down the barrel, examined the muzzle end, then exclaimed, "Christ! You've bent the bloody barrel. How the hell did you do that?" I told him about the trench-digging problem we had encountered and he laughed. Then became quiet and said, "Oh, bugger. You know we're out on the rifle range tomorrow, don't you? If you try to fire a round through that, it will blow up in your face. You'll have to change it at the armourers before we go to the range in the morning."

I felt some apprehension about what problems this might incur until I remembered that there was a fault with the bolt action on my rifle. It was not secure. A small piece had broken off the swivelling head of the bolt so that every time I pulled it back the whole thing would jump out at me. That was sufficient reason to exchange my rifle which I did the following morning. At the armourer's, I demonstrated the faulty bolt action and there was no hesitation about exchanging that rifle for a different one. That day on the firing range everything was fine and I scored well enough to be recorded as a 'marksman'. We were also introduced to the Stengun with which I did equally well.

A few weeks later, the day before we were due for that week's leave, my name appeared on Part 1 Orders. I was required to present myself before the CO next morning. As related earlier, at first I hadn't the least idea what I had done to deserve this. I made no connection between being on a 'fizzer' and that trench-digging incident with the rifle. When I asked one of the office clerks what the reason was he hinted that I was to face a charge of—"causing wilful damage to army property, to wit, one rifle."

I still wouldn't have had a clue what he was talking about but for that one word—'rifle'. Then it all clicked into place. When I had exchanged the old rifle with the faulty bolt action and drawn a new one I had been required to sign against the relevant serial numbers. The armourers had, in due course, checked the faulty rifle, found the barrel to be bent, checked their records, found my name and notified the authorities.

Next morning, in freshly pressed uniform and with came face to face with the Company Sergeant Major. He ordered me to "Shun" then

"Stan' at ayse" in a tone of voice that seemed to pick me up by the scruff of the neck and drop me again. He then growled in my ear, "You are on a charge, you 'orrible little man, for wilfully damaging army property, to wit, one rifle whose barrel got itself bent while in your possession." Being six feet tall the thought passed through my mind to retort, "Less of the 'little', Sarge." but this was not a good time to get frivolous or smart, certainly while he was so close and so intent on his duties.

Evidently, this session of Company Orders was being held solely for my benefit so, as far as he was concerned, I was just a bloody nuisance. Eventually the door to the CO's office opened and the clerk nodded to the CSM. The time had come. Ordered to remove my hat and belt, the CSM, standing close behind me, suddenly barked right into my ear: "Shun. Quimarch. Leff, rye, leff, rye, leff, rye. Alt. Leff-tun. One pace forrard. Rye-tun. Stannat ayse. Name." "22440769, Private Milnthorpe J, SIR!" I shouted out staring fixedly at the wall behind the CO.

The charge was read out and the CO, in a very grave and cultivated voice, said, "This is a very serious offence you know. Willful damage to army property just will not be countenanced. What have you got to say?"

I told him exactly what had happened, how we had been dumped out on the old tennis court on a trench digging exercise with no tools that would make any impression on that ancient tarmac. The only way to get started was to use our bayonets to lever some up. I had no idea a rifle barrel could be so easily bent. Next day, since we had to go to the range for target practice and the bolt action was faulty, I had changed the rifle for that reason.

He thought for a moment then turned to another officer sitting next to him. I could swear that a smile crossed his face.

"That was a most ingenious use for a bayonet," I heard him say. "I don't see that the damage was wilfully caused after all, do you? The man was just using his initiative."

The other officer nodded agreement so the CO turned to me and asked: "Are you willing to have the cost of the repairs deducted from your pay?"

"Yes, sir," I quickly replied.

"All right then—case dismissed," he told me.

The CSM bundled me out of that room as quickly as he had bundled me in and dismissed me. At the company office, I obtained a travel warrant and went off on leave wondering if such a thing had ever happened to any other soldier anywhere. I felt sure the officers who had been in that room would dine out on my story for quite a while. I could just see them turning to a neighbour at table and say in their plummy voices:

"Did I ever tell you about the squaddy who bent his rifle barrel by putting his bayonet on the end in order to dig a trench in the middle of a tennis court? Ha, ha."

As far as I could tell, no money was deducted from my pay for repairs to "One rifle, damaged, barrel bent at muzzle." Eventually I was to learn that rifle barrels were not made of hard steel which could shatter under certain circumstances. They were made of ductile steel that would wear out first.

Wild, wet and windy Wales

If the experience with that rifle had been a comedy of errors, there was another quite different experience coming that was to leave an equally lasting impression. Early in March we went on a two-week field training exercise to a Practical Training Area (PTA) in the Trawsfynydd area south of Snowdonia in Wales. We slept in leaky-roofed Nissen huts out on a very bleak area of moorland and spent most days engaged in field craft exercises and shooting practice. We learned the approved method for advancing in line, or in file and for crawling from cover to cover on our bellies in a lizard-like manner using knees and elbows, our hands holding our weapons out in front of us. We charged imaginary enemy positions, took up defensive positions and learned the correct way to lob a hand grenade.

My most vivid memory came from one particular exercise in which, dressed in Full Field Order (FFO) of packs, pouches, rifles, bayonets and water bottles, we were dropped off in groups of three along the Ffestiniog to Dolgellau road with orders to make our way westward across country to the coast road near Harlech. When we reached it later in the afternoon, we were to wait there for the lorry back to camp.

The country was very rugged. First of all, we had to find our way up out of the valley through dense pine-covered slopes. We did this by finding a stream that had cut a path through the tangle of branches and following it upwards. Then we met and had to climb steep rocky outcrops several metres high. Beyond lay a broad area of marshes which could only be crossed dry-footed by leaping from tussock to tussock. Finally, we had to haul our weary bodies up narrow, rock-strewn paths through a pass in the mountain range and down the other side to the Harlech road.

It was one of the most enjoyable days out that I spent anywhere during that first year of my national service. This was the kind of physical activity that I really enjoyed. There was also the sense of freedom at being left to use our initiative to find our own way, plus the wild beauty of the Welsh countryside. It was soul refreshing and an experience that was to remain memorable for many reasons in later years. It also intensified my affection for the Welsh countryside that had begun the previous summer in Pembrokeshire.

Off to be a signaller

Following a few days leave at Easter we joined the 1st Battalion the Welch Regiment at Sobraon Barracks in Colchester. It was at this point that Brian and I went separate ways for a month, he for training as a company clerk while I went on a signaller's course in Dovercourt near Harwich. On that course, the instructors taught us how to use field telephone exchanges and to lay field telephone lines and repair them when they were broken. We learned how

Welch Regiment badge

to operate the standard '31' and '62' wireless sets then in general use and the phonetic alphabet used when communicating with them. '31' sets were used within a company for communication between company HQ, platoons and sections, especially when out on patrol. '62' sets were for inter-company communication within a battalion. They were bigger and more complex to set up and use. The '62' sets could also be tuned to work with tank commanders when necessary.

A field training exercise completed our training. Kitted out with all the signals equipment we had been learning about, we marched the fifteen or so miles round to The Naze just north of Walton on Naze. Here, split up into sections, we were put through our paces laying telephone lines between exchanges and repairing them whenever instructors took it into their heads to cut them. We set up wireless communications between the various sections and practiced the correct wireless procedures. All this continued until well after it became dark so we spent that night sleeping rough.

It would have been fun but for one small issue that arose during the night. To prevent anyone from catching pneumonia while sleeping in the open, we were told to pair up, put one large poncho-cum-groundsheet on the ground to lie on and another one over us. The Welshman I paired up with turned out to be a very horny individual and not very particular where he turned for relief. He took some persuading that I was not available.

At the end of the course there was a passing out parade during which there was one curious little moment. The CO had arrived to inspect us all. When he reached me he asked if I had ever thought of becoming a regular soldier or applying for a short-term commission. When I replied that I had not, he replied, "That is a pity. We need people with your excellent sense of humour." This took me aback a little. What did he mean? What did he know about my sense of humour? Why was that particularly important for becoming an officer? If he had referred to 'intelligence' it might have made some sense but he only left me feeling rather bemused. This was the only time we had spoken to each other; what little I had said was hardly conversational or significant. If he knew anything about me and my alleged 'sense of humour' it must have come from the course instructors, probably Cpl Ron Church with whom I got on well.

Count-down to embarkation

The commanding officer of the Welch Regiment had meanwhile received orders regarding a move to Korea. The battalion was to relieve the reconstructed Gloucestershire Regiment. When the news filtered down to our level, I finally knew that my premonition a year ago on that farming holiday in Pembrokeshire was solid. The battalion would sail in the autumn. What I found even more interesting was this Welsh connection. When the news about the outbreak of hostilities in Korea was announced, I had been in Wales and now my premonition was coming true through being in a Welsh regiment and not the Glosters as first thought. Brian's only comment when he heard the news was " . . . to think that we are going to war with a bunch of pit ponies and cave men."—a somewhat bitter observation that revealed how apprehensive he was about the prospect.

The battalion would sail on September 9th but we were not destined to travel with it. Late in August we were transferred to the Dering Lines, the regimental depot in Brecon, South Wales. We spent a month there being jabbed, kitted out and otherwise processed for what lay ahead. I collected an infestation of 'crabs' from somewhere which entailed a visit to the Medical Officer, having parts of me shaved that had never been shaved before and then suffering the ignominy of having gentian violet painted over the area. Was this some twentieth century equivalent of the 'woad' that ancient Brits covered themselves with to frighten their enemies? Perhaps that was the idea, to frighten the crabs away, but as latrine 'graffitologists' knew, "It's no good standing on the seat. The crabs in here can jump six feet."

One morning, an Education Corps sergeant gave us a geography lesson. A map of the world hung on the wall and he began by asking, "Since you lot are all going to Korea, who knows where Korea is?" I stuck my hand up. It was the only one and I felt very exposed among all the other chaps. We had all been told we were being posted there months ago. Was I really the only one who had taken the trouble to find out where the blasted place was?

Inevitably there were mutters of "Big 'ead'", "Oh yeah, trust 'im to know" and other comments but no animosity in them. "OK where is it?" the Sergeant asked me. "Between China and Japan," I said. "Quite right," he replied tapping a point high up on the right of the map. He made some smart comment about 'grammar school education' which brought a laugh and embarrassed me a little but I had destroyed any illusion he might have had that we were all a bunch of ignoramuses on whom he could demonstrate his superior knowledge unquestioned. He would now be more careful.

After telling us about the route we would take to reach Korea and something about the ports of call where we might get shore leave he dismissed us. The upshot was that, in addition to my current nickname of 'Lofty' I now found myself being called either "Prof." or "Teach".

Toward the end of the month we received a few days embarkation leave. I had told my parents about the possibility of my being sent to Korea as soon as I had known myself and they had time to come to terms with the idea to some extent. We were able to enjoy these last days together before departure. Brian did not tell his mother where he was being sent until he was on embarkation leave and this caused her real distress since the news from Korea had recently been quite grim.

While at home I asked my father if he would let me have a few driving lessons; a possible situation could arise in Korea where I had to get the hell out from wherever I might be. If a vehicle was available, knowing how to drive it would be invaluable. He saw the sense in this and organised three lessons for me with a driving instructor he knew. I took to driving like a duck to water.

Back in Brecon one evening, we decided it might be a good idea to have crew cuts and proceeded to chop one another's hair off in the barrack room. The sergeant was none too pleased when he found out saying it was a very unhygienic thing to have done. However, since it was a fait accompli he let it go. Several visits were made to the Medical Room to receive typhus and cholera jabs which remained quite painful for a day or so.

Army life somehow seemed to insulate us from general public events because on 27th October 1950 a general election was held in the UK. I had been blissfully unaware of any campaigning going on. Clement Attlee's Labour government, which had agreed to send national service men to Korea, was shown the door and Winston Churchill became Prime Minister again. Obliged to support the USA in return for their ongoing support for the country after the war and for NATO, it appeared that Attlee's government had paid a huge economic price for taking part in the Korean conflict which had shattered his plans for Britain's post war economic recovery. This probably caused the discontent that helped Churchill's return to power.

On 29th October 1951 we were taken by truck into Cardiff and put on a train for Liverpool docks where we boarded the *MV Georgic*. According to notices around the ship it belonged to the White Star Line and when the cruising season was over served as a troopship. There were over 2,000 men on board including the 5th Royal Inniskilling Dragoon Guards, a tank regiment going to relieve the 8th King's Royal Irish Hussars, and drafts going to the King's Own Scottish Borderers, the Argyle and Sutherland Highlanders, the Royal Norfolk Regiment and the Welch Regiment.

So, by the end of October 1951, we were on the high seas bound oftentimes with a depressing relentlessness for foreign parts and war. The Welch Regiment, comprising around five hundred and thirty men and officers (and one white goat), had sailed from Southampton almost three weeks before on *HMT Empire Fowey*. They must have been nearing Korea as we were about to depart to join them.

2

THE MERSEY TO ADEN

29th October-10th November 1951

We are sailing . . .

Departure was delayed by dense fog that lay across the Mersey River. It didn't want to lift so the moorings were finally loosened and the *Georgic* moved away from the quayside out into the river. All we could see was a low lying grey murkiness with the birds at the top of the Liver Building just visible above it. Not quite sure how we felt about our situation and tired of the grey gloom, we went below to our small four berth cabin on D2 deck. Apart from Brian, the others in the cabin were Alec Fulcher from Shaftesbury and Bill somebody from somewhere. Strangely, I never did find out who he was or anything about him. He was that kind of person. The accommodation was cramped but we were clearly not to suffer much discomfort in the next month. The bunks were wide and the mattresses thick and very luxurious.

MV *Georgic*

Here and there, notices indicated that in the summer season she ran the Liverpool-New York route. Now she had been requisitioned to make this run to the Far East. It was evident that the *Georgic* was going to be a rather superior kind of troopship.

It was now 21:30 and nearing the end of our first day at sea. The general opinion was that we were already well down the Irish Sea and probably now heading for the Bay of Biscay, notorious for its rough weather and waters. We had only left Brecon that morning and it seemed quite incredible that we might already be one third of the way to Gibraltar.

Next morning, Reveille 'blew' at 06:15 over the public address (PA) system. After ablutions we paraded in the mess hall to be allocated jobs. The catering system on this ex-liner was table service and Brian and I were assigned to be waiters. We were a little apprehensive about what this would involve because, although the sea was relatively calm at the moment, the swell still caused the ship to roll. Carrying a loaded tray might not always be easy and I wondered what this job would be like in really dirty weather and rough seas.

Each day we served two sessions of three meals—breakfast, lunch and dinner so that all the men on board could be catered for. Each session lasted about an hour and a half. So far, the food seemed excellent and quite posh affairs even if they did take an age to serve up. Nothing as ordinary as sliced bread on this ship; we had rolls. Neither were we to put up with margarine; only butter was good enough it seemed and there was all the jam and marmalade one could desire to go with them.

After breakfast the tables had to be scrubbed and the floors swabbed down but after lunch and dinner we were only required to sweep the floors. It was hot, stuffy work and usually one hell of a rush to get everything done but certainly better than doing nothing at all.

Rumours went around that we would pass Gibraltar in two days' time but would not stop there. Port Said was the first scheduled stop but current tensions and the state of emergency in the Suez Canal Zone would probably prevent us having time ashore.

That evening the ship's cinema showed *"The Lavender Hill Mob"*, but there was only limited seating. We would have to wait for another showing for our crowd to see it. Prices in the canteen were astonishing. A measure of whisky cost as much as a beer back home, beer cost almost nothing, cigarettes were a quarter the price but for some reason chocolate and sweets cost much the same, which didn't make sense.

On Wednesday we found ourselves afloat on a vast blue-grey ocean, no land in sight anywhere. Off duty, we would stand by the rail and stare across it wondering if our vision could ever stretch far enough to see what lay on the other side. Something that endlessly fascinated me was the way the colour of the sea changed with the weather conditions and the colour of the sky overhead. This morning it was dirty gunmetal grey under an overcast sky but later, when the clouds cleared and the sun came out, it became a profound ultramarine blue. Also fascinating was the sight of the bow slicing through each gentle swell. The parting of the water to either side as the propellers thrust the ship ahead was a hypnotic sight that I could watch for hours.

The journey was becoming exciting. Though many chaps had lost their meals over the side, no qualms of seasickness had affected me yet. In that sense, it was good to have work to do, something to have to attend to, since the alternatives were to prowl around the deck or lie on your bunk to read or sleep. Korea seemed impossibly far away, a fantasy more than an ever-encroaching reality that would eventually have to be dealt with. Yet, with every second, every minute, every hour and day that passed we were relentlessly pounding our way out of fantasy-land toward that reality. In this regard there would be no respite, day or night.

The *Empress of Australia* passed us earlier, homeward bound from the Suez Canal zone and there was some excitement around 16:30 when land, probably the northwest coast of Spain, was sighted on the port side. As night fell we could see lights away on the horizon that indicated we were still near land.

When the sun rose on Thursday, we were forging ahead down the coast of Portugal. There was time to stare at it for a while before starting work. By 10:30, when breakfast duties were over, the ship's inspection was announced. This took place at the same time every day while at sea and lasted about twenty minutes. Section officers checked the men's accommodation areas while the captain inspected the main public areas. In the meantime, we had to stay on deck out of the way.

Around 11:00 an announcement came over the public address system, informing us that we were passing the mouth of the River Tagus and the entrance to Lisbon harbour. We hung over the rail to stare across to where a very blue sea was washing up on golden beaches beneath towering, exotically coloured and stratified cliffs. These were topped by cool pine forests decorated here and there with small villages of brilliant red roofed, white walled houses basking in the sunshine. We were tempted to dive off and swim ashore to explore this paradise.

Two dolphins followed the ship for a while this afternoon, leaping from the water and slipping back in with consummate ease and grace. We passed Cape Vincent at around 15:30 and it would be dark before we reached Gibraltar.

There was an hour of music over the PA system before the evening meal, a blend of easy listening swing classics and more serious classics that was very soothing. A short news bulletin followed with some encouraging items about the war in Korea but not much detail. Perhaps the war might be over before we got there. We might then end up as a garrison force in Japan. Who could say?

That evening after dinner we had our chance to see *"The Lavender Hill Mob"* starring Alec Guinness. Although I had seen it before it was still great fun and worth a second viewing. Besides, we were grateful for the chance to indulge in a little escapism for a while.

In the Mediterranean

Early on Friday, 2nd November, a somnambulist among us reckoned he had seen lights away on the port side in the early hours that might have been from Gibraltar but now we were out of sight of land. The

Mediterranean was as calm as a mill pond when we went on deck—very, very blue and very tempting.

Later in the day a barren looking coastline appeared off the starboard bow, probably Algeria and the notorious Barbary Coast. The weather was as in the best of summers at home and evoked memories of days of sea, sun and sand on the beach at Sandbanks or Studland Bay. Korea, and indeed the rest of the world, would have seemed quite remote were it not for the periodic news bulletins which reconnected us to the troubles mankind was creating for itself everywhere.

CO's Orders announced that we could adopt 'shirt-sleeve order'. We no longer had to wear ties or battledress jackets and could literally roll our sleeves up. This was very kind of him considering that the temperatures now exceeded anything we could ever have at home and we were almost dying from the heat. Typically, his order came thirty minutes after we had been instructed by our officer to remain in full battledress, including ties and despite the heat. Someone with influence must have taken pity on us and dropped a discrete word in the CO's ear.

We began to get instructions about how to behave when we reached the Suez Canal zone. There would be no shore leave and no trading with the native trading boats, or "bum boats" in military speak. Photography was also forbidden which begged the question, what might we possibly see from the deck of a ship passing through the Suez Canal that might possibly be of a militarily sensitive nature. And for whom? Us or the Egyptians? Did the authorities suspect that there might be secret agents of some kind among us?

Our officers were causing us some amusement with their nutty orders. We were expected to report for routine military training between our work periods in the mess hall. Now these were proving fairly arduous and time-consuming and the poor ventilation was making the mess hall a very hot, stuffy and enervating place in which to work. Usually we ended up too tired to sleep properly. The point was that we would only have half an hour in the morning and three and a half in the afternoon available for this training requirement and we were hoping that some person with influence would see to it that we were excused this additional military-type training.

That evening, leaning on the rail and looking out to sea, Brian and I pondered the fact that when we were working, when we stopped working, when we were able to relax a little and even when we were asleep we never stopped travelling. The ship's progress suddenly became disturbingly remorseless. We were in the grip of very powerful and incomprehensible forces and quite helpless in the face of them.

It then occurred to me that this was equally true of our situation on this planet anyway as it journeyed around the sun and as our Solar System moved around the centre of the galaxy. Powerful forces were constantly at work. The forces directing this ship and the purpose of this voyage were hardly more powerful and incomprehensible than these cosmic processes yet, in some way and for all immediate purposes, it seemed that the ship had usurped the place of all these events as if it were another celestial body that was equally beyond our control. Like our planet spinning in space, this ship was a small world of its own afloat on the ocean. The throbbing of the engines never ceased no matter where we were or what we were doing. It was particularly noticeable in our cabin where, like the maternal heartbeat for the unborn child, it might sooth us to sleep. If it were to stop in the night would we wake up and wonder what had happened?

It was our fifth day at sea. When we went up on deck the Algerian coast was still close on the starboard side. Clouds obscured the sun for much of the day and later the wind picked up and raised a heavier swell that made the ship roll more noticeably—really quite a pleasant sensation.

Two incidents spoiled the day. Someone had lent me a Leslie Charteris 'Saint' novel to read and I was well and truly into it by the time I went on lunch duty in the mess hall. Returning to my cabin, it was not where I had left it. Someone had been in and taken it which was very irritating.

The second incident happened while on dinner duty that evening. I slipped while taking a tray of dirty crockery back to the galley. The customary cheer echoed the resounding crash as the plates hit the deck and some of them smashed. One of the galley staff came out with a bucket to help collect the larger pieces. The rest would have to wait until the time came to sweep the floor. However, I had also managed to twist my right ankle.

There was a heated discussion in the mess hall this evening. Passions were stirred up when someone questioned why he had been called up into the army and not been allowed exemption. Everyone seemed to have something to say, mostly trying to find good reason why they should not have been called up let alone sent to war.

One fellow complained that his mother had been left with eight kids to look after single handed so he reckoned that he should have been given exemption so that he could work and help support his family.

"Of course," he said, "I don't mind fighting. Someone has got to do it, but surely not if he has to leave a badly provided for family behind."

"Well," I thought to myself, "Since he is getting paid while in the army, couldn't part of his pay be deducted and sent to his mother? If he had stayed at home it would still have been a struggle to make ends meet. So what did he mean exactly when he said he didn't mind going off to fight?"

Our sergeant who had been present, obviously a regular soldier, became rather fed up with the inane level of the discussion, said that no one had offered a reasonable justification for their opinion and left.

Early Sunday morning just before the first breakfast sitting we passed Malta on the starboard side. The sun rose at exactly the right time to flood Valetta harbour with light so that we could see quite clearly into the Grand Harbour. Then, like some exotic dream, the scene slowly slipped astern and we were left wondering what it might have been like to go ashore and have a look around. We had covered two-thirds of the distance from Liverpool to the Suez Canal. Everyone was aching to set foot onshore again but we would not get shore leave at any of the places along the Suez Canal and quite a few days remained before we got there.

Once again, awareness of the relentlessness of our progress became acute. It was one of those moments when the omnipresent pounding of the engines became oppressive and we wished they would stop, if only for half an hour.

Because the heat was very oppressive, work in the mess hall had now become a bore and a strain. We sweated so profusely that we wondered if there would be anything left of us to hang a uniform on by the time we got to Korea.

M.V. "GEORGIC"   Sunday, November 4, 1951

Troops Bill of Fare

BREAKFAST
Oatmeal Porridge in Milk
Grilled Breakfast Bacon
Fried or Turned Egg
Rolls and Butter
Preserves   Tea

MID-DAY MEAL
Soupe Beaucaire
Fried Calf's Liver, Smothered Onions
Lyonnaise Potatoes
Rolls and Butter
Fresh Fruit
Preserves   Tea

3-30 p.m.   TEA and SCONES

EVENING MEAL
Cream Reine Margot
Saute of Rabbit, Jardiniere
Macedoine of Vegetables   Mashed Potatoes
Cocoanut Custard Pie, Whipped Cream
Fresh Rolls

MV Georgic menu card

I tucked away a copy of the menu card as a memento of the catering on board. These were printed out each day and placed on each table, a little touch of White Star Line luxury.

None of us knew what many of the items were or what we would actually get. Justifying my nickname of "Prof", my slender knowledge of French helped a little when I was asked what some of the words meant. The wisecracks about these menus could be quite rude:

"Oi, Prof., Wot's 'Turned Egg' mean? Bad egg? On the turn? Buggered if I want that. An' oo's this Cream Rene Maggot?"

I translated for him as 'Queen Margot's Cream' and for my trouble got, "An' wot's that? Her face cream or summat?"

"No, it's a soup—probably a recipe that this Queen Margot liked, whoever she was."

Their imaginations also ran riot with 'Sauté of Rabbit Jardiniere'.

"Wot 'sort' of rabbit's that then, or do they mean 'Jugged 'air?"

"It's probably rabbit stew made from one bred in a cage, not a wild rabbit," I replied.

"Wot d'ya mean; we're eatin' someones pet?" another joker asked.

"Massey doin' of Vegetables? Wot's that mean then?"

"It's pronounced 'mass-a-doyne'," I told them,

"Oo's 'ee when 'ee's at 'ome?"

"I think it's a mixture of diced vegetables."

"Oh, not 'masseyed' then as in 'masseyed' spud?" And that brought a bit of a laugh.

"I don't think so," was all I could say.

We saw no land all the next day so must have been nearing the Nile delta and Suez. It was Guy Fawkes Night and would be celebrated with a whist drive and quiz but no fireworks. The fireworks would come soon enough we thought to ourselves.

Called on parade, we received more typhus and cholera jabs, the last of a series. The Medical Officer tried to give me a double typhus jab because the MO back at Brecon had failed to record the one he had given me in my pay book. I protested and managed to get out of it, for which I was very thankful. The typhus jabs were particularly painful. There was also a pay parade this morning at which I received ten shillings. It was not as if I really needed them because I still had sixteen shillings on me and, as I had found out, there were thieves on board.

The temperatures had once again soared and the sticky, sweaty conditions persisted. Depressingly, I managed to aggravate my right ankle and was also developing a cold. However, things perked up a little at dinner time when, as a token of appreciation, someone started a collection for us waiters and a total of £6 was gathered. There were fifty-six of us on waiter duty and we each received the grand sum of one shilling and nine pence. But the thought was there.

Port Said and the Suez Canal

Recently I had wondered what would happen if the ship's engines stopped. Early that morning we reached the entrance to the Suez Canal, the anchor was dropped and the pounding of the engines ceased. As I had expected, we woke up. At last there was respite from the relentlessness of our travelling. The silence on board, the absence of that continuous thumping vibration from the ship's engines, was quite eerie. Going up on deck that night, we saw lights on shore. As dawn broke, we saw that many other ships were waiting to pass through the canal, mostly oil tankers.

The ship lay off Port Said for about seven hours waiting for permission to enter the canal and proceed to dock. Only one-way traffic was being accepted, hence the delay. It was around 08:00 when a French pilot boat came alongside. Three quarters of an hour later, the anchors were raised and we moved into line with other ships proceeding toward the entrance of the canal. By 09:30 two Royal Navy tugs had helped us into a berth just beyond the ESSO terminal on the eastern side of the canal.

A brisk breeze was blowing which carried with it a curious combination of smells. After eight days out on the briny our nostrils had become accustomed to the clean, tangy air of the ocean winds and were now very sensitive to strange odours. All sorts of reasons for them were considered. Perhaps the garbage collectors had been on strike for a month, the cheese makers had suddenly discovered a new and more savoury process or the sewage system had backed up all over town. So exotic were these wind borne 'perfumes' that poets among us coined some delightful names for them—"Fragrance de la Trine", "Attar of Camels", or, even more appropriately, "Essence of Sewage." The truth was that the place stank.

The order not to trade with the bumboats proved totally irrelevant. They did not want to trade with us and remained tied up along the opposite canal bank. None came anywhere near the ship. Perhaps they had been warned off or, being Egyptian, were aware of the tensions along the Canal Zone and just decided to keep clear.

The crisis in the Zone had evidently increased when Egyptian mooring workers went on strike. This meant that only one convoy each day in each direction could be handled and no transits at night.

The usual mess hall duties had to be performed but with increasing difficulty. My right ankle had swollen and had become quite painful. As a result, I was becoming increasingly disenchanted with all the running about with trays of food and dirty crocks, with scrubbing tables and swabbing floors. A saloon steward believed the aggravation to my ankle stemmed from all the running about we had to do combined with efforts to retain balance on a rolling ship. The only cure was rest and he suggested I report sick and see the Medical Officer. But I decided to wait a little longer to see if the condition eased by itself.

Through the canal

When we awoke on the Wednesday morning our transit of the canal had begun. An aircraft carrier had joined the convoy ahead of us. The country on either side appeared very strange, stretching away into the distance on both sides without any distinctive features and no sign of habitation.

The Suez Canal is 101 miles long, 45 feet deep and 500 feet wide at water level. There are no locks along the entire length because there are no tides in either the Mediterranean or Red Seas and no mountain ranges to cross. Normally a passage of the canal took between ten and twelve hours.

The canal road ran along the bank on the port side while a railway line used the opposite bank. Beyond the banks lay great stretches of marshy lakes. In the distant west we could see the lateen sails of native boats. Occasionally we passed some locals washing themselves in the canal water with a piece of dun-coloured material. Afterwards they would dry themselves with it and then put it on. What a great idea to have a flannel, towel and shirt combined in one garment like that. They also made it very clear that they didn't like us and stopped their ablutions to give us what was euphemistically known as the 'brown arm' or 'short arm' salute with their forearms. It was returned with enthusiasm and a few interesting variations by some of our chaps, presenting exposed buttocks being one of them.

In several places the canal banks had become eroded and working parties were out trying to repair them. At one place some fresh concrete had been laid. As we approached, the ship's propellers pulled water from around the hull causing the water level to drop by about two feet. As soon as we were past, the water flooded back like a mini tidal wave. It was pretty clear what would to happen—and it did. That wave swept right up over the newly laid concrete causing the workmen to scamper about dodging the water as they tried to rescue their tools. Then they danced about waving their arms and shouting abuse at us. We had to laugh but we also felt sorry both for them and for the hopelessness of their task. There were at least a dozen more ships to pass by and each one would produce its own mini tidal wave to wash over their work.

Eventually the marshy lakes were left behind and a sandscape stretched away on either side. From time to time we passed buildings belonging to the Canal Company. They looked very cool, well kept and of a design that blended in well with the palm trees that surrounded them. Not long after, we passed a place called El Quantara where the canal, which had been dead straight up till then, took a slight curve to port.

Before long we observed that another canal ran parallel with ours, perhaps a place where convoys could pass each other before current tensions imposed a limit on the type and timing of convoys. At a canal side army camp, soldiers stood on the bank to watch us pass. Inevitably there was much good-natured, bawdy banter exchanged with them. "Get yer knees brown," they shouted at us. "Get yer skis on," we replied referring to the fact that we were bound for snow covered Korea.

When the canal curved slightly to the starboard, we saw curious looking structures ahead standing in the water on either side. Their purpose became clear as we approached. They belonged to a swing bridge that could be rotated to provide a road across the canal. This was the El Ferdan Bridge where there had been a confrontation between Egyptians and our soldiers a few days before and we could see where some of our soldiers were dug in and half concealed in sandbagged positions on either bank to guard the bridge.

Up until now I had only been vaguely aware that there was trouble here for the British government, not just where the canal was concerned but in our whole relationship with Egypt. I asked Brian if he knew what was going on and he remembered hearing or reading something about riots in Cairo and Port Said when five of our chaps were killed. There had also been bad rioting in Ismailia. Soon after that, a brigade of paratroopers had flown in from Cyprus to help garrison the Canal Zone.

Later I found that trouble had been brewing since October 1950 with the rise of nationalist sentiment. The Egyptians wanted to unilaterally end the Anglo-Egyptian Treaty of 1936 governing a British military presence in Egypt. Egypt also wanted to end the 99 year concession made to the builders of the canal and due to end in 1969. There were riots in Cairo, Ismailia and Port Said and this political tension led the government to send the 16th Parachute Brigade from Cyprus to occupy the Canal Zone.

A little later, the canal opened up into Lake Timsah, the smallest of the lakes that the canal builders had made use of. Over on the starboard side lay a sizeable township which one of the old timers said was Ismailia, the hot spot that Brian had mentioned where quite serious demonstrations had occurred. This led us to remember the many countries around the world where British troops were stationed. In many of them they were involved in action of some kind. Altogether we noted that our chaps were in Occupied Germany, Trieste—which the Italians wanted back, Gibraltar—which the Spanish wanted, Cyprus—which the Greeks and the Turks were squabbling over, Egypt—which wanted the canal for themselves, Aden, Kenya—with its Mau-Mau terrorists, Colombo, Malaysia—with its communist terrorists, Singapore, Hong Kong, Occupied Japan and now in Korea. And that list did not account for other colonies where a garrison was maintained. Anyone wanting to see the world only needed to join the British army or the Royal Navy.

From Lake Timsah we entered a short stretch of canal that led into the Great Bitter Lake. On the starboard side was a forces' holiday centre with neat-looking accommodation set amid lush trees and shaded lawns. There were sailing dinghies drawn up at the edge of the lake and a swimming pool but there was nobody around to make use of them. Probably the situation here had led to cancellation of all leave. It was easier now to understand why there had been no shore leave in Port Said and why the bumboats kept away.

At last we saw our first real sand dunes. Memories of geography lessons returned in which we learned how, through wind action these dunes could travel across the desert much like waves across the oceans. Away to the east on the port side lay a range of extremely barren, ragged looking mountains that seemed to stretch away forever. Was that Sinai, the country of the Exodus, Moses and the Ten Commandments?

Our course altered to the port side as we crossed the Great Bitter Lake. The water in the canal had been of a light muddy turquoise green colour but the lake water looked more like some primeval pea soup. It was reputed to be so toxic that anyone who fell in had to stay in quarantine for weeks. Continuing into the Little Bitter Lake and on to the last stretch of canal, we passed more groups of maintenance workers among whom were negroes and even a few white faces. A patrolling jeep carrying a group of maroon bereted paratroopers came along and stopped to watch us pass. They cheered, whistled and jeered at us shouting, "You won't be home for Christmas," or "You're going the wrong way," or "Do you want a lift back to blighty?" We shouted back, "Shut it, get out and give us a push." But soon, like everything else we passed, all this receded behind into the distance.

The aircraft carrier had made better progress than us and was already at anchor when we reached Port Tufiq. At the southern end of the canal, Tufiq contrasted pleasantly with Port Said. There were many trees and the houses were more western in style and spaciously laid out. Police in white uniforms and hats controlled traffic. Tufiq was one of two harbours at the head of the Gulf of Suez, the port of Suez proper being somewhere over on the starboard side and not clearly visible from where we were. Many other ships lay at anchor over on the Suez side waiting to join a northbound convoy.

Later research on the *MV Georgic* revealed that in July 1941, it had been a troopship and in convoy travelling east. Spotted by German aircraft while anchored at Port Tufiq, it had been bombed and set on fire. In 1944 it was salvaged, repaired in India, taken back to England for refitting and returned to service as a troopship.

Putting on more speed, we passed the carrier and proceeded on down the Gulf of Suez toward the Red Sea. Soon Tufiq lay far behind. Away on the port bow the line of rugged mountains continued. Later in the afternoon, we saw a twin peaked mountain that seemed quite detached from the others. A distinct knife-edge ridge ran between the peaks and we wondered if this might be Mount Sinai, but it was Mount Katherine at the southern end of the Sinai peninsula. We remained just in sight of land for a while longer but eventually it also receded behind us over the horizon. There was no land to be seen in any direction before the sun set on our starboard side.

The aircraft carrier appeared astern around 09:00. By lunchtime it had caught up with us, passed by and was out of sight again well before dusk. As far as I could judge, we were now sailing in a SSE direction down the very un-red Red Sea. In fact, it was a rich royal blue so the origin of the word 'Red' could have had nothing to do with colour. Perhaps it stemmed from 'reed'. There had certainly been a 'sea' of them on either side of the first part of the canal out of Port Said.

My ankle was not improving so I attended sick parade. The MO, a young chap with a pleasant manner, was quite concerned. Asking what my shipside job was, I told him that I was waiting on table in the O/R's mess hall. He said that would have to stop and wrote a letter to my CO to that effect, ordering two days complete rest.

The weather had now become extremely hot and Brian had already acquired quite a tan, something that he did very quickly given his dark colouring. I remained as white as a proverbial lily and had to take great care not to get sunburn. Someone idly wondered if a self-inflicted wound, such as allowing oneself to become badly sunburned, was grounds for being put on a 'fizzer'

The order was finally given for us to wear our tropical kit and the evening was spent trying to make it fit better. As things were, Brian and I both looked quite ridiculous in it. Brian's trousers were six inches too long and needed to be taken up but as he was quite useless with a needle and cotton all he could do was complain that the task was beyond him. I had to sort out my own gear before I could give him any help. We were also beginning to feel quite depressed that we did not receive any mail at Port Said. Was the address we had given our families correct?

Part 1 Orders informed us that we would reach Aden tomorrow, Saturday, November 10th, and there would be shore leave at last. Old hands on board told us there was little of interest and the NAAFI Club was three miles away from the docks. My ankle had improved for the rest but was still quite swollen. The weather continued very hot and humid and kept us in a continual sweat all day. Land appeared on the port horizon later in the afternoon, which, if my geography served me well, was probably the coast of Yemen which meant that we were approaching the southern end of the Red Sea.

On deck that evening, a group of the Welsh chaps in our detachment—it was made up fifty percent of English blokes!—gave an impromptu concert of their national songs. Naturally, being Welsh their singing was excellent and I enjoyed listening to them. An overcast sky with a warm dry wind helped us feel more comfortable and we lounged around stripped to the waist happy to forget that at dinner this evening one poor chap had found four dead maggots floating in his soup.

The sun rose over the ship's bows instead of the port side as on the past few mornings. This meant that we had changed direction in the wee hours and were now sailing east. A notice on Part 1 Orders stated that the post box would be cleared at midday so I rushed off to scribble a hasty postscript to the letters I had written since we left Port Said. I returned on deck to see a very strange looking coastline. Earlier we had sailed quite close to a string of dusty, dry and very rocky islands. They looked remarkably like heaps of rubble on a building site. Mountains now rose in huge masses or long serrated ridges out of a flat sandy coastline. Dark brown and black, they rose sheer out of the sand like the remains of monstrous, long-dead dinosaurs. There was absolutely no sign of vegetation or of habitation.

The approach to Aden (1)

The approach to Aden (2)

For the most part, the mountains lay some way inland but occasionally a massive outcrop managed to get its feet in the sea and as we rounded one of these Aden finally came in sight. The entrance to the harbour and the huddle of cream or off-white buildings beyond lay beneath a formidable undulating ridge of rock. The few trees that had been established along the harbour-side must have required constant watering to keep them alive. Then someone observed that Aden had not had any direct rainfall for twenty-two years and all the drinking water had to be extracted from seawater. That, I thought, would also have produced a lot of sea salt, an essential mineral in a hot country! However, it all looked so arid and dusty that if by any chance there ever were a real downpour here the whole place would just crumble and wash into the sea.

It was almost dark by the time we docked but that did not keep the bumboats away. There was no trouble with the locals here in Aden so we were allowed to trade with them. Nylons, headscarves, chewing gum, cigarettes, lighters, and a plethora of mass-produced embroidered articles were on offer and several chaps did business with them. One purchased a lighter in the shape of a camera on a tripod that was operated by a remote-control shutter release. It was very ingenious and made in "Occupied Japan". They could cost anything between three and ten shillings depending on your bargaining skills. Tomorrow we would have time ashore to explore our first Eastern port! At the moment it looked quite a charming place but then, all we could see were the lights of the port and their reflections in the oily water.

Shore leave at last

The bumboats came alongside very early next morning bringing with them little kids who dived for coins. Invective frequently filled the air when they discovered that one of the coins they recovered was only a penny covered with silver paper to make it seem like half a crown. Their use of colourful English was surprising.

After breakfast, one of the launches plying back and forth between the ship and the dockside took us ashore. It was good to set foot on land again but close up in daylight the place looked like a dusty slum. We took a taxi to the NAAFI Club but found little to do there. A small beach in a little cove had been turned into a swimming pool by closing it off with underwater netting to keep sharks out. There was nothing else of interest to keep us there so we walked back into town.

On reaching the main shopping street we were continually being stopped by someone wanting to sell something. They tugged at our arms with offers of fruit, chewing gum, lighters and many other items, all at inflated prices. English chewing gum was cheap though at a penny ha'penny a packet but fizzy bottled drinks were very expensive compared to their cost at home. Some stands carried week-old English newspapers of no interest for us but we did see other items that were not only attractive but attractively priced. Tins and boxes of chocolates and sweets, shirts, cameras and many other items might have seen us part with our ten shillings pay many times over but for the fact that we were going in the wrong direction, east to war, not west back home.

Wandering on we found ourselves in a native quarter where the air was dominated by the smell of stale urine and the raucous sound of Arabic music. Most of the shops belonged to tailors who sat outside to carry on their work. The rest sold cheap jewellery.

Aden currency was now issued by the East African Currency Board and on a par with English money. The East African penny was the same size and colour as ours but had a hole in the middle presumably so that they could be looped on a string to keep them safe. Their shilling was the size of our two-shilling piece, had a minted edge but lacked the hole. Paper money invariably ended up looking very tatty. Until recently, Indian currency—rupees and annas, had been the local currency. No one seemed to have objected to the change. We had been warned against changing our English currency into the local coin. If there was any of it left at the end of shore leave, it could not be changed back. The natives seemed unaware of this because we were frequently approached by some wallah who would show us a fistful of English coins and say, "I geeve you Eengleesh monee for yours, aye, Johnny?" and pester the life out of us.

3

ADEN TO SINGAPORE

11th November-20th November 1951

Going through the motions

That Sunday morning, soon after we returned to the ship around 11:30, sacks of mail arrived on an RAF launch. Shortly after that, two tugs began to manoeuvre us away from the moorings and we were once more on our way. We moved out into the Gulf of Aden heading for the Indian Ocean and the huge piles of rock, dirt and dust surrounding Aden receded below the horizon. The sea was like the proverbial millpond and the sun was set to scorch. Brian lapped up all that he could get but I kept in the shade.

As the sun set a wind arose and it became cooler. An almost full moon rose in the east. We leaned over the rail to watch and listen to the crash of the bow waves. They made a soothing noise. The balmy air and the glitter of moonlight took our thoughts homeward with more than usual intensity and to memories of warm summer nights on the beaches of Poole Bay. We were now beginning to realise much more clearly how far we had come from home and, with time zone changes, quite out of synchronisation with everyone at home.

Early the next morning, we saw the tip of the Horn of Africa recede off the starboard bow. We were expecting to reach Colombo on Friday morning. There were frequent cries of 'sharks' but invariably they were the wing tips several feet apart of huge, ominous looking manta rays. One came quite close to the ship's side and we could see its eyes on the end of stubby stalks. It gave them a mean and hungry look. Flying fish began to appear more frequently; whole shoals of them leapt out of the water to travel a few feet in the air like so many glittering, silvery streaks of animated sunlight before skittering back into the sea.

An attempt to resume a semblance of military training was made later in the morning. A lecture on infantry-armour cooperation was held in one of the saloons but the atmosphere was very stuffy and it was difficult to keep awake and pay attention. Some of our officer's efforts to 'keep us up to scratch' were strange. Were they afraid that we would be totally unprepared for the reality of Korea and the war conditions we would encounter there? Perhaps they were right to worry but they chose one rather useless way to address their concern. We had to iron our tropical uniforms before reporting for morning parade; it was always a total waste of time. Given the temperature and the way we perspired, all those neat creases fell out again within a few minutes of putting them on. It was doubtful if we would be required to do this for long. Perhaps what our officers really did not like was the way after dinner we lounged about reading, sunbathing or sleeping—lazy as lords and very comfortable.

The seas had picked up and the sky become overcast which made the weather more oppressive. The clocks were put forward and we lost another hour's sleep. Strange to realise that ever since passing Gibraltar our days had been only twenty-three or twenty-three and a half hours long. We were continually sailing into tomorrow. However, it would be made up again on the way home, if and whenever that might be.

It was so warm during the night that when we awoke at reveille it took ages to gather our wits together. Our cabin in the bowels of the ship on D2 deck had no natural light and the piped air-conditioning was not very effective. The atmosphere was much too close for comfort and we always woke bleary-eyed. We had also begun to sleep naked, no sheets or blankets over us. They irritated too much. The water from the cold tap was warm and useless to refresh us. Even a routine activity like going to the loo would have us breaking out in a sweat, the air being even stuffier in those cubicles. Not surprisingly, we got a dressing down on parade for looking untidy but the officer making the comment did not look any too smart himself.

After breakfast we were shown another training film. Called *"A Day in the Front Line"*, it featured troops from the Dorsetshire Regiment. We learned nothing additional to what we had been told and put through at Trawsfynydd and Buckingham Tofts. Afterwards, the MO came along to give us a talk about infectious tropical diseases. Lacking prior knowledge or experience to relate it to, his information went over our heads

Later in the day, detailed to a group ordered below to fetch some ice from the fridge, I descended into the bowels of the ship. Passing through a thick wooden door into a cold store, the temperature dropped to around 0° C. Upstairs it had been 40° C in the shade and quite stupefying so the sudden chill hit hard. Where before I had felt only sweaty and sleepy, suddenly I was completely awake. However, the return topside with the ice and back into that heat was another shock and I almost passed out. For quite a while afterwards everything remained completely out of touch.

Around 17:00 we passed a small, low, thickly wooded island with a lagoon at one end. The water in the lagoon was a light turquoise blue and contrasted sharply with the deep blue of the ocean. A brilliant white lighthouse stood out sharply above the trees. A steward said that it was a leper colony on one of the Maldives Islands, a chain that ran north to south off the southwest coast of India.

Brian had started to write home at last but letter writing was evidently not a strong thing with him. I only discovered this when he kept asking me how to spell a lot of quite simple words. Finally, he asked me how he should sign off. And he had a grammar school education?

We had yet another film show this morning, one on *"Motor Cycle Maintenance"* and the other on *"Good Driving"*. Both were interesting but hardly relevant for us. If you didn't know how to drive, you would hardly learn by watching the second film. However, it did help me to appreciate the driving lessons my father had paid for on embarkation leave. Such lessons could have been a very useful part of our training at Whittington Barracks.

Colombo Shore Leave

On Friday, 15th November, Ceylon came up on the horizon after lunch but rain obscured the view. After watching the pilot boat come alongside I went below and quickly fell asleep. When I awoke we were at anchor surrounded by merchant shipping from all round the world; a US freighter called *President Polk*, a very new-looking Swedish freighter named *Andaman* and a French liner called *La Marseillaise*. The harbour had been formed with a breakwater with two entrances to enclose a wide bay. Ships had to moor between huge marker buoys anchored to the bed of the bay. Refuelling barges and water barges were towed to where ships lay at these moorings. Many small craft were skimming around the harbour, their crewmen clad only in vests and loincloths and all of them soaking wet. Evidently it had been raining quite steadily in Colombo almost all day. Only one trader came out to us in his boat and all he had for sale were pineapples.

Passes were issued around mid afternoon. By 17:30, we had changed the money received at pay parade just before dinner last night and were ready to go ashore in Colombo. We joined the queue for the boats that would ferry us ashore. These were locally owned but the trip was free and we also had tickets to get us through the turnstile on the quayside. Being a waiter, Brian had priority for going ashore. I said that I was a waiter too and kept quiet about having been released from duty because of a swollen ankle. It was not questioned.

Getting into the boat was tricky. A considerable swell caused the boat to rise and fall about three feet at the end of the gangway. It was necessary to time things just right so that you had the least distance to jump. It was a slow business getting the boat filled and some chaps failed to time things well and came quite a painful cropper. All the while a soft warm rain was falling. It was pleasant, didn't bother us and we were soon as wet as the boatmen had been but it was a warm soaking and not uncomfortable.

On shore we found that many shops were still open, mostly jewellers who tried to entice us into their emporiums. Just for the hell of it, we entered one and were invited to sit down. The proprietor brought out tray after tray of rings, necklaces, and polished gemstones. It was all very interesting but, given that asking prices were anything from fifteen to fifty rupees and we only had five rupees each, his chance of making a sale was very remote.

When we finally told the proprietor just how much money we had he refused to believe us and we had the devil of a time getting away from him. Elsewhere, tea traders offered to send packets of duty free tea home for us, producing testimonials as to their trustworthiness but again their prices were too steep and our pockets too empty. There was one thing that we found strange, that at the end of every encounter like this we were asked if we had anything to sell—lighters, cigarette cases, even cigarettes. Again we had to disappoint them.

There were many fruit stalls around, mostly selling bananas, coconuts or pineapples. I paid the equivalent of one shilling and six pence for a large bunch of quite small, very sweet and tasty bananas which had a much better flavour than the bigger bananas now becoming available again in British fruit and vegetable shops. Brian paid four rupees for two tins of pineapple chunks to be eaten later when back on board ship.

Small boys came up to us with offers of "Jig-a-jig, Johnny, jig-a-jig?" or "Postcards, Johnnie?" which we again declined. Uncle Reg had told tales of life in India when posted there by the RAF during World War II. Small boys would come and offer him the carnal services of any of their female relatives, even their grandmothers, or postcards of them taken in erotic poses.

Tiring of this commercial merry-go-round we headed for the NAAFI Club. Our way lay along a promenade above a beach. It was raining again and the world seemed to close around us so that for a moment it was as if we were back on embarkation leave walking along the Undercliffe Drive in Bournemouth. To support this illusion, most of the buildings we glimpsed through the rain were European in style. A sense of reality quickly returned when a rickety old taxi rumbled past followed by a barefooted boy pulling a rickshaw. Nothing like them had ever passed along the Undercliffe Drive. We later saw many more rickshaws but they seemed smaller than in any pictures I had seen. The boys who pulled them could have become superb athletes had their circumstances been different. They were certainly fit and had plenty of stamina.

Battered looking electric trolley buses rumbled along the main street picking up their power through a single connection to an aerial power line. Those we were familiar with in Bournemouth connected to two overhead lines, one for the power and the other to earth it again. Brian reckoned that the earthing connection here must have been made through the trolley rails. We only saw one motor bus and that, much to our surprise, was a double-decker.

It was now about 22:45 and, having seen all we could manage on foot and given our limited funds, we returned to take the boat back to the ship. Brian received a letter from his mother and a cutting from a paper about our departure from Liverpool. It described our conditions on board as luxurious, which I suppose they were—especially for the officers. I could only imagine what they might have been on a regular troopship—doubtless of a much lower standard. Her letter also told him that Roy, his elder brother, had been stationed in this part of the world serving aboard HMS *Loch Glendhu*. We actually saw it lying at its moorings in the harbour but Roy had gone home on a troopship some time ago.

Only half the ship's company went ashore last night so the rest went off this morning for a few hours. More traders came around this morning to sell fruit and souvenirs. Elephants seemed to predominate, carved black elephants, elephant book ends and picture frames decorated with elephants. We read in a local paper how an elephant had gone berserk on a plantation somewhere and caused much damage. In another incident, two plantation workers had been mistaken for thieves and shot. The place sounded more like the Wild West than the Mysterious East.

Just before noon we were paraded for a roll call then dismissed. The gangway was hauled up, the traders moved their boats away and we were off on our ocean cruise one more. Then the sound of high-pitched shouting attracted us to the rail. One of the traders was still following us, its owner waving his arms about frantically while shouting and screaming a torrent of abuse. Some joker had tied to the rail the rope by which goods had been hauled up and money sent down. The poor chap was now being pulled out to sea behind us, bouncing around in the waves of the ship's wash. In the end he had to cut the rope to get away.

The news bulletin carried an item about the situation on the Suez Canal. Tensions appeared to be increasing as the Egyptians continued to raise pressure to gain control of the canal. It was becoming worrisome. Was this going to erupt into another full-scale conflict? The news from Korea was not any better; talks were stalemated around the size of a buffer zone between North and South Korea. The argument was about who should give what ground and where along the existing front line. There was also news that the Canadians now had a whole infantry brigade in Korea.

Next stop Singapore

Sleeping on deck had been permitted for the past three nights but we had not tried this yet, preferring to make the most of the superb beds on this ship. However, despite lying down naked with no covering, it was still too hot and muggy in our cabin for comfort and it had been another restless and uncomfortable night.

When reveille sounded at 06:30, we stumbled around as if we all had monstrous hangovers. Going up on deck didn't help either. The breeze was too warm and humid to blow cobwebs away and the physical enervation we felt was accompanied by a desperate mental inertia. These conditions made everyone become touchy and over-sensitive. Even Brian and I had an argument.

On Wednesday morning we had passed the northern tip of Sumatra into the Malacca Strait between Malaya and Sumatra and well away from the swell in the Bay of Bengal. We should reach Singapore sometime tomorrow where one and a half day's shore leave should give us time to see something of the place.

The MO delivered another of his cautionary lectures, this time on Venereal Diseases, the various types, their causes and prevention. Nowadays they are called Sexually Transmitted Diseases or STDs. It was informative and interesting to learn that if caught in time they were completely curable, not fatal as once believed. He also told us that contraceptives were available to those who thought they might require them. It was claimed that their use reduced the chances of catching VD. For my part, I had no interest in having casual sex of any kind. I was still far too naïve about these things and wouldn't know where to go, or how to begin.

This morning the sea was very calm and almost mirror slick. It was already intensely hot since this was the first sunny day we had seen since leaving Ceylon. There were many long, awkward looking native craft with outriggers and straw sails sailing about and a multitude of small islands lay off the port side. All were heavily wooded, the same drab olive colour as our tropical kit while the larger islands had houses on them. Some were partially built over the sea on poles while other houses were built right out in the sea with no direct connection to the land at all. Such houses had been built at the ancient lake village at Glastonbury as we had seen in our school history books.

By mid morning we had dropped anchor near a Shell tank farm on one of the islands at the entrance to the docks. The pilot boat arrived and other launches brought out sundry officials, some civilian, some brass from the army and air force. Just after midday the anchors were weighed and we moved slowly forward into the docks. We passed through a very narrow gap between two islands and entered a vast open seaway crowded with shipping of all sizes and nations. By the time lunch sittings were over we were securely tied up in dock.

The scenes on the port and starboard sides provided a great contrast. To starboard, across the water, power launches, pleasure cruisers and native boats lay quietly at their moorings. Behind them, white buildings with deep, cool verandahs were scattered amongst lush tropical foliage. All was peace and quiet over there in stark contrast to the dock scene on the port side which was one of enormous activity. Long, corrugated iron warehouses revealed another side to life in this port city. There was no natural beauty and tranquility down there. Chinese dock workers, both male and female, were everywhere outnumbering any Europeans around.

MPs were everywhere effectively removing any illusion we might have had that we were on a pleasant ocean cruise. A notice posted on Ship's Details informed us that four fifths of the population of Singapore was of Chinese origin. It was strange to think that we were en route to a land where we might be required to kill their cousins.

Mail was distributed and at last I received my first letter from home. An air-letter, it contained no news of any significance and certainly no answers to any of the questions that I had asked in all my letters. My initial reaction was one of confusion. I had tried so hard to keep my family informed of how things were with me so that they might not worry unduly but none of them seemed able to write back other than very briefly and superficially. I was very disappointed.

Singapore Shore Leave

By the time we were up and breakfasted, the harbour on the starboard side, so tranquil when we arrived, was full of activity, mostly with small native craft plying back and forth. The way they were propelled was fascinating. The boatman stood facing the way he wished to go, holding onto oars tied to sticks in the gunwales. To move forward they pushed the oars away from them and then down to lift the blades out of the water to be pulled back in readiness for the next stroke. The advantage of this technique was that they could see where they were going. When rowing a boat back home, it was necessary to turn and look awkwardly over your shoulder to find out if you were on course.

I moved over to the port side to watch what was happening down on the docks. An announcement came over the PA system—"All passengers disembarking in Singapore are to be off the ship in five minutes, complete with baggage, or they will stay on board until shore leave finishes." This prompted an explosion of activity. Chattering, squabbling porters swarmed up the gangway to collect the luggage lying about, mostly belonging to some of the women and children who were on board, no doubt the families of servicemen stationed in Singapore. None of the porters looked well nourished but it was astounding just how much they could carry. It would have resulted in a severe rupture had I tried to equal their seemingly casual feats of strength.

While waiting for Brian, still on duty in the mess hall, I talked with a chap I had met last night for the first time. Almost as tall as me, Alec Ahern impressed me as a very gentle, thoughtful chap and I quickly came to like him immensely. Brian had also taken a liking to him and last night we had decided to go ashore together.

It was almost eleven o'clock before Brian was ready. As we walked down the gangway he sounded off about how pissed off the waiters had been when, of over a hundred who had signed up to have breakfast on board, only twenty-four blokes turned up. The waiters had to hang about unnecessarily when they could have gone ashore much earlier.

At the bottom of the gangway, MPs scrutinised our appearance and our passes, nodded OK, and directed us to a row of trucks behind the warehouses—our transport into town. And what a ride that was! The roads were crowded with every imaginable form of traffic but our driver, foot flat to the floor and horn blaring, pressed on regardless. We had our hearts in our mouths for most of the time and little chance to appreciate the passing scene. Finally, we were dropped outside the services club in Beach Road.

Entering the driveway beneath an archway bearing the name Shackles Club, we wandered around to investigate. The Advice Bureau would accept letters and parcels to be posted home. There was a reading and writing room, a cafeteria, gift shop, dance hall, photographer, hairdresser and a court-yard overlooking the sea. I took the opportunity to have a haircut to tidy up the mop of hair that had grown on my head after the cropping it received in Brecon. After a quick bite to eat—sausage, chips, beans and a cup of tea, we left the Shackles Club and set off to see something of life in this city. Turning right into Beach Road, we wandered past the Raffles Hotel—much too sophisticated and expensive for us—and entered an area given over to clothes shops, jewellery shops, bookshops, cafes and goodness only knew what else.

The shops were no more than openings onto the street with their goods displayed all over the walls. If you dared to stop and have a closer look at anything, someone immediately came up and started urging you to buy something—anything! It was as testing a time as it had been in Aden and Colombo.

"Yes, Johnny, velly nice blooch. You like watch stlap? Velly good. Only thlee dolla." The prices were out of reach again and I often felt like saying, "Who do you think we are, Americans?" We wandered on and on just gazing at the scenes around us, immersed in the noises and swirling movement of people flowing past. The babbling confusion only seemed to intensify as daylight began to wane. Dusky people, all yelling or chattering like so many sparrows, swam past in the gloomy light leaving us quite bemused.

The smell of the east

A little further on we entered a Chinese market, an area of narrow streets and even narrower walkways between stalls where everything imaginable was on sale, or so it seemed. As night descended, this district became a fairyland: 'trees' of small acetylene gas flames enchantingly illuminated all the stalls. The wet calcium carbide must have been in a container beneath the stall. Were it not for the distinctive smell it would have been quite magical. The odour of carbide gas reminded me of when I had first discovered just how smelly it could be. While still at junior school, it had been possible for us to buy small quantities of calcium carbide. A tiny piece dropped surreptitiously into some unpopular kid's inkwell would cause the ink to froth over, send a delicious pong into the air and cause him a lot of bother with the teacher. Those were the days of dip pens, blotting paper and ink monitors in junior school and fountain-pens at the grammar school, soon to become redundant with the advent of ballpoint pens.

As we ventured further into this Singapore market another element in the atmosphere was discernible in addition to the carbide smell, one markedly different but still remembered from school days. When I was at junior school we would have known quite quickly when someone had farted or seriously soiled their pants. This other element that we were now able to smell was like that, decidedly faecal, as if everyone was suffering from the runs, not just people but any cats and dogs that were around too. If it were not that the principle food here was rice we could have sworn everyone had overdosed on beans. We agreed that it was the worst stench we had so far encountered anywhere. Port Said and Aden had smelt like rose gardens by comparison.

Eventually we discovered that this particular stench came from open sewers between the kerbs and the pavement along both sides of the streets. They were anything between two to six feet deep depending on the importance of the street and eventually emptied into a main sewer that ran between the Raffles Institute and St Andrew's Cathedral. This was obviously flushed out by the tide so that everything from food waste to human waste eventually fed the fish. We guessed that the smaller sewers would only be washed out when it poured with rain. Fortunately that happened quite often.

We soon grew accustomed to the smell as an essential part of the atmosphere in this corner of the Mystic East and were quite content to put up with it. We wandered around the market watching the activity of the stall-keepers and examining their goods. There were many small kitchens where a plethora of dishes were prepared. Passers-by could purchase whatever they fancied and sit on low stools to eat it.

To our eyes all the food tended to look like variations of stew. It was served up in small bowls and eaten with the help of chopsticks made from wood or plastic, eating tools that we had heard about but never seen in use before. We marvelled at the dexterity displayed by the diners.

Eventually, finding our way into a shopping centre known as Shaw's Buildings, I bought a souvenir at an Indian emporium: a silk headscarf that was embroidered with the word 'Singapore'. We then crossed the road to the Shackles Club. When I took the scarf out to have another look at it I was quickly approached by a complete stranger who offered to buy it for what amounted to twice the price I had paid, an offer that that could not be refused. That's business, I supposed.

After purchasing two huge bunches of small, sweet bananas for what seemed very little we returned to the transport back to the ship. Another journey like the earlier one, it was more fraught because it was now dark. But we arrived safely, gave in our passes and went to catch some sleep.

Day two ashore

We went ashore again just after 0900 this morning and took the truck into the city. This time we knew what to expect and managed to see more as we travelled into the city. Streams of people were moving about in all directions, most of them wearing pyjamas. We crossed over the Singapore River, crowded with sampans and stinking to high heaven. I suspected it was another part of the naturally flushing city sewage system. Not that this deterred small children from swimming around in it. Heaven alone knew how they managed to avoid catching some seriously infectious disease.

The Shackles Club was not yet fully open so we walked back to the area around St Andrew's Cathedral. Trishaws, a combination of a rickshaw and bicycle, were everywhere but different from those seen in Colombo. There the passenger seating had been behind the driver on a two-wheeled extension that was part of the main framework but here in Singapore the passenger carriage was on the side of the bicycle rather like the sidecar for a motorbike. Almost to a man, their Chinese drivers displayed gold somewhere among their teeth, sign of wealth that also indicated that either gold was cheap here or trishaw driving was a very profitable business.

Tattoo parlours were almost as numerous as the rickshaws and were even to be found in the cathedral grounds offering an amazing range of designs; some quite elegant and tasteful, others garish, horrific or just plain stupid. They could cost anything between two and ten dollars. Most of the tattooists we saw executed the designs using the old hand tools but a few had more modern electrically operated needles. Quite a number of the chaps on board acquired a tattoo while we were in Singapore but the idea held no attraction for me. I had enough natural embellishments scattered all over me already. I was born with them.

In St Andrew's Cathedral

St Andrew's Cathedral stood in the heart of the administrative and institutional centre of Singapore. With its Gothic style of architecture it looked typically English but a little larger than the average parish church back home. It stood on the opposite side of North Bridge Street from the Shaw's Building and the Union Jack Club and between the Raffles Institute and the main Administration Building. Lawns and a few trees surrounded it just as if it were in some English city. With its coat of white paint, it looked well cared for, fresh, cool and dressed for the tropics.

St Andrew's Cathedral, Singapore

Entering by the west door, we signed the visitor's book. Brian and Alec went straight on in but my attention was drawn to some plaques on the wall and I spent a few moments reading some of them. Turning to catch them up, I was just on the point of walking through the doorway into the nave when someone started to play the organ.

Suddenly, and very loudly, the whole cathedral was filled with the tune of a very old and well-loved hymn, "O God, Our Hope in Ages Past", one I had sung many times as a choirboy in the local Anglican church. As that tune registered fully in my consciousness, a most extraordinary feeling of exhilaration swept through me.

My legs then felt decidedly weak and I slowly moved forward to stand behind and lean on one of the back pews. The strong, tingling sensation coursed over my head, across my shoulders, down my back and along my arms. I could not move. Indeed I had no desire to move. My whole being had been completely taken over by an incredible surge of energy. Whether it was primarily emotional or spiritual—or both, I could not say. It was as if I had been totally consumed by some great, splendid, transcendental and utterly mysterious force. As I listened to that music, that old familiar tune, and as I recalled the words, tears began to flow down my cheeks. All sense of time was gone. For a while, I was in another place, another world, existing on another time scale. While this state seemed to last an age, probably only a few moments passed.

The music ceased but I remained where I was, standing still and listening as the echoes dispersed. Then, gradually I returned to an awareness of where I was. The sensations dissipated and the ethereal moment came to an end. I looked around for Brian and Alec. Evidently they had been quite unmoved by the organ music and were only interested in moving on. But for me, it had been a completely astounding experience to hear that hymn tune break out at precisely the moment when I set foot inside the main part of the cathedral. It was an experience that would never be forgotten. A verse from Psalm 23 seemed to echo in my memory,

"Yea though I walk through the valley of the shadow of death, I will fear no evil; for thou art with me, Thy rod and thy staff they comfort me."

There had been something immeasurably comforting and reassuring about this experience, as if I had been told that all would be well. In that moment I knew, beyond any doubt, that I would not die in Korea or even be seriously wounded. One day I would return home physically intact.

More smells

Eventually, I caught up with the others and we wandered aimlessly for a while looking at all the imposing buildings around and near Empress Place. The noxious smell we had encountered yesterday hit us again as we crossed over the 'pongy' Singapore River. It was still as jam-packed as ever with sampans and houseboats in a web of ropes and gangplanks.

We decided to visit another Chinese market and once more entered an area dense with stalls selling clothing, fruit, food and Coca Cola. Most of the time, the narrow walkways and the crowds compelled us to walk in single file. And the atmosphere was as asphyxiating as ever. When we reached an open space where the air smelt fresher we almost passed out with the shock.

Wandering on, we passed a shop where the UN Korea Medal and the British Commonwealth Korea Medal were on display. We would receive them one day. By now daylight was fading and lights were coming on. Huge neon signs lit up the main streets, one for 'Tiger' Beer, the local brew, being very prominent. Also, the festoons of acetylene flames on side street stalls indicated that our time ashore was coming to its end.

Singapore—cycle rickshaw

At last, by the GPO, we reached a bridge over the river and strolled back to the Shackles Club for something to eat. I then went to the writing room to write some letters. Later, wandering down to the water's edge at the back of the club I sat down to rest. Exhausted from all the walking, I must have dozed off. When I awoke and went looking for Brian and Alec, I was told that they had left with some other chaps. Spotting others from my unit who were on the point of leaving I tagged along.

We returned to the Chinatown bazaar area again. Every time we stopped to look at anything, even if it was only a packet of gum, the stall keeper exploded into activity, eager to show us every thing else he had for sale. But it was all for nothing. None of us had much money. Eventually, becoming tired of shaking my head, I headed back to the Shackles Club to catch a truck back to the ship and my bunk.

4

Singapore to Pusan

23rd November-30th November 1951

Further East

Reveille sounded at 06:30 but made no impression on me and I slept on to finally be woken by the 07:30 call for the first breakfast sitting. Calculating that there was still time to take things easy since there was always the second session at 08:30, I stayed put. Eventually I rolled out of my bunk, tried to stand up but collapsed into a chair and almost nodded off again. Then I woke with a jerk—but did not recognise him or remember his name. Grabbing my washing kit and towel, my next objective was to reach the washroom which lay up two flights of stairs. It was as much as I could do to stay awake and find the energy to move out of the cabin, get there, commence my ablutions and complete them. Those two days wandering around Singapore had left me with a very heavy non-alcoholic hangover.

The ship was already on the move and from the washroom porthole I could see tugs pulling us clear of the quayside. When I finally got up on deck we were well under way but remained in sight of land until about 11:30. The sea was very calm again; there was no swell and the gentlest of breezes slightly ruffled the surface of the water. It was a beautiful shade of turquoise, only changing when we reached deeper water sometime after dinner. Several small islands were passed on the starboard side. They probably lay off the coast of Borneo and all looked very isolated and lonely.

With sunset, a cool wind arose into which we could escape the stuffiness of our cabin. We expected to reach Hong Kong by Tuesday, 27th November. Once there, quite a few of the troops on board would disembark including one of the Welch Regiment drafts, but not ours unfortunately. Whether this would be a case of 'thank goodness' or 'bad luck' there was no way of knowing. We had picked up drafts from the Royal Navy and from the Royal Marines in Singapore, both bound for Kure in Japan.

No one could tell us if we would get shore leave in Hong Kong but rumour had it that we would and that the temperatures would be much cooler there. This probably meant that we would be back in battledress again. Against that possibility, after dinner I pressed mine so that it would be ready. Meanwhile it was still warm enough on board for me to sweat so heavily that my jacket was usually soaking wet. Stripping it off I lay on my bunk to continue reading Hemingway's *"For Whom the Bell Tolls"*, an excellent tale. The racy style, 'spicy' in places, made the characters came alive and Hemingway's philosophising also appealed to me. I knew that a film had been made of the book starring Gary Cooper but I was willing to bet that it didn't do the philosophical parts much justice.

Talking of characters, we had some prized specimens on board and no mistake. There had been a mania for having tattoos while in Singapore. One chap had a tattoo on his arm of a tired-looking soldier with the caption "Browned Off" inscribed beneath it. Elsewhere, he had the words "Korea—Never Again" embedded in his skin—and he hadn't even got there yet! It seemed an odd attitude to have but he was a peculiar character anyway, short tempered and his speech full of obscenities.

In the South China Sea

Reveille went at 06:00 this morning. The sergeant came by to remind all 'unemployed' persons that there would be a PT session at 06:45. We all went back to sleep. He returned at around 06:25 with the same message and we went back to sleep again. When he returned yet again at 06:40 we were still fast asleep and woke to an earful of abuse and the direst threats of what would happen if we didn't 'rise and shine'.

Over the last few months I had turned 'skiving off' into a fine art and had absolutely no intention of attending any PT sessions if I could possibly avoid them. I had hated them at school and that hatred had intensified since I had joined the army. So, despite not having been allocated another job, despite being 'unemployed', I still didn't report for that PT session. It was a fact that I was not doing anything much at that time to earn my pay.

It so happened that Brian and I climbed out of our bunks at the same time. As we stood up we both experienced a bout of giddiness but there was only one chair into which to collapse. I lost and slumped against the wall, then managed to steady myself sufficiently to grab my washing kit and crawl off to the washroom. Once there, I started to scrape the 'fungus' off my face. At one time this would have taken just over a minute to complete but now it seemed to be taking about ten. Either I was getting more conscientious about my shaving or I was more tired than I realised from the heat and all that exercise back in Singapore.

It was a beautifully cool morning on deck and fresh enough to finally wake me up. The sun was low in the sky to the east. The sea was dead smooth like a mirror and the reflected sunlight was blinding. A very slow, lazy swell set the bows gently rising and dipping as the ship proceeded on its course. The motion was soothing and pleasant. Hundreds of flying fish again skittered over the water as if they alone inhabited the ocean. We saw no other signs of aquatic life. It was a time in which to spend a few moments dreaming and soaking up the early glory of this day

However, it was soon time to come back down to earth, or the deck perhaps. The need for breakfast became increasingly urgent after which there was morning parade to attend. When that was over we were marched off to see another film, this one called "I am a Sniper". For once it was quite interesting. At 10:30 the ship's inspection took place, which meant that we stayed on deck out of the way.

We had a boat drill after the ship's inspection. These had taken place every Saturday while at sea. First there was an announcement over the PA system followed shortly after by the clanging of electric gongs. Six short blasts and one long one on the ship's siren was the signal that sent us all scuttling like rabbits into the guts of the ship to get our life jackets and then get back up to parade at our allocated boat stations. Once everyone had mustered and rolls been called we were dismissed.

Just a breeze!

I went below to read but by lunchtime the seas had become considerably rougher and it became increasingly unpleasant to stay in the small confines of the cabin so I went back up on deck. We were now well into the South China Sea which, by reputation, could be even rougher than the Bay of Biscay. The ship was going obliquely across the swell in a combined pitch-and-toss and rolling motion. As this motion increased, ominous creaking noises sounded all around us. It was as if we were on an old wooden sailing ship rather than a modern steel-hulled liner.

Then the wind really picked up whipping the waves and spray clear across the bows and it became too uncomfortable up on deck. Going below, I stood by one of the doors in the hull on C deck. A net was secured across it to stop anyone falling out. Normally the water level lay about fifteen feet below but now the waves were crashing right up almost to that doorway. This change in the weather and the sea conditions had come on quite suddenly but was very exhilarating. It guaranteed to blow away any tropical cobwebs that might have been hanging about.

Later, the wind drove a hard rain before it. Visibility became very poor requiring that the ship's siren be sounded every two minutes or so as if in thick fog. Whether it carried very far over the shishing sound of the rain on the water was doubtful. The clouds had also settled around us so that we appeared to be moving under a huge grey dome. Any boundary between cloud and sea had become very indistinct.

I went up on deck again to a position from where it was possible to look toward the bows and watch the effect the ship had on the waves. It was hypnotic to watch the bows rise up over one huge swell, hang there for a moment then plunge forward into the next. The water would split either side and lunge away from the ship showing a brilliant turquoise colour that contrasted sharply with the deep blue-black of the ocean around. Clouds of spray rose up to be instantly whipped away in the wind.

Beautiful as it was to watch, the motion caused most of us to lose our lunch and dinner that day. The galley had served up roast pork and all the trimmings for lunch after which I then went down to the cabin. There, despite the roller coaster motion of the ship, I managed to fall asleep only waking when the call for dinner came. I went up but only sniffed at a cup of tea and the apple pudding. Even that was too much. Getting up as nonchalantly as possible, I strolled outside and tore off quickly for the 'confessionals'. Despite my haste I became aware that in almost every one was occupied. Fortunately, one was still vacant and I quickly entered. I was just in time to make my 'confession', that I was only a fair weather sailor after all.

The rain stopped but the wind became much stronger. Brian and I went up to the open deck for a breather and within seconds were both thoroughly soaked by the spray breaking over the bows. It seemed as if the waves were trying to knock us down while the wind tried to lick the insides out of us. Nevertheless, it was better than being below decks. Down there our sense of balance could become completely disoriented. One moment, as the ship plunged into a trough, one felt as light as a feather and almost levitated to the ceiling. The next moment, as the bows rose again, it felt as if we would follow our stomachs through the floor onto the next deck. Trying to walk about was even stranger. As the ship rose, it was impossible to move at all. You felt extremely heavy and stuck fast where you stood, permanently bolted to the deck. Then, as the ship dropped again you felt released from this immobility and able to step forward again; but only to take a few silly little mincing steps onto thin air or rush at breakneck speed toward the nearest wall.

Under such conditions, moving on stairways could become very hazardous. If descending as the ship was dropping you just floated for a while and then stumbled down them at a rate of knots. If you were trying to climb the stairs you couldn't move as the ship rose. Then, as it dropped once more you became almost weightless and your feet scrabbled to keep their place on the steps. Only in the few brief seconds between each of these phases could you could make any safe progress. Otherwise, it was necessary to hang on to something firm. Attempts to write letters were doomed to failure because of this variable gravity and before long nauseous feelings began to grow again.

This day in the South China Seas was one that would long be remembered. It was such a sudden contrast to the conditions we had been sailing in for the past two weeks.

The next morning conditions at sea had not improved so I skipped breakfast even though my stomach felt very sore and in need of something to work on. Up on deck, the open area on A deck forward was out of bounds while the seas were so rough. I went below again and lay on my bunk. Returning on deck for a breath of fresh air, the wind had lessened and the cloud had lifted. Visibility had also improved sufficiently for us to see a small tanker off on the starboard side that seemed to be making extremely heavy weather of the conditions. The sea was still pretty wild. One moment the tanker would ride the crest of a roller and then plunge into the trough with its propellers thrashing the air. For a while, all we could see would be the superstructure. Then the bows slowly rose up over the next roller and the whole ship was visible again. What it must have been like for the crew aboard that vessel was beyond our imagining.

Back in the mess hall, Brian had discovered that the NCO on his table came from Boscombe, the district to the east of Bournemouth town centre. He was in the 5th Royal Inniskilling Dragoon Guards, the tank regiment going to Korea to relieve the 8th Hussars. What impressed me most about him was how much he looked like Brian, as if he were from the same family. He had the same black wiry hair, same profile, lips and deep suntan but his eyes were grey while Brian's were brown.

When the first lunch sitting was called I thought it would be safe to go and have something to eat but I was wrong. Just the smell of food was enough to have me rushing off to 'confess' my weakness all over again.

After lunch, Brian, Alec and I went up on deck where a group of us started a singsong inspired by the weather and the state of our stomachs. A few of our amendments to the titles of familiar songs will suffice to convey the mood we were in—"It's A Grand Night For Spewing", "A Slow Spew To China", "All I Do Is Dream Of Spew The Whole Night Through" and "Show Me The Way To Spew Up." We then crawled back to the cabin to snatch some sleep. At 16:00 I had a couple of tea buns, as the catering staff genteelly called them, and nothing untoward happened. I considered it would be safe to go for dinner.

At dinner I managed some soup, roast lamb, peas and mashed potato, as well as two helpings of rice pudding, a glass of water, two rolls and an orange. My stomach was still somewhat undecided how to respond to all this, probably because I hadn't consulted it first to see if it was ready to start work after the beating it had taken. There was just the slightest feeling that it could still play up. Alec's stomach was not feeling too comfortable either. But my stomach decided to accept the food I had sent down, thank God. By the time I went down to the cabin all signs of seasickness had completely disappeared. I went to sleep recalling one joker's cure for seasickness. "Eat plenty of jam," he said. "It tastes the same coming up as it does going down." A terrible idea!

This morning, while the storm had almost blown itself out, a huge swell continued to roll the ship about. We were told that there would be shore leave in Hong Kong so we retired below to get the smoothing irons busy pressing our jungle greens in readiness. It seemed that the weather in Hong Kong would be milder than expected and our battledress would keep for another time. I felt in fighting trim again when I woke up and looking forward to setting foot on terra firma again. Our shore leave would evidently commence at 14:00 tomorrow.

The sea remained rough but when we commented on this to one of the deck hands he just laughed and said that storm had only been a breeze. Maybe it had been for him but it was our first experience of such awesome conditions. The sea was the colour of wet tarmac and still looked ominous. The horizon, normally a smooth line, was saw-toothed because of the big swell that was running and a never-ending stream of white horses galloped past the ship.

We were still running diagonally across the swell and the combination of pitch-and-toss and roll reduced the morning parade to a total farce. The wind was blowing so hard that we had to hold our berets in our hands, holding them out for badge inspection. The officer had the nerve to tell us they were not clean but in these conditions, they could become tarnished again within minutes of being polished. We quietly treated his comments with the derision they deserved. With the ever-present threat of a drenching from the spray if we stood too near the starboard side, we were then lined up in threes on the port side and put through some basic drill movements. The massively heaving deck had a dire effect on our ability to control our movements. Rather than looking like a platoon of disciplined fighting men, we resembled drunks on their way home after closing time.

At pay parade—the last on board ship—I received the grand sum of £1 with which to go ashore in Hong Kong. It was worth noting that in twelve days time I would complete the first year of national service and get a further seven shillings a week. After dinner, we would be able to change money into Hong Kong dollars.

A room inspection was announced so we went below to clean up our cabins. In the end, the room inspection never took place. Stripping to the waist, I went topside to stand by the rail and let the last of the storm winds blow over me. Taking some deep breaths, I seemed almost to draw the very essence of the storm deep inside. Goose flesh appeared over my chest, back and arms and for a few minutes I felt really toned up. Returning below, my upper body was suffused with a lovely warm glow.

Hong Kong

When reveille sounded, word went round that we were sailing past a Chinese fishing fleet. Sure enough, when we went on deck there were hundreds of battered-looking junks stretching as far as the eye could see. One wag reckoned it was the Chinese communist navy but they were just fishing boats. Side on to the swell, they bobbed about like so many corks and looked incredibly unstable with their low bows, high stern decks and huge, unwieldy, multi-stayed sails.

Not long after some big islands loomed up out of the slight mist. We also spotted a destroyer ahead that turned out to be American. There were mutters of "Where are our lads?" indicating that there was no love lost on American services by the average British squaddy, a sentiment I found difficult to understand. Probably it was because the Americans were too fond of making big, glossy films about how gallant and glamorous their troops were in action and how they always won every time. There was also jealousy perhaps about all the money they always seemed to have.

A Chinese junk

More islands loomed ahead. They had a similar craggy outline to those at Aden but were much higher and covered with vegetation. They certainly looked less austere. Low clouds, once more threatening rain, softened their appearance. More junks appeared and there were some smaller craft propelled with a single oar over the stern. Large, creamy jellyfish the size of dinner plates floated past in the light blue water.

The ship's course was altered a few degrees to port and a few moments later we were able to look into Hong Kong harbour. More American warships lay there at anchor but we could see no 'red dusters' anywhere. Numerous double-decker ferryboats were plying back and forth between Hong Kong Island and the Kowloon mainland. Eventually a couple of tugs came alongside and helped us into a dock, port side on, at a quayside on Kowloon. The MV *Georgic* appeared to be the largest ship in harbour at this time.

Victoria Island and the Hong Kong waterfront lay on the other side of the harbour. Modern-looking warehouses and large waterfront buildings lay along the quayside but the hillsides immediately behind presented a different image. They appeared to be covered with shantytowns, untidy heaps of buildings that might have just been thrown there. Higher up behind them another change occurred. Dotted among the trees and even up to the crest of the hills we spied many very luxurious buildings, multi storied, white and clean. The access roads up to them must have been tortuous, given the steepness of the hillsides.

As soon as the gangplanks were in place lithe Chinese dockworkers swarmed everywhere. Several cars drew alongside bringing the usual procession of officials. Orders came over the PA system for us to attend a special parade at which to collect leave passes and change our money into the local currency. By 13:30 all passengers and troops due to disembark at Hong Kong had left and we hurried below to change and go ashore.

Hong Kong shore leave

Our first impression was that this was by far the most civilised of all the places we had seen or visited on this voyage. The air was almost as clean as at sea and the drains and sewers were covered. The streets were broad and clean and double-decker buses provided public transport. There was the usual variety of shops as in Colombo and Singapore but bigger and cleaner.

For a while, we were content to just meander around and inspect the shops selling the usual items—jewellery, watches, clothes, books and such. We bartered for sweets and fruit and found the prices to be very cheap. I thought that if we called in here on the way home, it would be a good place to buy presents at these prices. All clothing seemed to be remarkably and perhaps, on the way home, I could even kit myself out with new civvy clothes if I saved enough money.

Some shops displayed the most glorious silk cheongsam, a traditional, figure-hugging style of dress worn by Chinese women that had a slit up one side of the skirt; the colours in the embroidery were incredibly rich. But these were not for everyday wear in the street. They were far too beautiful and special for that.

Most of the women we saw were small and looked very lithe, with figures that would make a corset manufacturer weep for lack of business and make those who had to wear them envious. Their posture was so graceful that we enjoyed watching them as they walked along and wished we had eyes in the back of our heads to take in more of this exotic feminine beauty. The most common item of dress was a calf-length version of the cheongsam, a plain figure-hugging sheath with no sleeves, a high collar and a side slit up to above the knee, just high enough to occasionally reveal frilly-edged underwear.

Really, it was rather unfair to allow us soldiers, suffering acutely from what we called the "Three Effs"—"fed up, frustrated (or f*cked up?) and far from home", to be exposed to such slinky provocation. It was just as well these women were not in the habit of emphasising their bosoms. There were some women who chose to wear western style clothes and they did so very gracefully. Poorer women, and those who spent most of their time on the sampans, wore a uniform black or blue-black jacket and trousers. To our eyes, they looked like pyjamas and did nothing for them or for us.

Everywhere we walked we were surrounded by crowds of kids pestering us for pennies—ten cents in their currency. They all had shaven heads and were really quite engaging, friendly and not at all annoying. Some of them offered to polish and shine our boots as a "free" service but no doubt they expected a donation when they had finished. They clung to our arms as they importuned for business.

As in Singapore, many goods were available that we had not seen because of wartime austerities. They were only just coming back into the shops at home. Boxes of chocolates and many varieties of biscuits and sweets were abundant at quite reasonable prices. There were also many American-style milk bars, recognisable as such because we had seen them in American films. We were duly impressed by the huge jukeboxes that held twenty-four records of the latest songs and jazz pieces.

On the island

In the afternoon, we decided to go over to Hong Kong Island. The ferries went from Kowloon Post Office square, which was also a major bus terminus. Access to the ferryboats lay beyond where the buses were parked and we found that the fare for us was only ten cents, a concession for servicemen. Once on Hong Kong Island we discovered that, while the waterfront itself was lined with tall office buildings, they concealed a more densely built up and crowded street scene than we had encountered in Kowloon. Stalls lined the streets and there were many beggars about, all very reminiscent of Singapore, except that the place was still somehow much cleaner and decidedly less smelly.

Double decker Hong Kong to Kowloon ferry

Public transport was provided by double decker trams and single-decker buses, the latter presumably for the longer trips or destinations up on the hillsides. On the trams, those wishing to travel first class went upstairs by a separate stairway each floor having its own conductor. Taxis were all of British make but the private cars were almost all American, which contrasted strongly with what we saw in all the other ports of call, where many of the latest British models were to be seen.

After having a cup of tea for the magnificent sum of seven pence, we went to see *"Lullaby of Broadway"* with Gene Nelson and Doris Day. This was as much an excuse to rest our aching feet as to taste civilised entertainment again, probably the last for a year. As in a theatre, the seats had to be booked. Since there were not three seats together we had to split up. My seat in the rear stalls cost me one shilling and sixpence. The cinema was much like those at home, only smaller, air-conditioned and with more comfortably upholstered seats.

The film was very enjoyable, much like *"Tea for Two"*, which had the same stars and equally full of good songs. We were able to listen to the original American soundtrack while Chinese subtitles were projected onto a smaller screen below the main one, a neat way to do things. Trailers (promos) told us that an upcoming attraction would be *"Captain Horatio Hornblower RN"*. I wondered how the words 'landlubber', 'seadog', 'belay there', 'cat-o-nine-tails', 'keel-haul', 'bosun' and 'midshipman' would be translated into Chinese!

Outside once more, we noticed a huge billboard revealing that there were about seven or eight large cinemas in Hong Kong, all showing the latest releases and all having a change of programme every two or three days. *"A Streetcar Named Desire"* was showing at one of them.

On the way back to the ferry we passed the Cheerio Services Club and went in to see what was happening. We inspected the gift shop, watched the dancing for a while and then ordered egg and chips and a cup of coffee. It seemed that the Wiltshire Regiment was here in Hong Kong but we saw none of the chaps who joined up with us twelve months ago and who had been posted to that regiment.

As we crossed back to Kowloon, Hong Kong became a blaze of light. Neon signs in all shapes and colours covered the waterfront buildings, their lights reflecting in the waters of the harbour. High up on the hill the big mansions and tower blocks dotted the darkness with patches of brilliance connected by strings of fairy lights from the street lamps. Back on board we found we had mail from home, which was very welcome.

Off to War

It was good to sleep in a bunk that wasn't heaving about all over the place but I still woke feeling tired. Up on deck, the sky was clear and the view across to Hong Kong Island was sharper than it had been yesterday. A fleet of small sampans had gathered along the starboard side each containing an elderly woman dressed in the ubiquitous black uniform of loose pants and a high necked loose jacket. Almost invariably, they were holding a small baby while numerous other small children swarmed about her. One of these would be begging for money or food, holding out a net on the end of a pole to catch anything tossed down to them.

The whole scene looked rather desperate, especially when all they ever got were pennies and old bread rolls. One sampan unwittingly ventured too near the galley portholes and was showered with a bucketful of vegetable peelings that provoked a great wail of protest. Another sampan owner dared to tie his craft to the gangway hanging over the side of the ship. Even though it was not lowered far enough to be in use, one venturesome soul actually climbed up onto it. When a ship's officers spotted this 'invasion', he ordered that a hose be brought and turned on him. He got a shower and we had a laugh at the unfortunate fellow's expense.

Over on the dockside, we watched drafts for the North Staffordshire Regiment, the Middlesex Regiment, the Royal Army Service Corps and the Royal Artillery disembark. Having decided there was little of interest left to watch, I went below to write letters and read the newspapers my brother had sent to me. By noon we had cast off, been tugged out into the harbour and were once more under way. By the time the second lunch session was finished Hong Kong was far behind us. Pusan, South Korea, was our next stop in three days time. Strangely enough, the pilot boat was still with us, tied up alongside and bouncing along beside us. Unlike the motor launches that had brought pilots out at other ports, this was only a sailing boat. The crew was sitting in it, huddled uncomfortably in their waterproofs against the spray that was sent flying over them.

The news over the PA system told us that the truce talks at Panmunjom were nearing finality. If so, how would it affect us? Would we still join the battalion in Korea and be part of some kind of peacekeeping force, or be sent back to Malaya, or Egypt, or even back home? Only time would provide the answer to that. Then someone came to tell us that according to a notice on the Detail Board our draft would now certainly disembark at Pusan, not Kure in Japan, as we had once thought. There was no information about the thing which interested us most—how soon it would be before we were sent north to the sharp end? Another order instructed us to return to our old battle-dress uniforms tomorrow but to remain in shirtsleeve order, a sure sign we were entering a colder climatic zone. We were also told to have a pullover, a blanket and our greatcoats handy for when we arrived in Pusan. That sounded ominous!

Porridge, bacon and eggs were the menu for breakfast this morning which was much appreciated. The weather had definitely become colder so the change back to battledress was timely. One chap had all his hair cut off—as had happened back in Brecon—and started a debate as to whether this was a good idea or not. I decided it was. It would certainly deter lice if nothing else. One 'ancient' regular we picked up in Hong Kong told us that 'long hairs' usually managed to catch lice while on active service.

The wind rose again, the sky became overcast and the seas quite rough but it remained as fascinating as ever. We were quite alone on this ocean, not another vessel of any kind in sight, although there was a rumour that we might pick up a naval escort. Another rumour going the rounds was that all allied troops were leaving Japan and being based in Pusan. That would be a disappointment if true. I was hoping that, somehow, there might be a chance to visit Japan, perhaps on leave before returning home.

Land appeared on the starboard bow about 15:00. At first I was puzzled where it could be. Then, a little later, the penny dropped. This must have been Formosa (Taiwan), Chiang Kai-Chek's Chinese Nationalist fortress. So Red China couldn't have been too far away on the port side. I noticed that we kept quite close to the Formosan coast, probably no further out than two or three miles.

My latest reading was *"Moonlight in Gascony"* by Anne-Marie Walters, a vividly written story about the French Resistance during WWII. There was one moment when, recalling where I was, where I was going and why, I realised that this book was written before I had reached my teens and certainly too young to be called up to fight. Now, almost as soon as that war ended and I had become of military call-up age, here was another war to which I could be sent. It seemed so crazy—and in one respect disappointing—to find that the world had not yet had enough of war. However, at the same time there was a sense in which I was finding it all a huge adventure.

We had one more day of this 'cruise' left. It would seem strange to stand on dry land and see the same view for days and weeks on end. No doubt we would get used to it. The news from the front line was not so good. The fighting had become more intense and progress at the truce talks had stalled again. It seemed to be a case of two steps forward and one step back over and over again but exactly who was responsible for this silly diplomatic dance was never clear. The Commonwealth Division had been getting a quite intensive battering by the Chinese and a chap named Bill Speakman was expected to get a VC for something he had done a month or so ago. I wished we could get more detail about what was going on. I reckoned that the folk back home knew more about it than we did.

Great confusion arose when orders came to collect our kit bags and sleeping rolls from the ships hold. Everyone got in everyone else's way until a sergeant arrived to restore some sort of order but not before I got a push that introduced my head, smartly and painfully, to a metal beam that was part of a stairway. Back in our cabin, we tried to sort out our kit and get our tropical gear ready to return to the stores before disembarkation. This created great problems in the very cramped confines of our cabin.

Then an announcement told us that there would be a special ships inspection of the cabins at 0930 which put us in a real lather. It was a hell of a job to clean the cabin. With the four of us, our eight kit bags, our packs and four large bed rolls all taking up so much space, we were faced with a major logistical problem to get everything sorted out, repacked and stowed away tidily in time. Then the Sergeant came by and put me on a detail to clean out the washroom, polish the taps and clean out the latrines in time for the same inspection. That gave the other three chaps a little more room for manoeuvre.

Yet another announcement told us that there was to be a rigid blackout that night; no lights were to show from portholes or through doorways. This would be great fun, especially if we wanted to go up on deck. With no outside lights along the deck, it would be pitch black. The weather had turned windy, wet and cold again, a rather miserable change after those few weeks in the tropics. That blow in the South China Sea had not really been sufficient to inure us to colder conditions.

The ship must have picked up speed and we were now expected to reach Pusan early tomorrow morning. Evidently, after dropping us, it would pick up the 8th Irish Hussars, who are being relieved by the Inniskilling Dragoon Guards, and leave smartly for Kure. The Hussars were supposed to be celebrating Christmas in Singapore. They may just about make it.

That afternoon, sea kitbags were issued in which to pack our tropical gear. We were to hand them in at No.6 Hold by 16:30. While we were busy doing this, yet another order came to tell us that the MO was coming by to conduct FFI inspections in our cabins for which we would be required to strip completely. When he finally arrived, he examined us between our fingers and toes, under our armpits, looked through our hair—including that in our 'nether regions' and finally asked if we felt quite fit. A silly question really. We were suddenly sorely tempted to suddenly feel faint, or groan most miserably. All I said was that I seemed to feel eternally tired and just wanted to sleep. He moved on.

We put our watches forward another half an hour that night. They should have been put forward the same amount yesterday night but no one told us. This now put us nine hours ahead of GMT. Everyone was in a panic this morning when we found ourselves short of half an hour to get all our chores done. Details of our postal address in Korea appeared on the notice board:

Number, Rank, Surname, First initial.
1st Bn. Welch Regt. Draft—DAHZD
Korea. BAPO 3 (British Army Post Office 3)

Since we left Hong Kong, I was concerned whether the letters I had been writing would reach home in time for Christmas. Buying stamps and getting them posted had never been a straightforward business on board ship.

The Corporal crashed through the door at 07:00 with a new variation to the traditional wake up call,—"Rise and shine; the sun will scorch your eyeballs". We heaved ourselves up, stared at him myopically, muttered, "What?", and sank back into our bunks again to snatch another half an hour's shuteye. We finally got up when the first breakfast call sounded.

Up on deck the sea was very calm and a deep, icy blue. The sky possessed a crystalline clarity, but it was also bloody cold. We returned below to put on our 'winter woollies'. These consisted of a strange upper garment that reached down to our knees. It had a polo neck and short sleeves. The pants that went with them required holding up with braces, the result being that we looked more like people going for a bathe in the sea at Brighton in the days of Queen Victoria. But they were warm. Exasperatingly, in order to get them out, we had to dive back into our carefully packed kit bags, pull the required gear out and then repack the kitbags again, all this in the cramped confines of our cabin. Confusion reigned supreme once more.

The order came to strip beds, bundle bedding up in lots of ten and then take them to one of the holds. We walked along an endless maze of corridors and stairways, playing a kind of 'follow my leader'. We tangled with fatigue parties on scrubbing and sweeping details and actually did become thoroughly lost in the bowels of the ship. It was a grand case of "Don't follow me—I'm lost." However, everything was sorted in the end.

Up on deck once more, the coast of Korea was visible: an irregular, bare, brown, rocky mass spread along the horizon. I stood in silence and watched it as we drew nearer. So, eleven months after first being told that we were to be sent here, we had finally arrived.

Apparently, the truce talks were still deadlocked. The announcement that " . . . a suitable way to keep the peace, once settled, can't be found" was too cynical for words. It seemed that men with responsibility for determining how things are run in the world could only bicker and disagree like so many school kids. Would they ever grow up and leave the schoolyard mentality behind? It was now inevitable that we would join the battalion in the front line.

We were supposed to have docked in Pusan by 14:00 but at 13:30 we were still sailing along the coast. It looked a very rough, craggy land, the cloud shadows lending it a strangely mottled appearance. We were also sailing at 'dead slow ahead' because there were minefields about, or so yet another rumour had us believe. Where did these keep coming from?

Just before lunch, I joined a couple of chaps in my draft who were leaning on the port rail and staring at the coast. For a while we were silent, keeping our thoughts to ourselves, and then one of them turned and said, "You know, I don't think I shall ever leave that land. I only hope that, when I get my number, it is instantaneous." No one responded but in my mind's eye I recalled that moment back at St Andrews' Cathedral in Singapore when, as I was about to walk through the main doors the organist began to play that hymn. To restore some balance to the mood that had just been generated, I said, "Well, I've got a very strong feeling that I'm going to be all right. There is more in store for me before I leave this world than a plot of land here." I began to wonder if one's personal philosophy, beliefs and deeper expectations determined how one would come through a prolonged proximity to the kind of dangers we were soon to face. Was it fate's ironic way, that those with fiancées, good prospects, or even just extremely good natures, would be the ones with least prospect of surviving, while those with nothing clear cut about their future, those like Brian and myself, would come through unscathed?

I recalled the priest in Thornton Wilder's book, *"The Bridge of San Luis Rey"*, saying that one's life would end just after a really great and difficult crisis has been weathered, bringing with it a very clear change of mind and character. Maybe such an experience did indeed precede everyone's death but if that was so, by its very nature, it had to remain totally unknown until it actually happened. How was I to know whether such a moment would come for me while I was here? Deciding that it was not possible to know, the feeling remained strong within me that I would not die here in Korea.

5

WELCOME TO KOREA

1st December–8th December 1951

First Impressions

Just before 1500, I went on deck again to find that the ship was now sailing toward the coast. Ahead lay a big inlet and on either side many ships lay at anchor, both merchant and naval. It took some time to locate Pusan itself nestling at the head of the harbour. It seemed to be the same colour as the hills behind it and lay low at the base of the mountains.

The hills and small islands on the port side were clearly silhouetted against the glare of the sun. Bare mountainous cliffs towered over the sea, while along the top a line of trees resembled a strange procession of gaunt figures. The strata were very distinct, alternate bands of hard and soft rock forming the huge crags and gentler slopes between. Gaunt, barren ridges gave way to forested slopes while lower still were a few lush green fields; it was a weird land. As the sun began to set, the line of trees on top of the cliff became more sharply silhouetted and now looked, for all the world, like a scene from Gulliver's Travels; Lilliputians swarming all over poor old Gulliver's paunch as they tied him down. It was an odd association.

Ahead on the starboard side lay a rocky pinnacle; it rose sheer out of the water. Halfway up, a platform bore a few white buildings and a lighthouse. They stood out sharply against the ochre-coloured cliffs behind.

The ship stopped and the anchors were dropped. Were we waiting for the pilot to come out, or a dockside berth to become free? This was a signal for several boatloads of children to row out from the shore. They were dressed in a motley assortment of army gear as well as what looked like more traditional clothing.

An icy bite in the wind drove us below to get our windproof combat jackets. On deck once more, we were in time to see an old tug bring the pilot and a heap of 'brass' alongside. It also brought some mail but only three of our draft received anything.

The anchors were raised just after 16:00 and we began to move up the waterway towards the docks once more. As we passed the island with the lighthouse, I saw that it had actually been built on the first of a line of craggy pinnacles of rock. Out at sea they had lined up one behind the other to look like one island. The top of the foremost crag had been entirely removed to provide the platform for the buildings; it must have involved quite a feat of engineering.

Another boat pulled alongside bringing more mail. This time Alec, who had so far received no mail from home since we left England, had a letter postmarked 'Shaftesbury, Dorset, 31st October 1951'. He must have given his folk the final postal address.

The 'Skins' were informed over the PA system that they would not disembark until tomorrow but there was no indication when we would disembark. Maybe we would be spending another night on board sleeping in our bedding rolls on those very comfortable mattresses. Then another message over the PA system confirmed this. In the morning we would be moved off to a transit camp where we would stay for three days before moving up to the front. That struck me as rather odd. After five weeks on an ocean cruise, we were far from fit and I hadn't seen or touched a wireless set in three months. We certainly needed a few route marches and some drill sessions to limber us up again. If the truth were told, we had probably become quite soft.

We never reached the docks. We just moved further up the harbour and dropped anchor again and as expected, we enjoyed one more night of comfort. Our sleeping bags proved very efficient—too efficient in fact—and all four of us became overheated in the stuffiness of the cabin. We spent a restless night gradually removing all our clothing to end up finally sleeping naked. Outside on deck it would have been bitterly cold.

By 11:00 next morning the ship had moved in to the quayside and tied up. Korean kids were still alongside in their boats begging for food. Many US cargo ships were at anchor out in the harbour:—*Jericho Victory, Ethiopian Victory, Hobart Victory, Warwick Victory, Blue Grass State* and so on. There were three hospital ships as well, two American and the *Jutlandia* from Denmark.

American MPs swarmed all over the place. One who really drew my attention was a huge African American in an impeccable uniform, a shiny white helmet and a huge revolver in a huge leather holster; definitely not someone to argue with. There were also some of our chaps around and one, an officer in the Royal Engineers, was energetically ordering a gang of Korean dock workers around.

Pusan itself did not appear to have sustained much damage from the war but huge changes must have occurred through becoming a military staging post. It didn't look a particularly attractive place though, just a motley sprawl of brown houses over brown rocks that were difficult to distinguish from the brown hillside. A bluish haze hung over everything, presumably smoke from cooking fires in the houses.

56th US Army Band on Pusan docks

Just after lunch, the 'Skins' baggage party went ashore. Since the whole battalion had to disembark, it was anyone's guess how long it would take before our turn came. Two bands, one from the Republic of Korea Navy and the other an all black band from the 56th US Army, marched onto the quay to offer a musical reception. I was interested to see those sousaphones so unique to American bands. In addition to the traditional drums, brass and woodwind instruments there were saxophone players. ROK Navy band also had sousaphones, probably from having been modelled on the US bands. To our delight, the air was soon filled with sounds of big band swing, jive and boogie-woogie melodies.

It was hard to imagine a British army band letting rip with "When The Saints Go Marching In" with quite such verve.

Eventually the national anthems of Korea and Great Britain were played and a group of very pretty Korean girls in traditional dress came forward to greet the ship's captain and the CO of the "Skins", presenting them with bouquets of flowers and kisses. After a few more lively tunes including, much to my surprise, a vigorous rendition of the Eton Boating Song from the ROK Navy Band, both bands marched off.

At 14:00, the Welch Regiment draft was told to stand by to disembark, so we rushed to 'pack up and saddle up' as the Yanks would say. Finally ordered to the gangway, we made our way ashore. US troop-movement police directed us to a row of big American trucks into which we threw our kitbags and clambered up after them. With much starting and stopping, bumping, jerking and tossing about, we finally got off the docks and into the town.

Our observations about Pusan from the ship had been pretty accurate. It was a smoky, messy place, teeming with US and Korean servicemen and revoltingly smelly. Someone said the stink was because it was a Korean custom to spread the product of their 'Number 2s' on the garden as fertiliser. A case of "Waste not, want not—but gorblimey, stink a lot!"

Pusan and Seaforth camp

Military traffic cops stood at road junctions using whistles and the most casually disdainful arm movements to control traffic that seldom took much notice anyway. The rule of the road here was 'Keep right'. It took us some time to get used to it even though we were not driving. The American influence again.

Our route took us past several servicemen's canteens and cinemas. The sound tracks of the films could be heard outside over the roar of the traffic and that probably meant that those inside watching the film could hear the passing traffic outside. What they may actually have heard of the sound track could only be imagined. Everything was so frantic, so noisy and everyone seemed in such a rush.

Eventually, after bumping over dusty white roads, up and down hills, over bridges, past paddy fields and threshing yards and a USAAF airfield we reached Seaforth Camp, the British Commonwealth Transit

Camp. We scrambled out with our gear, were fallen in, marched off to the tent lines, allocated to one of them, told to grab our cutlery and mugs and then marched off to the mess tent for dinner. The contrast with the food we had on the *Georgic* could not have been greater. Tinned meat, carrots, beans and dehydrated spuds were followed by tinned fruit and plum duff with condensed milk. It actually tasted better than expected and tins of butter and jam were on every table. There was certainly plenty of everything and no reason to get up feeling hungry.

These tents had wooden frames with wooden doors and floors (like those later seen in M.A.S.H., the TV series set in Korea). The lower eighteen inches of the walls were of corrugated iron that gave them more substance. There were even two electric sockets for light-bulbs, an unexpected luxury. Two Koreans were fitting up a petrol-burning stove which, like the tents, was also made in America. The Americans had provided everything it seemed, even the food but not cigarettes. The NAAFI only stocked British brands of cigarettes and sweets.

On my way back to the tent, I met a chap last seen on the signals course in Harwich. We were both surprised to see each other here. At that time he had been intended for the Devonshire Regiment but ended up being allocated to the Glosters. A month later he was out of England to finally end up here in Korea three months ago. He was lucky that it took so long since he also missed being with that battalion last April during the fateful Battle of the Imjin. He told me that others who had been on the course with us were with the Welch Regiment up in a notorious region on the western end of the front line to the north of Seoul. He reckoned we would be moved up there pretty soon but would probably have two weeks of refresher training and allowed to acclimatise before being committed to full service at the 'sharp end'.

Called out on parade, we marched off to the stores to each collect a camp bed and five blankets. When we returned, there was much competition to get a bed space near the fire. The beds proved quite vicious to erect and mine managed to take a small lump out of one of my fingers in the process. We finally got ourselves organised and pretty cosy; the only thing lacking was a radio with which to catch up on local and world news.

Before it got dark we had a look round the camp. It had been sited at the base of a hill on paddy fields once cultivated for rice. Ditches had been dug and bridges built over streams, presumably with the help of the Korean labourers who swarmed everywhere and obviously employed to do the labouring work. Korean women worked in the canteen to serve the meals. Probably many of them were civil war refugees who had been 'cleared' as friendly and given work to keep them out of the way. We tended to forget that the Korean war really was a civil war.

Our first official visitor was the camp RSM. He came by to give us a pep talk and outline what sort of behaviour would constitute offences and the punishments they would incur. He confirmed the return address to be put on mail we sent home and said that if that address was used by our friends and family, mail would reach us wherever we were. One wag quietly commented, "Even in Heaven, Sarge?" but it drew no response from him. Just to let us know we were really back in the army and not on a break from a cruise on 'Daddy's big ocean yacht' called the MV *Georgic*, he outlined details concerning parades, guard and fire picket duties and times of meals. Then, just to rub it in, he told us we were confined to barracks until our programme was organised.

Our pay would be in the form of a paper currency—British Armed Forces Special Vouchers, popularly called 'BAFs', in units ranging from three pence to one pound. They would only be accepted in Commonwealth Division canteens and were not to be given to any Yanks. He refused to be drawn on any matter concerning how long we would be here, or whether we were to go north next Tuesday. Finally, he said that there was a film show in a tent near the NAAFI that we could go to if we wished and bade us goodnight.

The camp cinema was in a huge tent and the film that evening was a Western, *"Best of the Badmen,"* starring Robert Ryan. Apart from the fact that the projector kept fouling up and the film breaking, it was quite enjoyable, especially when in saloon scenes a barmaid appeared in a very low cut gown. This provoked howls of appreciation from a clearly sex-starved section of the all-male audience.

It was an unreal sort of experience to emerge from seeing a film that contained scenes of those Western style trains with their cowcatchers and wailing sirens and then hear the very same sound reaching us from the direction of Pusan. Once we noticed the sound, we seemed to hear it all the time as a kind of background music.

There was much movement on the nearby airfield and I wondered where all the planes that were landing and taking off were coming from and going to. It was all such a dramatic change from the existence we had 'enjoyed' for the past month yet, at the same time, because of American films we had seen in the past, it all seemed vaguely familiar.

We had to pinch ourselves to realise we were not coming out of a cinema in an English town but really were here in Korea at last. I was quite bemused by it all. It was as if I had just been born and was having difficulty taking in and making sense of a totally new and separate existence in a strange new environment.

A couple of chaps went over to the store to collect a five-gallon can of petrol so that the stove could be started. If petrol could be used for space heating like this, there was clearly no shortage of it here. We placed a bucket of water on top to heat up overnight to have some warm shaving water in the morning. So, while it might have seemed a daunting prospect to be in a tent at a very cold time of year, we would sleep warmly enough. We had all drawn sleeping bags and five blankets from the stores.

For a while both Alecs, Brian and myself got into quite a deep discussion wondering if our present circumstances bore any comparison with those of the chaps who went off to fight in the last war. Before they actually went up to the front, they would have been keenly aware of the urgency of what they were involved in. The enemy they would face represented a very immediate danger to the country and their homes and family and there was a great need to restore peace and sanity in the world, especially in Europe which was so close to home.

However, here in Korea it was difficult to find or feel the same sense of importance or urgency. The reasons why we were here were not at all clear to us. Very few were interested in domestic politics let alone international politics and could not see this conflict in Korea as being much more than a local civil war. It did not directly threaten our homes, our families or our country. It seemed rather petty and unnecessary to put us into the same kind of dangers that our fathers or elder brothers had faced just a few years ago for no easily understandable reason or cause. It was very difficult to know how to relate to it all other than with a parody of the old saying that went, "Ours not to question why, just to do—and maybe die." We had been sent here to fight by our 'leaders' and maybe we would fight, should the occasion arise, until those leaders, or those 'others' with power and influence, came to see how senseless it all was.

Another aspect of our situation that bothered some of us was the fact that we were only doing our national service. We were not regular soldiers who had signed on with a clear understanding that the possibility of seeing active service was part of the job they had undertaken to do. Neither were we paid as much as regulars, yet here in Korea we would be required to run exactly the same risks, do much the same kind of work and for only half the pay. It seemed a very cheap way to raise an army to meet a so called international commitment. But this line of thinking would get us nowhere so we decide to put it to one side.

Were we the only ones in the tent thinking these thoughts I wondered? Many of the others were talking about 'bad men' and 'murderers', a conversation seemingly inspired by the film we had seen and the fact that one of our number was named Ryan. He was being unmercifully kidded about it. The only problem was that they were all sitting on my bed and I had to ask them to move off before getting into it and 'becoming myself'. This reminded me of our corporal in the barrack room at Whittington Barracks who once said to me, "I always look forward to getting to bed. Then I cease to be a number and become myself for a few hours."

It was Monday morning and we overslept reveille by half an hour—in a new camp too! We were very glad of that bucket of warm water on the stove. Using helmets as basins, we climbed back into our beds to shave in comfort. It was certainly better than going out into an icy cold morning to do it. The breakfast call came at 07:30 and we trooped off to find a very sumptuous meal waiting for us; shredded wheat and warm sweet milk—the first time this had been on offer since we joined up—followed by boiled bacon, scrambled egg, bread, butter, jam and tea. It went down extremely well.

By the time we had returned to our tent and tidied it up the sun was high, the sky was clear and it was warm enough to take our jumpers off and bathe in the sun's warmth. It seemed we would only need our jumpers first thing in the morning and in the evening as soon as the sun started to go down. A sergeant came by, told us to grab our British army issued duffle-coats and be ready to take them to the stores where we would exchange them for much warmer, fur-lined parkas.

There was also talk that commando style boots with rubber soles and a heavy tread would be issued. They would certainly be more waterproof than our ammunition boots. We were still wearing the same old things issued to us months ago for English conditions but even then, on that hike across the mountains in North Wales, I had found out that they were not waterproof. After hanging about for over fifteen minutes, we were informed that the duffle-coat–parka exchange would take place later. There was yet another FFI inspection which I passed without problem but this MO didn't bother to ask us if we were feeling fit.

Mail arrived and someone had news that the government was considering increasing national service to three years. This provoked tremendous discussion and argument. Comments of a nature that MPs back in Westminster would not have liked to hear flew around the tent. The government must have been desperate to find enough troops to man all the stations where Britain still had obligations. However, there was no way of knowing if this story was, or was not, true. And there was no news of this in either of the news-papers available here.

The four page British paper, the "Korean Base Gazette", gave a brief account of the latest news and UK sports results. The American paper, patriotically name "The Stars & Stripes", was sixteen pages and had good coverage of the news we were interested in. But their sports news meant little to us. Just as Americans were not interested in soccer or cricket we were not interested in gridiron football, or baseball, or basketball.

'Old hands' circulated stories about conditions up on the front line and said that British losses were very small; any of our chaps who were unfortunate enough to get taken prisoner were generally being well treated. I wondered how on earth they knew that. There were other stories about Chinese 'Banshee style' attacks which were pretty suicidal, even though the odds were usually 100 to 1 in their favour. They had overrun a King's Shropshire Light Infantry (KSLI) position this way and fourteen of our chaps were killed. Such attacks were the ones to be wary of, times when it would be wise to run like hell if necessary.

It seemed that the Chinese only won when they used crushing odds like that. They even advanced through their own shell fire to gain the advantage of surprise. There were tales that only the first wave carried weapons. Those that followed carried extra ammunition and would pick up the weapons of their dead comrades and carry on. What incredible cynicism this indicated on the part of the Chinese commanders. We all wondered how they persuaded their men to do this. Were they drugged up to the eyeballs or just a lot of zombies?

While the Glosters had been practically annihilated a few months ago, it had cost the Chinese dearly to get that victory. Their offensive lost momentum, objectives were not reached, casualties were high and the UN forces had time to plug gaps in their lines. And all because the Glosters had held out so stubbornly for so long. Apparently, when the odds were nearer 6 to 1 our troops were more than a match for the Chinese.

We heard more talk about Bill Speakman, the chap who was up for a Victoria Cross for his performance in a battle in late October or early November. He was with the King's Own Scottish Borderers (KOSB) when they were holding a position up north around a place called The Hinge, a little to the west of the Imjin where it flowed down from the north. The story we heard was that he had taken a dram or two of some alcoholic refreshment before things started to get warm. In a mellow state of mind, he got really pissed off when his drinking was interrupted and a lot of his mates started to get wounded. It was proving difficult to get these wounded out so he finally lost his cool, grabbed a box of grenades and went outside to throw them at the Chinese as if they were explosive cricket balls.

Returning for more grenades and a few other chaps, he went back out again and carried on the fight. If that account were half true it would have been a formidable sight for both his mates and for the Chinese but, whatever the truth may have been, according to the report his extraordinary action bought enough time for the wounded to be got away. Although he was wounded in the leg he also got out safely.

It has been said that old soldiers never lie but neither do they always tell the plain truth. We were quite aware of how they liked to polish up their stories to impress 'rookies' so we had learned to take these stories with a pinch of salt, including this one about Bill Speakman and the drink. But it did appear that he did not have a good record for behaviour, which may have been why he was posted out of the Black Watch to the KOSB and ended up in Korea. It was difficult to get to the truth behind these stories. Anyway, on this occasion his behaviour was such that it merited his being cited to receive a VC and medals don't get more distinguished than that.

Speakman was flown back to Korea from Japan on 30th December 1951 to receive the ribbon from General Ridgeway, the UN commander. He received the medal itself from the Queen in an investiture at Buckingham Palace on 27th February 1952.

For some reason I became aware just how much at peace with things I was now feeling. Eighteen months ago I had been enduring intense pangs of love-sickness of the sort that Alec Fulcher was now experiencing for his girl back in Shaftesbury. I now felt much older, more so possibly than if I had stayed in 'civvy-street'. Now, out in the world, I was having 'the corners knocked off' as the saying went. Probably this feeling was natural considering all that I had seen and experienced since being called up.

I recalled the first full parade we had been on at Bulford Camp. It was a church parade where we had marched off behind a military band to the garrison church. A strange sense had come over me that we were reincarnations of Roman soldiers who had once marched across these very plains two thousand years before. Turning my head slightly toward the chap marching beside me I quietly muttered, "Quo vadis?"(Latin for 'where are we going?') Inevitably, his reply was "Wot?" But the sense of timelessness remained. The unreality of the situation I experienced then came upon me again here in Korea and it was a blessedly peaceful moment. Until some loud mouthed git disturbed me with, "Wot ya dreaming about now, Lofty?"

Lunch was sensational—turkey, tinned peas and carrots, followed by fruit pudding. The service was not quite as refined as it had been on the *Georgic* but this kind of food was equally enjoyable. We reckoned that it must have come from either the United States or Australia. But turkey! And it wasn't even Christmas yet. In the past, at home we had only ever had poultry of any kind for Christmas Day lunch. Even during the war my father seemed to know someone among his rural customers who had been able to supply him with a chicken. Poultry had been very much a once-a-year treat for us but here it was becoming a more frequent part of our diet.

My supply of airmail writing paper and envelopes was running out. The only option left, since the NAAFI had none for sale, was to use the Forces Letter Forms which would be delivered post free if "On active service" was written where the stamp normally went. However, at the rate I had been going, one of my usual letters would probably require several forms. A numbering system would have to be used for each individual air mail form that I used so that, when they were delivered, they could be opened and read in the correct sequence. I had already been numbering my letters so that my parents would know if one failed to arrive. Probably all I needed to do was add a letter behind the number to indicate how many forces letter forms were part of the same letter. The next time I went to the camp post office I took a good fistful of these pale brown forms.

At pay parade we received fifteen shillings worth of BAFs and were then marched off to the armourer's stores to draw rifles. They were the same old No. 4 Lee-Enfield 303s we had back in Britain and were very dirty. The armourer told us they had been 'salvaged' from the 'Glorious Glosters', so it felt appropriate for us to have them. The parade, and cleaning those rifles, took up most of the afternoon. Then it was time for dinner.

After we had eaten we at last handed in our duffle coats and collected the new parkas. These were beautifully made and very luxurious. Deep olive green on the outside they were snug and had roomy lined hoods. Evidently these had come courtesy of the Canadian government. We would probably be very glad of them because stories had circulated that winter temperatures could drop to around zero Fahrenheit up north, well below freezing point. We also drew wrist mittens, two extra pairs of socks and an inner sleeping bag. The kit we were now getting was very good and just in time too. As we discovered later, it was of much higher quality than that issued to our chaps who were here from the beginning of the war. We wore the parkas to the cinema for warmth while watching that evening's film—*"The Frogmen".*

Guard and fire picket duties were free of the usual bull that went with them back in Britain. Our boots and badges still had to be shined up but the emphasis was really on keeping a sharp eye out for intruders and trespassers. The order of the day was that if a challenge was not answered correctly "Shoot first and ask questions after". Of course, if anyone were shot there would be an enquiry which might give cause for concern, even if the guard were exonerated. The thought of actually being in a position where we might have to shoot at someone was a little difficult to take in.

An order came to be ready to move out at half an hour's notice any time after 0600 tomorrow morning. Provided the line hadn't been sabotaged again, we would be going by train to join the battalion at A Echelon which was some three miles behind the front lines. We would stay there for two weeks of refresher training before going up to front line positions. This news put everyone in a great tiz-woz again as they set to getting their gear ready.

Last night, the stove went out and we discovered just how efficient our sleeping bags were. It was so cold when the reveille bugle sounded that we stayed put until just before the time to go for breakfast. We had stayed up into the wee hour discussing, for the umpteenth time, what we thought we were doing here in Korea. As before, no one had any clear ideas about this and by the time the subject began to lose interest the stove had started to go down. We refuelled it but failed to put in enough to last the rest of the night.

For the next hour or so after breakfast, we finished packing our kit, then lounged around playing cards or sleeping until called out on parade and taken for a stiff march up the hill and back. Presumably this was the beginning of the process of licking us back into shape again. The lower slopes of the hillside were intensively terraced and many were turning green with young rice plant shoots. Small houses dotted the hillside. They were built around three sides of a beaten earth yard and surrounded by clumps of poplars and beeches. Higher up the slopes burial mounds had been built on small areas levelled out of the hillside. Most were quite simple but others were neatly defined with borders of stones or small bushes.

The view from the top of the hill was spectacular. Pusan harbour was clearly visible and seemed even more full of shipping than when we arrived. We also overlooked the airfield. For a while, we watched huge transport aircraft, fighter bombers and jet fighters continually circle, land and take off. We were already used to the non-stop roar of all this activity.

Having been marched to the top of the hill, the sergeant, like the Grand Old Duke of York, marched us back down again, returning us to camp in time for lunch of cold meat and salad followed by tinned peaches, apricots and pears. The colour sergeant came by to tell us that, at 1800 tomorrow, we would be leaving for the docks to board a ship that would take us round to Inchon on the west coast, about eighteen miles from Seoul. Everyone below the rank of sergeant would travel in one of the holds. So much for a train ride north. Perhaps the line had been sabotaged after all. That was the trouble with a civil war: you could never tell if the local people were on your side or the enemy's.

Much later, I learned that there were a very substantial number of communist troops and sympathisers in the northeast mountains of South Korea. Many had been cut off by the success of the Inchon landing where the amphibious landing had gone ashore in September 1950 allowing the UN forces to retake Seoul, cut the supply route to the North Korean troops and throw them into complete disarray. It was the astounding success of this operation that had probably isolated many of the communist guerillas. They were now very active committing acts of sabotage to hinder the allied war effort and a huge campaign had been initiated to clear them out.

The Inchon landing and afterwards

I remembered reading about the Inchon landing at the time and thinking what a master-stroke that had been to relieve the pressure on UN forces bottled up around Pusan. As a result, during the winter of 1950-51 the UN forces recaptured South Korea and pushed on into North Korea, almost to the border with China. I had also read how General Douglas McArthur, at that time the UN Commander, had wanted to pursue the North Korean army as far as it took, even into China, to demolish them as a force and to reunify the whole Korean peninsula. But this caused him to butt heads with President Truman. He was dismissed and replaced by General Van Fleet. Even top generals were required to take orders, or else.

The Chinese, regarding MacArthur's aim as a threat to their borders, threw in an army of so called "People's Volunteers" to support the North Koreans. The result was a long, bitterly cold withdrawal by the UN forces as the communists re-took North Korea. According to South Korean intelligence, this so called People's Volunteer Army included some crack regiments of the Chinese Red Army which had been present in North Korea for quite some time.

In April 1951 the Chinese mounted a huge Spring Offensive to drive south and recapture Seoul. By this time the Commonwealth Division was in place below the traditional southward invasion route that lay down the Samichon River valley and across the Imjin River. There were considerable gaps in the line of defence either side of the Glosters which allowed the Chinese to virtually surround them and remove them as an effective fighting force.

However, the resistance the Glosters put up caused the Chinese to pause and their spring offensive came to a halt. During an October-November 1951 campaign called Operation Commando, the UN forces slowly pushed back, regained strategic territory north and west of the Imjin and the battle lines finally consolidated in a more or less NE to SW line across the old 38° N frontier, the one that had been drawn up at the end of WWII by the Russians and the Americans.

Later I learned that the 3rd battalion, Royal Australian Regiment (3RAR) had an almost similar experience further east at Kapyong. Their resistance also broke the momentum of the Chinese advance. The Glosters and the 3RAR both received US Presidential citations for gallantry. Today, what is remembered as Gloster Day in England is celebrated as Kapyong Day in Australia where it also comes the day before Anzac Day—two days of drinking, feasting, marching and remembering for the Diggers.

It had been intended that we spend that afternoon zeroing our now meticulously clean rifles but this was cancelled when it started to rain. Once more, there was nothing to do except laze around reading, playing pontoon, writing letters, sleeping or indulging in mild horseplay. Four of us tangled playfully on my bed and succeeded in snapping off one of the legs. That night it had to be propped up 'port side midships' with a bucket.

After dinner and returning to our tent, we found that the contents of our petrol can had been syphoned out. Fortunately the can had been left so a search party went to get some more from the fuel dump. No one fancied having to spend the evening sitting around in sleeping bags to keep warm and we were relieved when the search party returned safely without encountering any trigger-happy prowler guard.

When the stove ran out of fuel again, another search party had to go off to find more. Since the can was kept outside the tent in case of fire there was always the risk of its contents being filched. Two attempts were foiled when we tied a cord to the handle of the petrol can at one end and to a tin with some stones in it on the other that hung inside the tent.

A little later a sing song started up, mostly Christmas carols, then many of us decided to shave while we had some hot water. Last night quite a number of shots were fired and some unfortunate intruder was actually killed. It was very sad but orders to "shoot first" just had to be obeyed. We hoped our sleep would not be disturbed by any more shots.

That night I slept very warmly in my combat suit, parka and boots beneath five blankets. This was from sheer idleness since I did not want to unpack my kit again to get my sleeping bag out. It saved much trouble when reveille sounded.

After breakfast and a trip to the stores to return our beds and three of our blankets, we were taken to a rifle range to zero our rifles. This was a very rough trip over roads full of pot-holes; we were shaken around like peas in a tin. The roads were also bone dry and passing traffic kicked up clouds of dust that an icy wind then blew in our eyes. That wind was as sharp as razor blades and our faces felt as though cut to pieces.

Despite the dust in our eyes, we did see a typical Korean elder on our way to the range; he was an old man with an incredibly wrinkled face, long wispy white hair and a long sparse beard. He was dressed in flowing, baggy, white clothes and wore what looked like a small black top hat precariously perched high above his forehead and secured with a cord under his chin. It looked many sizes too small but perhaps that was the fashion for him. It reminded me of the custom among certain Jews of wearing a little box containing lines from scripture on their forehead.

Finally we reached the range battered, shaken, frozen, blinded and choked. Once we had recovered a little from the journey and warmed up, zeroing our rifles proved to be good fun. My rifle was firing a bit high of centre—between eleven and one o'clock—so I now knew enough to make allowances should I ever really have to use it.

The return journey to camp was as bad as the journey out so we were glad to get back for the hot meal that awaited us. Unfortunately, almost before we could draw breath, our officer announced that there would be a rifle inspection after lunch which threw us all into a panic trying to get the rifle bores clean enough to satisfy him.

6

A slow boat to Inchon

5th December–8th December

Heavy Moving

Called early to have tea that afternoon, we were warned to be packed and ready to move out by 17:30. Some Korean kids came by and offered to clean our boots. I guessed they were about ten years old but they still put incredible energy into their work. One told me he had lost his dad in the war. Their charge was only a packet of biscuits or two packets of chewing gum and we never saw them eat any of the stuff they were given. Evidently, whatever they managed to get went back to the mother who then shared it out. Family loyalty would seem to be a very strong institution here.

By 17:20 rumours were buzzing around again. First, we were going to Kure—that night. Then another story had it that we were not going until tomorrow, and on it went. Eventually the sergeant came by and scotched all these stories by telling us that he was waiting for the OC troop movement to give him the nod. It didn't look as though we would move out now until around 20:30. So we scrounged another can of fuel, lit the stove again and settled down to play cards, or just talk.

Finally, at 19:15, the order came to move down to the truck park. And what a performance that was. In just one journey, in the dark, we had to carry all our gear—our packs with all our personal things such as washing kit, writing paper, eating tools and books etc. wrapped round with a roll of two blankets and a ground sheet, our rifles and two kit bags filled with our winter clothing. It was a bulky, heavy and extremely awkward load. By the time I reached the truck park every muscle in my arms, back and neck felt sprained.

We then had to hang around in the dark waiting for the order to get on the trucks. There were four drafts moving out, for the King's Shropshire

Light Infantry, the King's Own Scottish Borderers, the Royal Leicestershire Regiment and for the Welch Regiment, about six hundred men altogether. There were eight trucks but when our turn came only one was left to take our whole draft of about forty men, complete with kit. Chaps were lying under and on top of each other and their kit. It was an incredible jumble and once aboard no one dared move for fear of hurting someone, or losing their balance and falling off. In no time at all we were all suffering with cramp somewhere.

The trip to the dockside was as unpleasant as that to the rifle range; icy wind, clouds of dust, bumps, sudden shuddering stops, jerking starts and loads of moaning and groaning. Twice we had to stop at level crossings for trains making those weird, haunting, western-film-type siren noises to pass. Eventually we pulled up at the quayside and found ourselves opposite the one where the *Georgic* had pulled in a few days ago. Another hospital ship, the *Consolation*, was out there in the harbour along with the *Jutlandia*.

SS Hong Siang before it became HMT Empire Longford

The ship we were to board was the HMT *Empire Longford*, a small, scruffy looking craft. The Borderers were the first aboard and then, because we were somehow in the way, we were ordered on next and into one of the holds. The Shropshires were in the mess hall so goodness knows where the others were billeted. We were sharing with a Canadian draft, volunteers who had come over on the *Longford* from Kure and part of a special Korea Volunteer Brigade. One had been in England during WWII and stationed at Aldershot where some of our draft came from. It was a chance for them to do some reminiscing. As for me, no sooner had I found a place to unroll my sleeping bag and get into it than I was fast asleep. Sometime in the night we cast off and sailed out of Pusan harbour.

After some research, I discovered that this vessel was built in Newcastle in 1912 for the Melbourne Steam Ship Co. Ltd. and named '*Dimboola*'. She was sold in 1935 to the Ho Hong SS Co, Singapore, renamed '*Hong Siang*', and used as a freighter on the China coast. Acquired by the military in 1951 and renamed *Empire Longford*, she carried stores from Singapore to Korea and between Korea and Japan. One thing was sure—she was not designed to carry a large human cargo. Two years after we sailed in her she was sailed to the UK and scrapped in Dover. Visualise the ship in the above photograph painted white to see her as the troopship we sailed in.

One year to go!

This was the last day of my first year of national service. We woke this morning stiff but quite refreshed. Yesterday had been a hard day and we were all more tired than we realised. With only one tap in the showers and two in the OR's washroom for three hundred chaps, it took ages to get a wash, but we got there in the end. I managed to scrape part of my beard off but it was cleaning my teeth properly that finally woke me up.

Brian and Alec went off to find out what mess orderlies had to do. By a most extraordinary coincidence, they had ended up with exactly the same jobs they had on the *Georgic*. As we climbed the gangway yesterday evening, we were given a berthing card showing our embarkation number and mess table number. Some cards had born the additional information—"mess orderly". Anyone could have got those cards. It was a completely random allocation and that made it even stranger for Brian and Alec to get cards bearing this information. Brian moaned when he read it and reckoned he would have enough experience to apply for work as a waiter when he got back home.

Down in our hold, we were told to get into groups of ten. Breakfast for each group came in a large box which contained enough tinned food to feed ten men for one day, or five men for two days, or three men for three days. It was a very versatile system and very American. Evidently the British Commonwealth Brigade, being officially part of the US 8th Army, is catered for by the Americans. If this box of combat rations was anything to go by we should do well even in the front line.

There were tins containing sachets of sugar, tea, milk powder, sweets and chocolate; tins containing water sterilisation tablets, matches; tins with individual portions of cheese, jam, margarine, blocks of oatmeal and vegetable cubes; tins of sausages, corned beef, bacon and peas. Finally, packets of hard biscuits had to substitute for bread. In fact, the quality was excellent and we made a good meal, leaving enough for lunch and tea.

Among a multitude of other accessories in that box was a very small but very neat and effective tin opener. I still have one in my possession. It is stamped with 'US KOOLAIRE 1951', still works well and is almost foolproof compared with more expensive tin openers. All you need are strong fingers.

Hunger having been well satisfied, I was curious to know the direction in which we were sailing. The sun had risen over the port bow so we must have been going SSE, which I found rather curious. If my geography served me well, to get to Inchon on the west coast we should have been sailing first WSW and then turning northwards. When Brian returned from his mess duties I asked him what he thought. Using his watch dial with the 12 lined up with the sun, he agreed with me that we were indeed sailing SSE. But that was where Japan lay!

Around 11:00 we sighted land ahead. It had to be Japan, but where? Kure? Nobody seemed to know. We passed between tree-covered islands and dropped anchor near one of them. Great conical mountains covered with fir trees dominated the landscape. The weather was also much warmer, more like a pleasant autumn or spring day at home and there was no chill in the air, which was comforting. The ship swung on the tide and far off astern we saw several tall chimneys belching smoke, a sure sign of some form of heavy industry. We knew there could be nothing like that at Inchon because the war would have ruined it all. We concluded that this must be Japan.

It was time for lunch so gathering our group together, the sausages, bacon, chopped vegetables, cheese and biscuits were sorted out between us. It was good and sufficient and once again our hunger was agreeably satisfied. It could only have been improved had we been able to heat it up but there was no way we could light a fire on a wooden deck even if we had fuel.

The sound of the anchor being raised brought us all up to the rail; we were sailing off between more islands to eventually enter a fair sized industrial port. Much shipping was plying back and forth, mostly antiquated and dilapidated looking Japanese steamers. Many factory chimneys belched black smoke that hung in the air. The harbour seemed to stretch quite a distance and we passed several large Japanese and American cargo ships. Finally we hove-to and dropped anchor. The Canadians on board were able to confirm one thing for us. This was not Kure—and they would have known because that was where they had embarked on the *Empire Longford* in the first place. So, in the absence of an atlas or any announcement over the ship's PA system, we could not really know where we were.

As it happened, the ship had no PA system anyway and the issuing of orders required that the orderly room staff run all over the place to spread the 'gospel' as it were. Once they tried to organise a boat stations drill using runners to carry instructions around. Since the ship was hopelessly overcrowded, it was a complete shambles. Besides, had anything happened there would not have been enough lifeboats.

Recoaling—Japanese style

Quoting from my letter home:

"The gangway was lowered and boats came alongside bringing swarms of [Japanese] on board, poor little rat faced people who, when walking, reminded one of a lot of monkeys. The majority wore ex Jap army caps, even the women who came aboard, and they wore black, plimsole type shoes with separate compartments for the big toes. I supposed these enabled them to grip with their toes better but I couldn't think what.

When a large barge filled with coal pulled alongside the penny finally dropped. The Empire Longford was coal fired and had only carried enough to get from Kure to Pusan with the Canadians, drop them off and return. Presumably, the trip up to Inchon had not been part of the original sailing plan this time, so the captain had to return to Japan to pick up more fuel before commencing the longer journey.

The method of refuelling was interesting. A series of platforms had been slung down the side of the ship just beneath the chutes through which the coal was to be loaded. The lower the platform the further out from the hull it projected to create a series of steps down to the coal barge.

It was dark before loading coal actually commenced and flood lights had to be hung out over the side to illuminate the work. A man stood at each end of each platform thus forming two lines from coal barge level up to the coal chute while about a dozen others remained in the barge. They proceeded to rest a round basket against their legs and use a short handled hoe to fill them with coal.

These were then picked up and passed up the line from one person to the next until those at the top could chuck its contents into the chute and thus down into the ships coal bunkers. The empty basket would then be thrown back down into the barge to be refilled. It was a primitive method and dirty work but it was amazing how fast they went at it.

Once they got into their stride the pace never slackened and they never seemed to tire. They were still at it three hours later. With such stamina no wonder the Japanese had made such a fearsome enemy during the war in the Far East."

Tea had come and gone—tinned pears and condensed milk, rich fruit cake, tea and biscuits spread with margarine and jam. For supper we had more biscuits, margarine and jam, with bully beef. In the darkness, the harbour was ringed with lights and offered quite a spectacle. For a while I got into conversation with a couple of Canadians about where they came from and how they came to be going to Korea. Others held a song and dance session on top of the hold. Then it was time to get into my sleeping bag and hope that we would still be here in Japan in the morning. If we are here we can't be anywhere else I thought.

Anniversary

It was the 7th December, 1951, and the anniversary of my call up. A year ago, at 14:00, many of us were on the train to Salisbury to begin this journey to the other side of the world. A year ago I was on a truck to Bulford Camp on the Salisbury Plain to start my training in the PBI. A year later I was on an old ship going to Inchon on the west coast of Korea and to war, the reason for all that training during the past year. A few of us who met for the first time a year ago had a little get-together just to commemorate that time and all that had happened to us since. Brian and Alec Fulcher had gone on a clerical course to become company clerks, I had become a signaler and Alec Ahern had been promoted to lance corporal, which we all agreed that he merited.

This morning at 07:00 the sergeant poked his head into the hold and shouted, "Come on, it's seven o'clock. Breakfast is at 07:30 and you needn't bother to wash and shave."

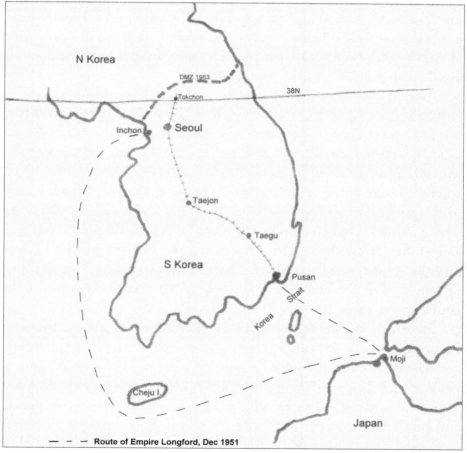

The route of HMT Empire Longford, December 1951

That was a most unusual wake-up call and, if anything was guaranteed to prove once and for all that we were not in barracks in England that was it. We took him at his word and even by 1030 very few of us had shaved. It had been another warm, cosy night even though it had been spent on a hard surface in the hold. When we climbed up on deck we saw we were out at sea again.

Up at the galley, eating tools in hand, we collected our breakfast; in one mess tin a gooey substance that the cooks told us would answer to the name 'Porridge' if we were polite to it, bangers and mashed potato were dumped in the other one. Collecting tea, biscuits, real butter and jam we proceeded to the mess deck. It was a meal guaranteed to make us realise just how lucky we had been to travel on the *Georgic*. After breakfast the hold was swept and tidied up ready for an inspection. It was such a cursory affair it might as well not have happened. I then decided to have a shave to avoid being grabbed for spud bashing duty.

Around 11:00 we passed land to starboard. According to Brian's wrist-watch compass we were proceeding in a WSW direction and had been for quite a while. For some reason we assumed it was not Korea but we were wrong. Just after lunch a map was posted up outside the orderly room showing us where we had been, where we were and where we were going. The land we had passed was Jeju Island, a part of Korea that lay off the south west corner of the mainland. The port where we had taken coal on board was Moji which lay on the western side of the narrow channel between the Japanese islands of Kyushu and Honshu. Our time of arrival at Inchon was also posted as the morning of Sunday 9th December, but we had yet to take a more northerly course to get there.

For lunch we were given roast beef, cabbage and potato followed by stewed prunes. Was the MO getting worried about the regularity of our bowels? For a time I joined a game of whist then, after reading for a while, I started on my daily letter home. This was interrupted when some Canadians came by and we got talking. They were a nice, easy-going bunch and quite amusing in the casual way they talked about the army and going to war. If they were issued with any kit they felt they didn't want, or couldn't be bothered with, they either threw it out or gave it away. Ammunition pouches, tin hats, bayonets—if they thought they wouldn't, or didn't want to use them, out they went. One of them gave me a neat canvas breech cover to keep the dust and grit out of the working parts of my rifle.

However, there was no doubt that the Yankee commanders looked after the creature comforts of their troops very well and we would benefit greatly from that. This reminded me that my ammunition boots were beginning to fall apart and an appointment to see the CQMS when we reached the battalion would have to be given priority. Would footwear in my size be available that would better withstand the strain of active service? A pair of those Yankee combat boots that came halfway up the calves would be fine.

During the night there was an incident whose after-effects rippled through much of that day. Someone had discovered where the beer was stored, broke in and took a few bottles in an 'accidentally-on-purpose' sort of way. When some Canadians heard of this exploit, being broke and unable to buy any beer, they decided to raid the store too. It so happened that Brian and I were sleeping near the hatch cover that had to be removed. It was allowed to drop onto Brian's back. Naturally this woke him up very suddenly and he delivered a terrific yell right into my face. This woke me and we sat up to find three Canadians and one of our chaps standing there.

Before they could take anything, an MP came along to find out what the row was about. Seeing the Canadians standing there, he asked what they thought they were doing but those chaps disappeared as if their pants were on fire and got clear away. The MP's pursuit was totally frustrated by all the bodies lying around the hold.

Throughout the morning, our sleep, or whatever else we were doing, was interrupted by visits from various superior persons. First, the troop deck sergeant, then the ship's Quarter Master Sergeant (QMS), the OC troops and finally the purser all arrived to pester us with questions about what had happened. We were not able to be of much help to any of them. We were also supposed to give evidence at the orderly room but nothing came of this idea.

The MPs managed to recover four cases of beer that the Canadians had actually succeeded in pinching. Later, the Canadians made another raid on the beer store and got away with six cases that were never recovered. One of them was stupid enough to drink a bottle before going to breakfast where the QMS smelt it on his breath and had him arrested. He was charged but got away with it somehow.

There was little discussion about the whole affair and interest fizzled out until we heard how one of the French Canadians on board had threatened to kill any MP who tried to take the matter further. He had even loaded his rifle and put a bullet in the breech. Fortunately nothing happened. Those French Canadians had a reputation for being mad, nasty bastards if crossed.

7

Joining the Battalion

9th December-20th December 1951

Inchon & Seoul

We arrived off Inchon during the night. After reveille, the corporal grabbed me to guard the hatch to the beer store. A quarter of an hour later it was announced that we would be disembarking at 10:00 so I was dismissed from duty to get my gear together which then had to be taken up on deck. Everything was shrouded in a dawn fog and we waited until the sun rose high enough to burn it off.

A large pontoon was towed out and moored alongside. An hour later a big US landing craft came alongside and we were ordered to climb down onto the pontoon and clamber on board. Once again progress was seriously hampered by all our heavy packs and kit bags; it was a tedious and tiring business. The intention was to try to get all six hundred of us on that craft at the same time, kit and all. A Yankee 'Lootenant' on the bridge kept yelling out "Mooove down thaire, ra-eet on daown. Thaire's plainty of rooom." There were muttered protests. One group started to "Moo" and there were the odd shouts of "Gid along liddle dogie," and "What is this, a cattle drive?" However, he didn't succeed in getting us all ashore in one trip.

The way Yanks pronounced the rank of lieutenant as 'lootenant' always made me smile. It sounded as if they were referring to someone who lived in a toilet. Probably our way of pronouncing it 'Leff-tenant' was equally amusing to them. However, the American pronunciation was more accurate since it derived from *lieu* (place) and *tenant* (holder). Since our word 'loo,' meaning toilet or bathroom, is of uncertain origin and probably not in their vocabulary, Americans may not have understood that allusion.

By 11:45 we were disembarking at a long, sloping, improvised jetty. US army trucks waited for us at the top and I nearly broke my back again with all the weight I had to carry up to them. Inchon looked a mess; seawalls were breaking up, small craft remained where they had sunk or high up on the mud flats. Landing craft, jeeps and Yanks were everywhere.

Remembering the trip to the firing range in Pusan, we were not at all cheered by the knowledge that we had a five-hour journey ahead of us. Once again, we were packed in like sardines but this time only fourteen to a truck. The fact that each person's kit took up the equivalent space of another two people meant there might just as well have been forty-two chaps on board.

We sped out of Inchon on the Seoul road as if the Chinese were after us. Surprisingly, it was still in good repair so we were not battered about as much as we had been expecting. Acres of paddy fields lay on either side and children cheered us wildly as we drove through small villages. But all this changed as we approached and finally reached the Han River to enter Seoul itself. Of the three bridges that had originally spanned the river, two were complete wrecks and the central span of the other had been repaired with wooden ramps. It was the only one in use.

The city itself had been pretty well razed. The tide of battle had flowed through it four times in less than a year. The North Koreans came through in June 1950; the UN recaptured it in September 1950 after the Inchon landing. After the Chinese entered the war the North Koreans came back through Seoul in January 1951 while the UN counter operation pushed them back again in March 1951.

The blackened remains of houses lay on every side but people were still searching for what they might find. A few shops had managed to reopen to sell leather revolver holsters, flags and brilliantly coloured silk scarves but where were the tourists to buy such things? Some women were out and about dressed in the very bright Korean traditional dress but many more were in uniform and on traffic control duty.

Our route out of the city ran northwards beside a railway line. For much of the next stretch we competed with a long freight train pulled by a coal-fired engine that belched black smoke high into the air. At first we kept ahead of it but eventually, after straining its guts up a long incline, it took off and thundered past us.

Some miles on, at a place called Uijongbu, we turned left off the main road to travel along narrow, unsealed, military roads that were hard and very bumpy. It wound up one valley and down another, round bends in hillsides with sheer hundred-foot drops on one side. Every time a vehicle approached from the opposite direction, our hearts leaped into our mouths lest we plunge over the edge, or slide into the ditch.

This did happen to the truck behind us. Remembering that the rule of the road was to 'Keep Right', that truck had to pass to the left of another on a gradual left bend. We watched as it slid slowly into the ditch and canted over onto its side at a sixty degree angle. The chaps on board were quite shaken up but no one was hurt.

While waiting for the truck to be pulled back onto the road we saw our first officer from the Welch Regiment. Major Comer, officer commanding HQ Company, drove past in a staff car. We passed other trucks that had recently overturned but saw no casualties. The problem was with the roads which, being bare clay and stones, froze overnight and became slippery. As the sun rose they thawed but remained very slippery and extremely treacherous. Later, we heard that the battalion water cart, driven by a chap named Squires had slid off the road and down a fifty-foot slope. It came to a stop about three feet from a minefield. He had crawled out unhurt but the battalion had no water cart for a couple of days.

Gloster Valley scene, December 1951 [1]

Gloster Valley scene, December 1951 [2]

The countryside we passed through ranged from flat valley floors heavily terraced into paddy fields to impressively high and grotesquely rocky mountain peaks that tailed off into long undulating, steep sided ridges. These hills rose abruptly out of the paddy fields. Up here near the front line the paddies had, of necessity, been neglected. With the war going back and forth as it had, there had been no time or opportunity for farmers to cultivate them this year. The hillsides were covered either with stunted pines, scrub oaks, or masses of long wiry grass. Since it was winter time only the pines carried any green colour; the rest was all dull brown of every shade and hue.

From a soldier's point of view, this was superb country in which to build and camouflage defensive positions but a real bastard if one had to go on the attack. It would be exhausting. Those forty-five degree slopes looked formidable. From stories heard about the attack on the Glosters' positions last April, the Chinese soldiers must have possessed incredible stamina to pour over them as if they hadn't existed. The thought of possibly coming into combat contact with them in this sort of country made us all rather quiet and thoughtful.

Finally, passing over a high range of mountains, we dropped down into a valley. Soon after passing two signs—"56 Replacement Training Camp" and "A Echelon", we knew we had reached the end of the long journey back to the battalion. Things were about to become serious again. The trucks turned off the road, bumped along a track and stopped about fifteen yards from a group of tents.

We tumbled out, hauling our kit after us. A sergeant led us to a tent where we dumped our gear and waited. It was now about 18:30. There was a chill bite in the air. We were also dead tired and must have looked it because, after being given some surprisingly good grub, we were told to go and get some sleep. To our delight, mail was waiting for us and we were more than happy to first spend a little time reading it.

The holiday is finally over

It was Monday, 10th December 1951. Reveille sounded at 06:45. Orders were given to get ourselves in shape—properly shaved, boots and badges polished and ready for muster parade. Wow! We were back to the old 'bullshit' with a vengeance. This astonished us considering that we

were now only a few miles from the front line. Our bedding and kit had
to be laid out as per the standard pattern, the tent swept out and the sides
neatly rolled up.

On reflection, this return to a familiar military regimen was really
quite important. The casualness of the voyage out on the *Georgic* and
the unavoidable laxness on the *Empire Longford*, indicated that a sense
of discipline and cleanliness needed to be restored to stiffen morale and
prevent disease spreading which, given some of the 'types' among our
number, could happen quite easily. We would be here for twelve days on a
refresher course before going to the front.

The battalion had only been in the front for about two weeks so it was
all very new to everyone. The company presently here in reserve and going
through a refresher course in weapons training and field craft, especially
the latter was C Company. We had arrived in time to join them before
going up front to relieve another company due for a period in reserve.
Brian and I were allocated to No. 3 Section, 7 Platoon.

Just across the valley was the hill where the Glosters suffered that
appalling defeat just a few months before. Panmunjom, where the truce
talks were being held, was less than twenty miles further over to the west. A
searchlight there shone straight up into the sky at night to indicate that the
talks were in progress. Presumably that would also prevent it from being
mistakenly bombed or shelled.

The sergeant informed us that our forward companies occupied a
notoriously difficult position called "The Hook" on the western side of the
Samichon River valley, the major line of approach to Seoul that the North
Koreans had come down in June 1950. The Commonwealth Division had
been given the task of blocking any further attempts to march on Seoul again.

In April 1951, when the Chinese mounted their major spring offensive,
the Division had made a gallant stand. The line had held and throughout
the summer and into the autumn, the front line had been slowly pushed
back north across the Imjin again. The Division now held a very strategic
line northwest of the Imjin from the Samichon River valley up to a hill
called Little Gibraltar. I would have loved to see all this on a map but that
was not to be. Only the officers had maps.

So far, the battalion had only suffered one death. On the 30th
November, Pte J. Corcoran had wandered off a path and been blown up

by a mine. Then on the 9th December an A Company patrol met with stiff opposition and suffered ten casualties. The battalion had been mainly engaged in sending out patrols to a hill known as 169, the objective being to take prisoners for interrogation. But the Chinese had turned the tables on one of these patrols and set up an ambush, hence the casualties.

The QM informed us that much of our kit would be exchanged soon. Instead of our itchy battledress we would have Yankee windproof combat suits with hoods, long flannel underpants, puttees, poncho groundsheets and rubber-soled frost-proof boots with wire gauze insoles, which were supposed to be infinitely better than our ammo boots,. I had to wonder if the stores would have boots to fit my size eleven feet.

It had been bitterly cold when the bugler awoke us at 06:45 hours the next morning. Breakfast came first and then a shave in hot water provided by the cookhouse. Boots and rifles were hurriedly cleaned, bed spaces tidied up as best we could and off we raced for muster parade at 08:45. The corporal in charge of No 3 Section, 7 Platoon, was Cpl. 'Tiger' Davies, a thuggish looking character who expertly used crude language about almost everything. But he also had a great sense of humour. He liked to make out that he was as tough as nails, one of those "I'll not be beat [sic] and will bloody well let you know it" types. But he could be very thoughtful and funny, as I was to find out.

The first order of the day was documentation. The platoon sergeant took down all the particulars about us that he required for his own reference. We then struck our tents and re-erected them beneath the reverse side of a hill to lessen the risk from possible air attack. The reverse side always sloped away from the enemy and usually faced south or south east on our section of the front.

When this was completed and everything tidy again, we hung around waiting for the battalion commanding officer, Lieutenant Colonel H.H. "Dixie" Dean, to arrive and welcome us back to the battalion. In the end he didn't come but Brigadier A.H.G.Ricketts, commander of 29 Brigade, did appear and proceeded to give us a cautionary talk on how we should conduct ourselves here. After lunch, Major Hallows, the battalion 2i/c arrived, deputising for the CO. He welcomed us to the battalion with a short talk on the regiment's honourable history that we were expected to maintain. We were then treated to a cup of tea and an issue of rum. While not a drink that I really liked, I nevertheless drank it for the warmth it stimulated. We were told that rum issues would occur frequently throughout the winter. Needless to say, in practice they were few and far between!

Talking of commanders, I later discovered that the Commonwealth Division Commander was Major General A.J.H. Cassels, CB, KBE, DSO, (Gentleman Jim). He had under him two British Brigades, one Canadian Brigade, two Australian Regiments, one New Zealand Artillery Regiment and an Indian Field Ambulance and Surgical Unit. This required him to report to five governments via a command centre in Sydney. As a result, he was unable to enjoy the flexibility and independence in command to which he was accustomed. He also probably irritated his US superiors with his habit of always wanting to know 'Why?' whenever asked to commit men to an operation! And why not?

It was on Tuesday morning, after muster parade, that we eventually marched off to the training area. Getting back into shape for what might lie ahead when we really joined the rest of the battalion in the front line was very necessary. We were required to maintain an 'anti aircraft' formation, which meant keeping about five paces apart and in single file much of the time. Our path wound up hill and down again, round spurs in the hills and across the entrances of small valleys. Most of the time, these paths were barely discernible in the scrub oak hillsides. It crossed my mind just how easy it would be to stray off one of these 'paths' and unknowingly enter an unmarked minefield.

Several Chinese graves were passed marked with a lath on which a few Chinese characters were written. One or two of the graves had been disturbed and we could see part of a human skull at one end and the remains of a pair of shoes at the other. It seemed the Chinese were not very concerned about taking their dead back for decent burial. So much for the value they placed on human lives.

That afternoon the company commander informed me that on December 22nd I would go to the HQ Company signals platoon. Brian was to stay with C Company it seemed. This caused us both some angst for we had developed the sort of friendship that would have us prefer to stay close so that we could look out for each other. We were what the Aussies called 'mates'. I couldn't help feeling concern because, at one time on the ship he had admitted to a 'belief' in palmistry. He had his palms read while on leave and been told that he would be wounded here. However, like me, he was absolutely sure he would return home safely.

We both knew that this parting of the ways had always been on the cards from the time that I had been sent for training as a signaller and he to become a company clerk. The time had now arrived for me to be that signaller. It was also becoming clear that, because of this and particularly because of my training in the use of 62 sets for inter-company communication, it was highly unlikely that I would ever be sent on patrol. The nearest I would probably get to action would be as a front-line company HQ section signaller. It seemed that in this battalion I possessed some 'rare' skills and was quite valuable.

On Wednesday morning, taken once more on that brisk five mile trek to the training area, we were given a refresher course on the Bren gun. We were also introduced to use of the mortar. This was followed by a lecture from a Canadian officer on the winter clothing we would be issued with and another from the MO on the use of field dressings. In the afternoon, the application of field dressings was practised then we were put through some strenuous field-craft exercises—how to find and use camouflage and how to find cover and then advance using it as stealthily as possible.

Given the dire reports heard about Korean winters, the weather was milder than anticipated. Then it began to rain and we ended up slopping around in mud while my right boot continued to do its damndest to lose its sole. I fervently hoped the new boot issue would take place very soon.

That evening after lights out, while answering a call of nature, I tripped over. In the darkness, attempting to keep my balance, I placed my right hand on the edge of the hot stove and acquired a beautiful blister some half an inch by two inches along the edge of my palm. "That is going to be most useful", I thought sarcastically to myself.

We must have looked a sorry sight this morning, half asleep, yawning our heads off, dirty, smelly, unshaven and having left everything in the tent in a total mess as we stumbled off in the dark to get our breakfast. The ground was not very even either and the frost had rendered it rock hard. It would have been so easy to twist an ankle. Then dawn broke and the view across the valley to Gloster Hill became clear.

Out on the training area the art of erecting barbed wire defences and digging trenches was demonstrated. For lunch we were each issued with a box of American C7 rations ('C' for 'combat' presumably and '7' for the particular version perhaps). Each box contained a tin of savoury meat, or something similar, a tin of sweets, sachets of coffee, milk and sugar, a tin with crackers and jam, a packet of other accessories such as cigarettes, matches, toilet paper, chewing gum and more sachets of coffee, milk and sugar. There was also another of those clever little tin openers inside, so simple in design, yet so effective. These rations were excellent and we were well pleased with how effectively they satisfied our hunger. The sergeant told us that they would be issued quite frequently in place of cookhouse-style food, but not every day.

A view of A Echelon, December 1951, 355 in distance

The afternoon was spent digging and wiring a defensive position on the hillside before marching back to camp. My bayonet had remained firmly in its scabbard! Thankfully, the pace was not as brisk as it had been that morning. We all felt thoroughly tired but very cheerful.

The temperature did not rise very quickly with the rising of the sun. We were fast learning to become speed shavers because the hot water drawn from the cookhouse did not stay hot for long. For some reason our razors felt as though they were peeling our skin instead of cutting hairs. By the time we went on muster parade the sun was quite high and perversely the sergeant always had us line up with it in our eyes so that it was impossible to see a darned thing properly for some time afterwards.

The temperature began to rise, which cheered us, but the wind still blew cold enough to be felt keenly by our hands and faces. We had decided not to wear our string vests and parkas in an attempt to try to toughen up a little being of a mind to save them for when it got really cold.

There were more field-craft exercises and another opportunity to zero our rifles. With the odds likely to be against us if the Chinese made a determined attack, these 303s could be very slow-firing weapons with which to defend ourselves. They were OK at fairly long range when you had time to pick a target, sight up and gently squeeze the trigger. But at close quarters, a Stengun would have been more useful, either on single shot or rapid fire. It seemed that the Chinese preferred their assault troops to carry sub-machine guns. They were called 'burp' guns from the 'rude' noise they made when fired.

After C7 rations for lunch, we 'played' stalking and concealment exercises much like the games of 'Cowboys and Indians' played with friends on a gorse-covered piece of common land near my home during the war. For a moment this memory made it difficult to remember where we were and the serious purpose behind what we were doing.

When the sun went down later that afternoon, it became bitterly cold again. Back in camp we had a petrol stove in the tent like the one we had in Pusan. For some reason the controls didn't work properly so it roared away at full blast and sounded like an aircraft taking off, the whole contraption becoming red hot from about six inches off the deck to about half way up the chimney. We all huddled round it in the evenings.

That night, I was detailed for prowler guard duty and was fortunate to draw the first 'stag' between 19:15 and 21:30. We were detailed in pairs to ensure that if one chaps brains froze in the bitter cold there would be someone to maintain guard. But our bodies still copped the chill, despite the fact that it was not yet the coldest time of year.

In January and February the temperature could drop below 20° F (-7° C) but hopefully, by that time, we would be acclimatised to the situation and know how to cope with frozen water cans and water bottles in order to wash and shave. At night we now placed our jerseys, shirts and trousers under our sleeping bags so that they were relatively dry and warm to put on when we got up. Otherwise, anything the least bit damp and left out overnight became as stiff as a board. Every morning so far the bristles on my shaving brush had been frozen stiff and my face-cloth like a piece of sandpaper, even though it was slippery from not having been washed properly in ages. I hated to think what colour my towel might have now become had it not been dark green to start with.

Understatement sealed the fate of the Glosters

Around Gloster Valley Dec. 1951 with R Imjin on L

A view over Gloster valley—R Imjin on left

There had been a full moon over the past three nights. According to 'old soldiers' among us, the Chinese preferred to launch their attacks on such nights. These 'Banshee' attacks, as they were known, usually came on the full moon, wave after wave advancing through their own shell and mortar fire. The first wave carried grenades, the next sub-machine guns while succeeding waves brought up ammunition and retrieved the weapons of their fallen comrades to carry on fighting. They seemed to have no transport or radios, all orders being given by bugle or whistle.

The story went that last April, when the Glosters were besieged just across the valley from where A Echelon now stood, on hearing all the bugle calls from the advancing Chinese side, their drum major ordered his buglers to play all the British army bugle calls in order to confuse them. Apparently this had the desired effect causing the Chinese to stop their bugle blowing for a while. The Gloster buglers succeeded in buying a short respite in the battle. What a great story to illustrate the irony in the British sense of humour.

Later, two stories illustrated another facet of the British character, the capacity for understatement. At the height of the fighting on Gloster Hill, the commanding officer, Lieutenant Colonel J.P. Carne, went missing. The adjutant was worried and searched for him everywhere. At last the CO reappeared carrying a rifle. Asked where he had been he replied, quite calmly, "Oh, just shooing away a few Chinese."

While there might be humour in that moment, far behind the battle an event took place that was not at all funny in its consequences. In the afternoon of Tuesday 24th April, the American divisional commander asked the British brigadier, "How are the Glosters doing?" The brigadier, also well schooled in understatement, replied, "Things are pretty sticky down there." To the American's ears, this did not sound too desperate so he ordered the Glosters to hold fast and await relief the following morning.

That sealed their fate. On the Wednesday morning the adjutant heard the news. "You know that relief force?" Col. Carne told him, "Well, they're not coming." Cultural differences were a deciding factor in the loss of a battalion.

Corporal 'Tiger' Davies

After finishing my stint on guard at 21:30, I got into conversation with our corporal, 'Tiger' Davies, and didn't get to sleep until 01:30, which should indicate how interesting the conversation became. Very likely this was because neither of us had ever met anyone like the other before. I found out much about him because he loved talking and boasting of his achievements—and they were many.

Orphaned at an early age, he had soon learned that he had to fight his way alone if he was to get anywhere. He had experienced almost no family life or education and everything he had was earned the hard way. Now at the age of 33, he told me that the army was the best paying job he had ever had. However, he had managed to save enough to get married and have kids. His wife had been a student at Leeds University and was now a nurse. It was obvious from the way he spoke of them that he loved her and their three children dearly.

His lack of education and rough path through the early years had left him without a refined bone in his body. He was invariably crude, uncouth, blasphemous in the extreme and capable of being quite pitiless should the need arise. The way he settled disputes with anyone he was in charge of would be to say:

"We will do it this way, MY way! I'll not have any argument from you or anyone else. What I say goes and if you object I'll take you round a corner and plant a bunch of fives on your nose that it will make it look like a daisy. If you try to hit back, I'll thump the living crap out of you. OK?"

With that kind of talk 'Tiger' was someone you felt compelled to respect. Yet, despite almost no education and a very tough early life, by sheer determination, he had learned to read and write. And he had a surprisingly deep understanding of people.

These 'psychological' insights had also been gained the hard way and could be very fair and sensible in ways not always necessarily, or exclusively, found in more educated people. For example, before we went out on a long march, he would gather us round and say,

"If, as we go along, you find you need to have a piss, don't tell everyone. They will then realise that they want one too, so keep it to yourself and wait till we have a rest halt. The same goes if you feel thirsty or hungry or tired. Keep it to yourself so that you don't spread unease among the section."

This was very sensible, rational, practical and intelligent advice to give and left one wondering how a Welshman who looked more like a cross between a Mongol and an Arab came by such understanding.

'Tiger' was full of contradictions but he did make one mistake with me, probably because he had never met anyone quite like me before. He expected that I, like everyone else, would hero worship him but I did not and would not. But I would trust him if we ever saw action together and got into trouble. I believe that he had a formidable instinct for survival and I would always obey his orders because of it. His practicality and his independence, which he continually boasted about, were quite admirable. In so many ways he was a fabulous character, the sort of common soldier who would normally only exist in stories.

However, I was not to stay in his section at the end of this training period but Brian would. It was some comfort to know that his section corporal would be such a capable man. But what else would one expect of a man who had fought in Burma, Egypt, France, Germany and Finland while in the Airborne Regiment, who had twice been captured and twice escaped and had now come to Korea?

Later he would rib me about my grammar school education but there was the end of it. In a sense he respected me probably more than he might admit because I had the education he had been denied.

With guard duty over and my conversation with the corporal over for that night, I crawled into my sleeping bag without bothering to undress.

I awoke with my clothes still on and found that I just had time to have a shave before breakfast instead of after it. The day was again spent in the training area doing much the same as yesterday but lunch was a good old British army stew instead of C7 rations. Later, back at camp, we attended a pay parade at which we each received twenty-five shillings worth of BAFs. I spent some on chocolate and biscuits to provide some sort of supper. We were also told that tomorrow, being a Sunday, will be a 'rest day of sorts'—whatever that might mean.

A sort of day of rest

I was late getting to breakfast. The sergeant nabbed me to help repair and re-erect the dining tent. Later that morning we were given Bren guns and Browning machine guns to clean after which I attempted to have a 'bath' in half a drum of hot water.

After lunch, wanting to get a better understanding of where we were, I walked to the top of the hill above the camp on the northern side. Off to the west and below me lay a wide curve in the Imjin River. Three pontoon bridges had been built across it and one was teeming with activity. Some way off to the right on the south side of the river, flashes of flame and puffs of smoke revealed where some of our artillery were positioned. They were busy sending 'greetings and good wishes' to the Chinese. The sound of those guns provided a continuous background noise every night. Beyond the river lay successive ridges of grey and brown hills, not a building of any kind in sight. Neither were there any signs that the land was being farmed in any way. The war had put paid to that.

Mail arrived after lunch and it was a relief to know that my letter with change of address had reached home in time. Following afternoon tea we mustered for a church parade. I hated these parades with a passion right from the very first one that I had to attend at Bulford Camp. The association of religion and the military, particularly in times of war, was to so hypocritical that I believed attendance should have been made optional long ago.

There had been a time when, failing to turn up for one of these parades, I was brought before the company commander on a 'fizzer', not for failing to attend a church parade as such but for failing to attend the muster parade held prior to it. I was sentenced to serve one day performing menial duties in the officer's mess cookhouse—peeling spuds and washing up. What else?

Anyway, this parade was soon over and we went back to our tents to write letters, read, or play cards. After dinner 'Tiger' starting boasting again and his blaspheming became truly awesome. He happened to notice the tea stains in one chap's tin mug and started to give him the most extraordinary verbal dressing down. But I caught a look in his eyes that made me realise he wasn't really being serious. He was just pulling rank and having some fun at the poor chap's expense. If truth be told and you had seen a character like him in a film, you would have laughed out loud at this small scene. At the time though, I recall feeling quite disgusted about it and began to walk out of the tent. He called out, "Aren't you going to stay and talk to me tonight?" I just kept walking.

Later that evening, while I was writing a letter by torch light, 'Tiger' came over to me with a letter he had just written to his wife and asked me to read it. I was rather surprised but did so out of curiosity to see how well he could write. In the end, I was impressed. He was able to express himself with a sensibility that almost bordered on the poetic. I imagined that this was from the part that loved his family so passionately. As expected, his punctuation skills were poor but mine were not always crash hot. However, what he had written was fluent and there was real inspiration and feeling in the way he had worded things. He was a queer mixture and no mistake. I wondered if it would ever be possible to really get to know him properly.

I told him I thought he wrote with real feeling and he seemed pleased by this. He went back to his bed returning with his journal opened at the page for the day we had disembarked at Pusan. There, amongst other things, I read an image destined to stick in my memory for ever:

"Arrived and disembarked at Pusan, South Korea, the asshole of the world. And to think that in a few days time we will be 500 miles up it."

Another restful day

After muster parade this Monday morning, I reported sick and was sent by ambulance to a medical reception centre four miles to the rear. The MO told me I had developed a sweat rash and I was 'treated' with gentian violet. Returning to camp in the ambulance, I spent the afternoon catching up with correspondence. There were only six of us left in camp; all the others were out on the training area again so we had to fend for ourselves at lunchtime. We found a frying pan, some bread, some butter and a couple of big tins of beans and had beans on fried bread cooked on the petrol stove.

When the others returned that afternoon, mail was distributed. I reflected on some of the news contained in mail yesterday. Here we were, right in the middle of some of the biggest news-making events anywhere and we knew very little about what was going on. What we did eventually learn came in letters from our homes thousands of miles away or in newspapers that some chaps received. This was the only way we knew what was happening at the truce talks being held about twenty miles away.

Something that irritated me, and would continue to do so given my interest in geography, was the fact that I had no concept of the topography of the region where we were. Where were the highest points we kept hearing about in relation to each other? How did they relate to the Samichon and Imjin valleys? Where was our front line and where was that of the Chinese?

The officers knew. They had maps. It would have been good if they gave us an outline of how things lay here. Some of us had been educated well enough to appreciate such things. It seemed that the only difference between the officers and us was social status and that could be extremely irrelevant out on patrol. The Chinese would certainly have no respect for such niceties of English social structure, except if and when they captured any of us perhaps. It was the officers who would probably get the hard interrogation.

According to statistics, the River Imjin should have been frozen to a depth of about nine inches by now but the weather was still comparatively mild so there was no sign of ice on it.

We meet the men in armour

This morning we were ordered to 'stand by our beds' so that the major could conduct a quick inspection. We then marched off up the valley to where six of the new 50-ton Centurion tanks manned by men of the 5th Royal Inniskilling Dragoon Guards were waiting at the bottom of a hill.

We listened to a lecture about the tanks and learned that they were armed with a 20-pound gun, a BSA medium machine gun projecting from the turret, a Browning machine gun on top of the turret, a bomb thrower that was rather like a 2-inch mortar and a Bren gun kept handy inside the turret. They carried a crew of four—a driver, a signaller, a gunner and the tank commander.

I asked about the wireless equipment the signaller used and was told that there were three separate systems; one for communication with other tanks, a "19" set for communication with regimental HQ, similar to the 62 set, and a "31" set which worked to the infantry units. A telephone on the rear of the tank allowed anyone outside to communicate with the crew. There were fixed periscopes set around the turret for the commander and a moveable one for the gunner. They usually carried 62 shells for the 20 pound gun, belts of ammunition for the machine guns and bombs for the bomb thrower. The engine had four forward gears, two reverse gears and petrol consumption varied between one and three gallons per mile. The maximum speed they could reach was between 20 and 27 miles per hour.

Ordered to climb aboard the outside and grab something to hang on to, we were taken for a very exhilarating ride up, down and around the hills. This revealed just how powerful a piece of mobile artillery these tanks were. Since tanks had seldom been employed in such hilly country before, useful lessons were being learned about their capabilities here in Korea. In fact, during our 'joy-ride' they took us up some extremely steep hillsides that would have taxed us sorely to walk up.

After the ride, we were given a demonstration of part of their firepower. When one of the bomb throwers misfired, the bomb fell about 115 yards away and a few yards in front of the tank next to the one we were behind. We all ducked smartly for cover. When I got up, the company commander was rubbing his jaw with a rather rueful expression on his face. When I naively asking if he was OK, he grinned and motioned toward the muzzle of my rifle. He had bashed his mouth on it as he ducked.

Back at camp we were put to work cleaning the grease off a consignment of new Bren gun ammunition magazines. Luckily there was plenty of paraffin available so the job wasn't too difficult. Later we were brought up to date on patrol protocols to be adopted in the Korean countryside. Naturally they would be rather different from those employed back home where there were no paddy fields or low walls between them.

The corporal then asked me to help him check the kit of a chap who had been taken off to hospital suffering from asthma. The MO reckoned he should never have got past the first medical exam, or been called up at all, but somehow he had. At least he had a free ocean cruise out of it, maybe another if he went back by ship.

After dinner that night, several of us got together to sing Christmas carols. We were all in a sort of wistful mood and needed to indulge it in order to more easily cope with emotions. Outside, the night was very clear and the stars bright in the sky. Orion the Hunter would rise over Gloster Hill every evening as it got dark while the 'Seven Sisters' rode high above. They were exactly the same as folk would see back home. But we saw them some nine hours earlier, or fifteen hours later if you forgot the International Date Line.

More mishaps

The next morning after muster parade, we marched off to the range again. This time it was for a talk on and demonstration of the firepower of weapons such as the Vickers machine gun and the 3-inch mortar which we infantry chaps would not normally use.

There was another moment of terrified excitement when a mortar misfired and its bomb landed ten yards away. Again, we ducked for cover very smartly. This time the company commander was elsewhere but I heard that he nearly had a heart attack. The old saying goes that misfortunes seemed to come in threes so we were left wondering when the third mishap would occur and what it might be.

When the 'excitement' had died down we were told how field artillery was used to support the infantry. The Commonwealth Division had a New Zealand detachment of 25 pounder guns here while the Americans had much larger pieces of artillery further back from the front line that could be called on should they be required.

This was all very interesting but when a fog came down it became too bloody cold to be standing around listening to someone talk to us. We were put to work once more practicing section attacks on selected features of the landscape followed by a talk about land mines and the procedure for locating them with our bayonets. We had to practise crawling forward on our stomachs carefully prodding the ground ahead of us to locate any hard metallic object that might lie concealed in our path and be potentially lethal. It occurred to me to ask the sergeant how one could tell the difference between a mine and a rock beneath the ground and was promptly told to "stop being a smart arse and get on with it". But it was still a reasonable question to ask.

C7s were given out for lunch. My box contained corn beef hash, crackers, cocoa powder, sugar, coffee and milk. What a mixture. Then we marched off to another part of the range to practise firing two-inch mortars and the safe and accurate tossing of hand grenades. A picture of Bill Speakman came to mind. Was this where the third mishap would occur? I later found out that the same thought had actually crossed several other minds.

Field training continued with much rapid advancing in extended lines or arrowhead formation up and down hillsides, across valleys, seeking cover as we went and then charging up a hill with fixed bayonets yelling, in as murderous a voice as we could manage when almost completely out of breath, such silly cries as "Oh ho—Mahommed". What silly bugger thought that one up we wondered? Why not "God for Harry, England and St. George". On second thoughts, since we were in the Welch regiment perhaps it should be "God for George, Cymru and St. David," but that didn't have quite the same ring to it. Then it was all over and we were utterly 'shagged'. To cheer us up and make sure we were able to stand up again, the company commander told us how pleased he had been with our performance. This was, I supposed, a 'good thing'.

I was now becoming increasingly grateful that I would soon be going to the HQ Signals Platoon. This basic PBI stuff was too much like hard work. Much to our relief, we were picked up and transported back to camp by truck instead of having that long footslog back over the hills.

Back at A Echelon, those of us who were joining HQ Company were informed that this would happen on the morrow. Earlier in the day we were talking together and had agreed that the platoon commander was no longer very interested in us. He no longer cared whether we performed this or any other exercise properly. In fact, all our superiors in C Company seemed to have lost interest in us. The evening would be spent getting our gear packed up.

News from Panmunjom said that only one more point remained in dispute at the truce talks and then they might be signed. While there was a sense in which that was very good news indeed, it begged the question as to what that would leave us doing here? More training? Not a good prospect!

After another singsong that evening during which I could only croak, having caught a cold, an argument broke out about which guys were stronger—those with hairy chests or those without. This then proceeded on to similar but more indelicate questions. My pressing desire was to get on and write a letter but I was too exhausted to do anything but sleep. Meanwhile, 'Tiger' Davies had decided to go 'feral' and had dug himself a hole in the hillside to sleep in.

8

On The Hook

21st December-New Year's Eve 1951

Moving to the Sharp End

Everything was one hell of a rush when reveille sounded and not just because us fellows going to BHQ had to get ready to move. The whole of C Company was moving up to the 'sharp end'. Brian and I would not be seeing much of each other for a while but such were the fortunes of war. There were many farewells to be said, including to 'Tiger' Davies whose observations had amused and interested me so much over the past few days.

There was breakfast to eat, a rifle to clean, gear to be packed and taken to the appointed place and for once we all arrived at muster parade shaven and properly dressed. The CO marched round inspecting us and then stated how disgusted he was to find that hardly anyone had bothered to polish their boots. "What is Korea supposed to be, a 'jankers bullshit' detention barracks?" I thought.

Those of us going to BHQ were ordered to fall out and marched all of one hundred yards to meet Major Comer, the CO of HQ Company. We then had to hang about for over an hour waiting for our transport to arrive. The NAAFI van arrived but it only had cigarettes, chocolate and biscuits but no writing pads.

Trucks eventually arrived to take us to our appointment with the sharp end. We crossed the River Imjin via a rickety pontoon bridge. The Yankee engineers who had constructed it were certainly not backward in letting everyone know it was their work. A very large sign announced that it was called Widgeon Bridge. for reasons that would forever remain a mystery, other bridges in this sector had also been named after North American wild fowl such as Teal and Pintail. Two other pontoon bridges had been built parallel to the one we crossed and we wondered if something was wrong with them since no traffic used them. Perhaps they were there to facilitate a rapid withdrawal south if the Chinese initiated another major offensive again. Eventually we learned that building anything like a permanent bridge across the River Imjin was doomed to be swept away by the floods that came with the thaw and the spring rains.

Teal bridge across the R Imjin

Once across the river the bulldozed military roads were a mess; they were wet, muddy and very slippery, exactly as had been shown on TV before we left England. We were now seeing the real thing for ourselves. These conditions could tear the guts out of vehicle engines as they growled their way around the hills.

Eventually we saw the Welsh (Welch!) battle flag flying from a mast head—a red dragon on a green field against a white background and knew we had arrived at battalion HQ. It crossed my mind to wonder what the Chinese might be thinking now they found themselves facing an enemy with such an auspicious symbol on their flag. They considered dragons to be omens of good fortune, not emblems of horror and evil as in the west. Later I learned that the Chinese were indeed in considerable awe of the Welch battle flag.

As we drew in to the parking lot, we saw Lieutenant Colonel H.H. 'Dixie' Dean outside his caravan preparing to hold CO's Orders, the army equivalent of the local magistrate's court for small offenders (those five feet and under?) There must have been some very special cases coming up for him to be taking it. Usually this duty fell to the company commander. We were pointed in the direction of the signals bunker there to wait for Captain Dyer the signals officer. He was a lanky, fair-haired chap with a pretty easy-going manner and an elegant voice that reminded me a little of the English film actor George Sanders. Together with Les Baker, a short, dark haired chap who came from Portsmouth, we were detailed to help run the battalion HQ 62 control set. It was a relief for both of us to know that, for a time at least, we would be in relative safety near the battalion commanding officer.

After lunch the sergeant took us up to the top of Pan Buri hill from where all the forward company positions could be seen. He pointed out Hill 169, occupied by the Chinese and the cause of much bother. Evidently, a very curious situation, almost a gentleman's agreement, had arisen over it until recently. A Welch patrol would occupy it by night and withdraw at first light when the Chinese would move in to sit there through the day. That had apparently remained the situation until, one night, the Chinese decided to ambush the patrol going out to take over.

The sergeant now chose a site where we could dig a bunker for ourselves and stayed to help get it started. To lessen the amount of work, he had chosen to go into the side of an old Chinese crawl trench that had been blocked off at one end. We were very impressed by the amount he did and the speed at which he worked. He had obviously done this sort of thing before. There were no suitable materials with which to make a roof so we just suspended our groundsheets over the hole and when it got dark, crawled inside. The sky was absolutely clear and it had become extremely cold but we till managed to get some sleep.

Settling in

The first morning in BHQ brought a new experience. Reveille was blown at 06:45 just before dawn. With it came the order to "stand to". "Stand to" always took place at what was termed 'first light' when the sky to the east started to lighten. It also took place at 'last light' as the sun began to set. These were traditionally times when, visibility being at its most uncertain, the enemy could be expected to put in an attack or an attack would be mounted. Warmth was once more noticeable by its absence and we stood there shivering for over three quarters of an hour before being 'stood down'. This would be a twice-daily part of our life in the front line.

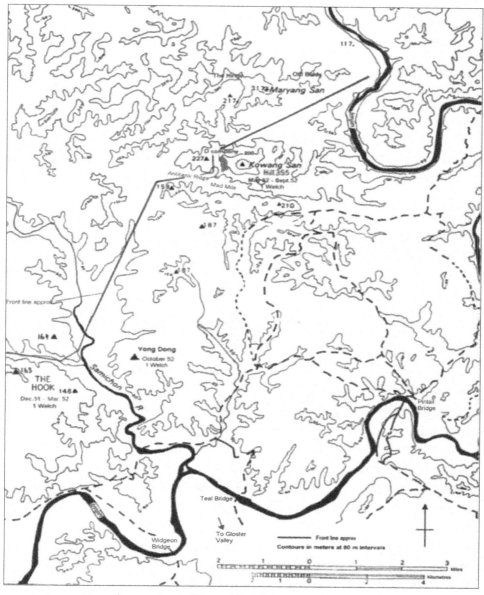

Comdiv section of line: Welch positions 1951-1952

After going down the hill to the cookhouse for breakfast, we returned to make our dugout more shipshape and homely. No sooner had we completed the digging and about to put a roof over it than the sergeant came along to tell Les that he was being posted up to A Company in the front line. I had to say cheerio to my last contact with the draft I had joined up with a year ago. The sergeant eventually returned to give me a hand with the dugout, even commenting that he might now move in with me. However, a lanky Welshman named Will Griffiths turned up and moved in instead. By the evening we had obtained and positioned some fairly straight and stout branches as the basic support for a roof but still had to spread our groundsheets over them for shelter that night. In another three days it would be Christmas.

A succession of huge flashes attracted my attention to the distant hills across the river valley to the right of our position. Republic of Korea (ROK) artillery was sending whistling messages of seasonal greetings and "glad you are here" appreciation across to the Chinese. After the flashes were seen, the sounds of the guns firing and the shells exploding took about ten seconds to reach me. Then, the 4.2 inch mortars of the Royal Artillery based at the bottom of our hill joined in, a succession of crisp crunches reaching our ears as their contributions were sent flying across into no-man's-land to give the Chinese on 169 something to think about.

It was important to get the bunker finished today. We had help from two Korean porters who went off to look for as many decent sticks as they could find. When they returned, these were laid close together across the beams we had maneuvered into position. They then went off again and returned with a quantity of rice straw to lay over the sticks to close up all the gaps. God only knew where they found it but it provided good insulation and stopped the earth that we piled on top from falling through. With that, the roof was finished. It would not be waterproof if it rained but that was not a consideration at this time of year. The most important thing was for our living and sleeping conditions to be warmer than they had been for the last two nights.

There was still much to do to make this place into a home away from home. The roof was only four feet above the floor and I was six feet tall so getting dressed, indeed doing anything would remain extremely awkward if things were left as they were. We dug a pit about two and a half feet deep and three feet square at the entrance. Here we could stand upright yet remain under shelter. Later, this was extended right back into the bunker. A number of other things needed to be done to make the place into a comfortable hole. The walls were squared off and cubbyholes carefully cut into them for storing small items. I made a small brush from a short stick, some springy twigs and a length of telephone wire and used it to sweep the floor and find out where it could be levelled off. Then the donkey-work was done and we were pleased with our efforts. Now we needed a way to heat the place up.

Monday, 24th December 1951

Today, my letter home started . . . *"It is Christmas Eve and hard to believe just how far away the rest of you are. Yet, all things considered and in a perverse sort of way, this experience is proving to be quite interesting, even enjoyable. Perhaps my ability to relate to the situation in this way is a blessing but it means that my quirky sense of humour is still not permitting me to take it at all seriously.*

My mother had started numbering her letters as I was doing with mine to her. I received letters numbered 1 and 4 which had me wondering where letters 2 and 3 could have got to? Later I replied to my brother David's letter and thanked him for sending me newspapers. He had also sent me a 'Film Diary' as a Christmas present for which I was very grateful.

It had become quite difficult to write as frequently as before but not for lack of time. For some reason, the necessary mental energy seemed insufficient to devote to it as before. My attention was all being consumed getting to grips with my job and this strange way of life we now had. The past few days of training had also been very grueling. David's diary was useful for entering the odd memory-jogging note but sadly, I lost this diary somewhere along the way.

However, at that moment it was also true to say that no matter how dire circumstances might prove to be, I would not have missed the experience of being here in Korea one bit. One day it would be possible to look back on it all, laugh at some of the things that had happened, or might have happened and be quieted, saddened and much wiser for others. They would pass before my mind's eye as if watching a film. There had already been times when I had looked at our circumstances here in this way, despite the emotions that I might have been experiencing at the time. But was there any other way to be? Whether it would always be a 'good thing' or not I was unable to decide. However, there came times when this feeling of sitting on a fence, unable to jump down on either side and throw myself fully into what was going on proved intensely disagreeable.

My brother had asked if the places we visited on the way out were anything like they appeared to be in books. I replied that they had but those pictures inevitably left out much significant detail. They could only convey a small portion of the experience of actually being in those places and able to look around. Pictures might prepare you for sights of the stalls with their acetylene tree lights in Singapore's China Town market but could not convey the reaction one had when encountering the putrid smell arising out of the sewers, or what it was like to be caught up in the teeming crowds of Hong Kong. They could only provide an introduction so that when you ever arrived in a place you had read about there would be less chance of getting overwhelmed, or perhaps lost. Pictures could titillate the appetite to visit these places but could never substitute for the actual experience.

Between 04:30 and 05:30, I had a 'stag' on guard duty. There had been reports of Chinese patrols creeping around on the last two nights but nothing happened while I was on duty. It was bitterly cold and I was extremely glad when my relief turned up. It was good to crawl back into my sleeping bag for another hour.

After breakfast we worked on the remaining tasks to complete our bunker. My brush was much admired, even envied, and for a mad moment the idea of going into business to make and sell them seemed a possibility. All they required was a straight stick about twelve inches long, a handful of springy twigs picked off a bush and a length of telephone cable to lash the whole lot together. Anyone could make one really! All it required was the idea and a little time.

My spell on duty in the signals bunker came between 12:00 and 18:00 but there was nothing happening anywhere. Our section of the front was suspiciously quiet. At that time all telephone connections were in excellent condition and this meant that the wireless network was quiet, only to be used if an emergency arose. However, the wireless network still had to be checked twice a day at 'stand to' to make sure that it was in working order should we come under an artillery barrage which might break any of the phone lines.

The chaps who had come out with the battalion told us that things had been relatively quiet up here at the sharp end for the past three weeks. News from the truce talks frequently spoke of an imminent deadline for completing the discussions. It was never mentioned who was actually laying down this deadline, the Chinese or the United Nations negotiators. Meanwhile, all this signified was that the prospects for settlement had deteriorated again. Hopefully the deadline would be extended. Every night the radio was tuned to Radio Kure for the latest news and the officers were constantly on the phone discussing the situation. There was expectancy in the air that we might suddenly be plunged once more into the full-scale battle situation that had existed earlier in the year. That would really be a shame now that we had made our bunker such a comfortable place to live in.

Christmas Day 1951

No mail came for me today and we continued to add improvements to our bunker, putting a central prop in for the roof, shelving for our kit and a fire. We made this from a metal mortar bomb box with one end bashed out and a hole in the lid over which we placed a chimney made from tin cans. The only available fuel was petrol which we put in a small tin inside the mortar box.

Lighting it with a long twist of paper was a very precarious business it required much care. Once lit, it burned very well, too well in fact because we could not control the draft. As a result the flame went right up the chimney and came out at the top. Naturally most of the heat followed it. The whole thing was extremely dodgy and potentially very dangerous.

By mid morning it began to snow. We were going to have a white Christmas after all. About eight inches of the stuff fell before the skies cleared late in the afternoon and the sun came out for a while. What a transformation. All those brown, muddy, war torn hills became bright and clean in their coat of fresh snow. Ridges and hills that were not normally clearly visible were now highlighted so sharply that it seemed as if one's eyesight was suddenly supernatural. All the roads showed up brown in the whiteness and it took little imagination to realise how slippery and treacherous they would now be.

A year ago the South Koreans and Yanks were very actively fighting a hard, gruelling campaign across this sort of country and in these conditions. It must have been a real bastard situation for them. In the autumn and early winter of 1950, when I was getting over my lovesickness and working for that jobbing builder, they had been hemmed in down south around Pusan. The landing at Inchon had changed all that, cutting the communist supply lines and allowing the UN to break out and drive the North Koreans back across the 38th parallel again.

That evening we discovered just how lucky we were to be at battalion HQ. The Christmas dinner served up by the cookhouse was superb—turkey with stuffing, roast and mashed potatoes and cabbage, followed by Christmas pudding. Beer, cigarettes, sweets and nuts were also provided. It was all so unexpected. We would not have done as well if we had been at home with our families. The commanding officer, "Dixie" Dean, came to see us. A short, stocky man, he was obviously well 'oiled' and his words were almost Churchillian in tone and delivery –

"We are here—to do a job—and—we—will do it.—So far—I am very pleased—with everyone—and—it is my earnest hope—that you—will—maintain this standard.—A very—Merry Christmas—to you all."

This was followed by "Three beers for the CO, Hic, hic, hic—booray." The 2IC then arrived to apologise for not having Taffy IX, the white goat regimental mascot, in attendance. The Goat Major had gone to bring Taffy from B Echelon but had been unable to return because of the snow.

Someone then started to sing and within seconds, everyone had joined in. The quality of the singing was superb as could be expected from Welsh voices especially when informed by beer and nostalgia for home. But I was feeling an urgent need to get away from all this merrymaking. While the meal had been excellent, the company had now become very boozy and noisy. I found myself in no mood for this. Making the excuse that I had to relieve the chap on signals exchange duty, I left and returned to my bunker for some peace and quiet. Besides, I was developing a cold, was not in good voice and couldn't join in the singing which I would normally have enjoyed doing.

Fire fighting fun

That evening we tried lighting the fire again with the same result as before—the flame and most of the heat emerged outside from the top of the chimney. We urgently needed to find a way to control the draught and tried placing another tin box across the end to close the gap. When the petrol in the little tin was exhausted, Will refilled it but while replacing it in the mortar box, managed to spill some. The box was still warm and the smell of vapourising fuel very quickly filled the bunker.

Suddenly becoming very apprehensive, I started to back out through the doorway. When Will attempted to relight it there was an almighty 'whoosh' as the petrol fumes exploded. A flame chased all around the bunker before ending up in the corner of the roof where it set fire to some of the rice straw. Clouds of acrid smoke descended on us like dark avenging angels and I quickly dived outside, my eyes streaming. A flurry of parkas, blankets, bedding rolls and other assorted items of kit followed me as Will, with remarkable presence of mind, began to throw them out. Smoke billowed out through the doorway and I could hear Will yelling and coughing. I dashed around like the proverbial 'fart out of a bottle' and eventually managed to find a can of water. Taking a deep breath, I charged back into the bunker to throw it up on to the flames in that corner of the roof and succeeded in extinguishing them. We had the blissful experience of sleeping on a cold muddy floor that night.

On Boxing Day, the mail drought cleared up with a vengeance. Letters 2, 3 and 5 arrived from mother together with others from my father, an uncle, my old Sunday school teacher Mr Grey, a card from my brother and a letter from Yvonne, a girl who lived two doors away.

The sergeant informed us that the temperature had dropped to below 14° F (-10° C) last night. What a great night to try and burn one's bunker down. Then it began to snow again. Being off duty for a couple of hours, Will and I got permission to walk up to one of the forward companies to see some of our mates. I thought of the familiar carol about Good King Wenceslas and his page. It was a long, cold walk there and back but good exercise. All sorts of rumours were going around, one being that, if the conflict here ends in a truce, the Welch Regiment would be sent to Malaya. Not that it was a better place to be because communist 'terrorists' were causing much trouble there. Where these stories originated remained a complete mystery

Around 11:00 a slight thaw set in and the paths became streams of mud. My boots were soon soaked through with the increased danger that the sole of one would come right away from the upper. The CQMS knew all about the state they were in but had been unable to do anything about them so far. Every time we met and before I said anything he would say, "Yes, yes. I know. You are about to lose your 'soul' any moment now. Perhaps you need to see the Padré." I also had three pairs of grey woollen socks that, having been washed several times, were now far too small for me to wear comfortably. I would have to speak to him about those as well.

That partial thaw brought a quite dramatic change to the scenery. The snow on the eastern and southern slopes of the hills melted away but not so on the western and northern slopes. It was like a topographical "Black and White Minstrel Show". By 15:00, it started to freeze again and through the night, the temperature dropped progressively below anything previously experienced. Fortunately, when on exchange duty we were able to keep warm enough.

Despite the smoky smell, we were also able to keep warm in our bunker, but it was another matter entirely to keep warm while on guard duty. A hazard that required caution at night was that the ground was frozen rock hard. Every step had to be taken with great care. It was too easy to end up slipping and sliding all over the place in the dark. Also, if your boots were damp, they could freeze stiff on your feet. And God help you if your socks were also damp. The cold could then become very painful.

The daytime thaw had partially loosened the snow covering the scrub oak. At night, as it froze again, some would drop to the ground creating the suspicion that someone was moving around out there beyond the wire. However, this served one positive purpose. While on guard in the dead of night, with the temperature having fallen sharply again, these wintry noises were what kept us alert. There were continual whispers of "What's that?", or "Who's there?", then "Eh?", or "Shhhh." Otherwise, we were almost continually preoccupied with the condition of our feet and trying to keep warm.

The only other things that commanded our attention at night were the stars. They seemed to be much brighter than I could ever remember and the sky seemed to be a darker, more brittle black. Only three constellations were familiar enough for me to pick them out: the Seven Sisters, the Plough and Orion. I always looked for them and it was in these moments that I could easily slip into a moment or two of deep contemplation. It was so still, the night so intensely quiet, so full of mystery.

More fire fighting fun

Back at the bunker, Will lit the fire again. Then, as before, when he tried to renew the fuel, yesterday's flaming experience was repeated. This time the roof did not catch fire but just smouldered for a while. Unfortunately, as Will was chucking kit out of the way, his parka fell across a small petrol lamp we had made and was quite badly damaged. The QM would be none too pleased about that.

I stayed outside for a while to let the smoke and the stink disperse. The hills and valleys around were obscured by the falling snow. Gazing into the storm, I drifted off into a reverie once more and just stood where I was, allowing my thoughts to drift where they would. For a while, an absolute peace suffused and surrounded me. Waking to the reality of where I was and why was not pleasant. In that moment I saw war as the ultimate and least intelligent way to resolve human disputes. Was there no other way to deal with issues of pride, ambition and strongly held ideals and beliefs and the suspicion and fear thy engendered?

Now, here in Korea, yet another outbreak of this madness had ended in a military stalemate and negotiators from both sides were in Panmunjom trying to bring this wasteful method of settling differences to an end. They had at least returned to the more civilised use of talk which should have been employed in the first place. Even if the two sides were still provoking each other, this was still a better way to proceed. Hopefully, reason and common sense would win out. But why had a deadline been laid down for their completion?

Apparently there were three basic sticking points at Panmunjom—the actual Armistice Line itself, how to maintain the Armistice once it was signed and the procedure for exchanging prisoners. There were 220 miles (354 kilometres) of front line to consider and the western end was causing difficulty for some reason. There was a proposal that a buffer zone two and a half miles wide be created taking in territory on both sides of the front line. It was positioning for this that would lead to the third active stage of the war late in 1953 after the relatively quiet time throughpout most of the year.

The prisoner exchange issue was complicated by the fact that many North Korean prisoners in South Korea did not want to be repatriated but the North Koreans were adamant that they should be. In May and June 1952 there was serious rioting between die-hard communists and anti-communists in the POW camp on Koje Island near Pusan.

Every night, if it were clear, we would look to the west of our position. There, at the site of the truce talks, we could see the searchlight shining vertically into the sky. There was a feeling that if ever it were not to shine it would presage a return to full hostilities, that we could expect another full onslaught from the Chinese like there had been eight months ago. Last night, while on guard duty between 22:00 and 23:15, that searchlight had not been visible. It was very eerie, very disturbing. The ancient Israelites, fleeing with Moses from Egypt into the Sinai Desert, might have felt much the same had the 'pillar of smoke by day and fire by night' that guided them in their wanderings suddenly not been there. Later, much to my relief, the searchlight beam reappeared once more. Perhaps, I thought whimsically to myself, they had to send off for more candles,.

Spotter planes were very busy during the day. According to the sergeant, they were based at an airstrip near a place curiously named Fort George that lay within a great horseshoe bend in the River Imjin at the end of the Gloster Valley. In fact, these planes had been around a little more frequently all over the Christmas period to report on any enemy activity that might warrant an air strike.

Along this section of the front air strikes were invariably mounted by Mustangs from the Royal Australian Air Force, events that were quite exciting to watch. Usually a flight of five planes, they would fly over in single file and as they crossed into no-mans-land would peel off one behind the other and dive quite steeply for some target. All we could hear would be the crackle of cannons and the thump of bombs exploding. Sometimes we saw a huge cloud of black smoke rise into the air and knew that napalm bombs had been dropped. When they exploded they scattered a blanket of flaming petroleum material all around. The thought of being anywhere near one of those when it went off conjured up awful images. Some rockets also carried napalm filled warheads and, in some quarters, were called 'Flaming Onions'.

Deepening the trenches

An order was issued to the whole battalion; the standard of all positions on the Hook had to be dramatically improved as quickly as possible. This meant that the most important command bunkers had to be deepened and roofs reinforced to withstand artillery bombardment and this included the signals bunker. Barbed wire defences had to be checked and reinforced but the most tedious job of all was to deepen all crawl trenches to a depth of six feet.

Currently, they were anything between three and four feet deep, probably much as they had been when taken over from the Chinese. Unfortunately, at this time of year, the ground was frozen solid. Deepening them would require much backbreaking work with a pickaxe before anything could be shovelled out. It was a mind numbing, physically exhausting activity and I had my share to do. In the course of doing so, I sustained a self-inflicted injury.

This particular morning, being pleasantly warm and sunny, I took up pick and shovel and started work just outside the exchange. After about half an hour of steadily picking away at the frozen ground and making what seemed little progress for the energy expended, I was feeling pretty shagged out and took a short breather. It was my misfortune not to notice that I had been working my way closer to a point where a bunch of telephone lines from the exchange crossed the trench about three feet above it. They were firmly tied to pickets on either side. Wearily picking up the pick to resume work, I raised it above my head and swung it forward. The next thing I knew was that the centre of the pick, the part where the handle attached, had smacked me hard on the forehead just above the left eye. It had snagged the telephone lines and been catapulted back to score a 'bulls-eye' over my left eyebrow. Dropping the pick, I subsided into the trench, one hand over the point of impact, waiting for the surprise to wear off and my wits to return realising that this would take a few moments. The real shock would no doubt come later.

Slowly, I regained enough strength to stand up and take stock. Judging by the blood pouring down my face, I had sustained a decent gash. Thankfully, neither of the pointy ends of the pick had hit me. If they had, I would really have been in trouble. My knees feeling very shaky and needing to get to the Regimental Aid Post (RAP) down the hill, it was all I could do to stumble down to it. The duty orderly cleaned the wound up with some antiseptic, told me stitches would not be needed, stuck a plaster over the wound and gave me a couple of aspirins to ease the ache that would follow. I quietly thanked God for giving me such a thick skull but knew I would not be so grateful for the thick head I could expect. After about ten minutes sitting quietly in the RAP, I felt able to walk back up to the exchange to see if anyone was having a brew up. Clearly, my trench digging was over for that day but a strong sweet mug of char would go down a treat.

By dinner time the dull ache over my left eye had greatly eased and I was able to do my stag on guard between 22:00 and 23:15. Putting it mildly, it was bloody cold but did ease the slight residual headache. The night was very clear and the astral spectacular did much to make my spell on duty bearable.

Will was posted back to A Echelon and a chap named Philips took his place. He ridiculed our fireplace and set to work to install a new firebox and a better method for supplying fuel to it. He used an old jerry can as the fire box, a few holes at the base to let in air and had the chimney rising from the spout. He 'found' a length of rubber tubing and a long thin piece of metal tubing through which fuel could be siphoned to drip into the can. By fixing a makeshift clamp across the rubber tubing, the rate of flow of the fuel and thus of combustion could be easily controlled. It was very ingenious and extremely successful. Once going, the whole jerry can glowed with heat. It was almost too much in such a confined space but I could put up with that if it meant no more explosions.

New Year's Eve 1951

While on exchange duty, the CO came by and asked for the 32 set to be tuned into the frequency being used by two platoons of Australian infantry positioned next to us. They were to mount a 'harassment' attack on Hill 169. Unfortunately, my relief came before anything started so I never found out what happened.

One of the advantages of the 62 set was that it could be tuned into various radio stations, particularly those that broadcast in English. In this way we were able to keep up-to-date with events both here in Korea and around the world. Month old papers only had interest for details of domestic news.

Altogether, it was a quiet and quite boring sort of day. A few spotter planes flew over and another, which someone said was used by the brigadier, went round more specifically over our positions. However, for me it was a day marked by a feeling of extreme weariness. Utterly fagged out and still experiencing residual effects from yesterday's blow to the head, I went off to my sleeping roll and slept. In comparison with all the activity back on the training range for those ten days after we arrived here, it was fortunate that life in battalion HQ was remarkably easygoing. There were long periods with very little to do but this inactivity proved even more tiring than that last day of field craft exercises.

Late on New Year's Eve I wrote home:

"Dear Mum, Dad and Dave,

It is fifteen minutes to 1952. I am sitting in the signals exchange bunker at the Pan Buri Command Post Hill, two miles north of the River Imjin and six hundred yards from the front line. Brian is about three hundred yards away as near as I can estimate and Panmunjom is about twenty miles to the west. We are listening to Radio Australia on the 62 set. The programme is of music to see the "old year out and the new year in", or so the announcer says. So far we have listened to songs and pieces performed by Bing Crosby, Judy Garland, Artie Shaw, Les Brown and Doris Day.

You will remember that this time last year I went out with Mike and Martin [school friends] and then came home early because they couldn't make up their minds what they wanted to do and I had got fed up with them. But listening to this music, which is slow and romantic, fills me with longing to be home at a dance. Then, when it gets more lively I just want to go completely nuts and jive all over the place. I would also love to be listening to this music in more civilised surroundings, instead of sitting in a hole in the ground at the other end of the Earth, drinking tea brewed in a black tin can over a jerry-built, petrol-fired space heater, the music coming over a military transceiver with fluctuating reception.

There are four of us here listening to the music, the duty exchange operator, who is waiting for his relief to arrive at midnight, the signals corporal in charge of the battalion HQ exchange, a chap waiting to go on guard and myself. The agony has just been piled on for us with the sound of Ray Anthony singing "Sentimental Me".

The minutes are slowly ticking by. There is still plenty of fuel in the jerry can and the bowl of hot water placed on the stove this morning is still there. Since 08:00, it has been used by about nine or ten people to wash in. Hot water is precious you see. Wireless earphones dangle everywhere from stick pegs driven into the walls and now the strains of "Truly Fair" can be heard. Old newspapers, comics and boxes of assorted rubbish litter the place but at least it is warm and all we have to call home at the moment.

Some officers are proving very annoying at the moment. They will insist on making phone calls in the middle of a tune we would like to listen to and then the set has to be turned off while the call is being put through. But it has been good to learn that the communications systems within this battalion have been complimented as the best anywhere in the division. That compliment came from the commanding officer of the Royal Artillery unit supporting 29 Brigade and it has to be said that communications with them are among the most important of all.

I've been replying to letters from a lot of people tonight—four so far. Another letter number "5" from you arrived today with "Not D Coy. Try C Coy." written on it. It is dated 14th December but what puzzles me is that on Boxing Day I received a letter numbered "5" and dated 11th December. I think you lost track of your numbers and it should have been number "6" because your letter number "7" dated 16th December has arrived today.

It is now 23:15. Ray Anthony has signed off and the announcer is giving the call sign of the station. Now the strains of "Auld Lang Syne" are coming over. The relief exchange operator has arrived and the process of handing over is being completed. Outside, the artillery is rumbling away and according to one chap who just poked his head in, "Bags of flares are going up all along the line." I suppose that is how the 'squaddies' up front are celebrating the arrival of 1952. I just pray that it will be a better one than last year.

The CO has just rung and asked to be put through somewhere so the wireless set has been smartly turned off. It is now 0005 a.m., the date is the 1st January 1952 and I am going to bed.

I should sign off with "Good morning" but will leave it as "Cheerio for now". All the best to you in this New Year.

9

New Year Begins

New Year's Day to 31st January 1952

Batteries and Boots

The dawn brought no change to the usual routines of the day other than my having to lend a hand moving the battery charging engine. Batteries had to be provided and maintained for lighting the bunkers of the CO, the duty officer and the exchange. Until now, this task had been performed at the foot of the hill where the charging engine had been positioned but this was proving unsatisfactory. Batteries had to be disconnected, taken down the hill, recharged, carried back again and reconnected. It was a real chore and we decided to move the charging engine up the hill and charge those for the hill up there.

However, the batteries that had been supplied to us were in a shocking state. Badly knocked about and maintained, the electrolyte in them was almost pure water. Not that we would have drunk it, but even when they had been put on charge for eight hours they no longer held a charge that lasted for more than two. The inconstancy of the power supply led to increasing complaints from the CO, the Provost and the Signals Officer so we rigged up a different system. Since we had to keep the charging engine running twenty-four hours a day, we thought it should be possible to rig up a direct lighting system. The batteries were left permanently installed in the respective VIP bunkers and connected directly to the engine. They were thus being charged and discharged at the same time. It worked very well until the time came to refuel the motor. This needed to be done every four hours irrespective of what was going on. Fortunately there was usually enough 'juice' left in the batteries to keep lights going while refuelling was carried out.

It appeared that the CO of C Company had a patrol out in no-man's-land and had forgotten to inform HQ about it. He had compounded this error by failing to notify everyone when it was returning. As a result, chaps at one of the machine gun posts heard and then spotted figures creeping around outside the barbed wire perimeter and were on the point of opening fire on them. Fortunately, someone had the good sense to check with company commanders of front line companies to see if anyone could confirm their sighting. How close things came to a real tragedy will never be known. Some of the chaps on that patrol were in my draft so it would have hurt to know that they had been shot up by our own gunners.

It was news to me that company commanders could initiate patrols without first consulting with the battalion CO. C company CO was the one who had bashed his face on the muzzle of my rifle as we had ducked for cover that time when a bomb from a Centurion tank bomb thrower had misfired. On Christmas Day evening he had taken over the 62 set in his company signals bunker and tied up the air space asking to be put through to various senior members of HQ staff. We knew they were all otherwise engaged celebrating and it was highly unlikely that they would come over to the exchange just to speak to him over the radio. The duty operator, in order to determine what priority to allocate to his requests, had asked why he wanted to speak to them. The major said, "Oh, I only wanted to wish them the compliments of the season you know." The signals sergeant, who was in the exchange at the time, nearly had a fit when he heard this and decided to weep with mortification instead.

Why the old buffer hadn't used the telephone we never found out. Perhaps he had also been celebrating too well and was the worse for drink. The sergeant then told us that this major, an oldish chap and a bit of an 'old lady', maybe in his late forties or early fifties, was pulled from behind a desk in the War Department in London to take command of a company. Goodness only knew why because he was also quite podgy and never looked very fit for the sort of life we were living here. His manner and actions, as on this occasion, were sometimes quite 'doolally'.

The CQMS had at last received some new footwear for me—a pair of Boucheron boots. Canadian made, they were similar to US army combat boots with half calf length leather uppers but gumboot style bottoms. He told me that they were the only boots he could get in my size since the commando boot pattern supplied to everyone else did not come larger than size ten. These boots were really quite good, a bit on the large side at size twelve but that was no problem. At least they should keep my feet dry. He was also able to supply me with a pair of 'long johns' to help keep my legs warm when on guard duty at night. Regarding the boots, he also commented, "You are as bloody difficult to fit up with boots as was that chap Speakman who won a VC here a little while back". I wondered where he had picked up that little bit of information. It must have been from someone in the divisional stores who was out here at the same time as Speakman.

We had a pay parade today at which I received the usual £1. It just covered my NAAFI bill so my finances were back where they started. I was now due for a pay increase of three shillings a week so later that morning went to see the pay clerk about it. I asked that he increase the allotment from my pay sent home to my parents for safe keeping until I was 'demobbed'.

Sometime during the day I had the oddest impression. I had been here at battalion HQ for only ten days but it felt like ten months. It was strange how quickly one could settle into such a totally new way of life, as though one had always lived this way.

That night, for some reason the duty exchange operator was so utterly tired that, were he to be left alone, he would probably nod off. If caught sleeping on duty he would be for the high jump in a big way and no mistake. So, feeling wider awake than he, I stood in for him while he went to sleep in the corner of the bunker for an hour. Just after 01:00, there was a hell of a rumpus. Both the telephone switchboard and the wireless were running hot and my sleeping friend had to be woken up to help handle the traffic. Unfortunately, I failed to note down what it was all about.

Who are we? Why are we here?

Down the hill below the signals exchange lay the Welfare Unit whose task was to find ways to keep everyone's morale high. They had set up a loudspeaker over which sweet music could be directed up over the hill each evening. I liked to stand outside the exchange and listen to these gentle sounds borne on the breeze. Although it was usually quite a pleasant thing to do, on this particular occasion, a profound sadness overcame me as I stood there listening to the music and gazing out over these bare, blasted, brown hills still patched here and there with snow.

The contentment I usually derived from listening to good music or contemplating natural beauty was absent. Now, savagely aware of where I was and asking why, a deeper question emerged. Suddenly I had absolutely no idea why I existed at all, not just here in Korea, but why I was alive on this planet in the first place. The part my parents played in this didn't come into it at all. What was I? Who was I? Why was I here?

There were probably many traditional religious or spiritual ways such a dilemma would be counseled, but none of them seemed capable of meeting the depth my questioning had suddenly reached. I could no longer consider a supreme, super-humanised God as having anything to do with this. Such an idea seemed an utter nonsense. The irrationality of religious belief, in our case Christian belief, became more apparent when one recalled how, in the world war just over, the Germans, Italians, British, Americans, French and countless others caught up in the conflict, all acknowledged this same God and all thought the Divine Strength would be given solely to aid their side in the conflict. The same applied where the God of these opposing forces was the Jewish Jehovah, Allah, Brahma or the Great Whatever; they were all different names for the same concept.

In the end, I was burning up to know why I was here in this three dimensional body on this three dimensional planet, why I or anyone else had come into existence in the first place. Why did the Cosmos exist? Why had we as a species been created? What was the point of it all? Was this 'God' so badly in need of something to do that he created the Universe, set the whole unimaginable process going that created our galaxy, the Solar System, the Earth and then allowed Life, in all its forms, to gradually evolve on it?

My questioning went far beyond merely asking why life and the state of the world were the way they were—in such a mess. It asked why a universe, a world, or life of any kind existed at all.

I Think Again

Later, just after midnight, something happened that made me reconsider. Some might say that 'God' decided I needed a slap on the wrist for questioning his and my existence. I had to fill the charging motor fuel tank and the large, very full twenty-five gallon jerry-can proved just a little too heavy and awkward to handle easily. Some petrol slopped over the still hot engine. It caught fire and the flame leapt across to the can that I was holding. Luckily the top was off or the consequences might have been far different than they were but the surprise led me to slop more petrol, this time over my right hand. As a result, during the time it took to put the can down safely, the back of the three middle fingers and part of my thumb were quite severely burned. Blisters developed that grew increasingly painful. Later, when I finally got to bed, they prevented my getting off to sleep for quite a while. When sleep finally came, I slept all through 'stand to' and breakfast, finally getting up around 10:30 to wash and shave as best I could.

I had taken much care to dress the wound with a field dressing but after lunch, decided it would be wisest to report to the RAP and have it properly dressed. The result was that my three middle fingers were bandaged together, a very awkward arrangement. Unfortunately, a small piece of grit, which had not been properly cleaned off, remained lodged between two of my fingers and the bandage kept it there to irritate.

However, when all was said and done, my injuries were still much lighter than those sustained by another chap who, some time back, had a can of petrol blow up in his face. I never learned exactly how this happened but with the blisters and then the scabs, he was in real agony for the next few weeks as his face repaired. But he survived and fortunately, kept his sight.

Our section of the front line was humming for a while as A Company mounted an attack on hills 169 and 137. The radio was running hot with requests for artillery support from the tanks dug in along the hillsides and among the forward trenches. Administering all the radio traffic created a huge problem for us signallers. It was almost impossible to keep the log books up to date with all the messages passing through the exchange. Everyone everywhere was on air at the same time, getting in each other's way and making a hell of a lot of noise. We had no watch with which to record the time on the messages that had to be written out for delivery by runner to this or that officer. Bearing in mind that this operation by our chaps was only a small harassing manoeuvre, it didn't bear thinking about what our situation would be like if the attack had come the other way.

Earlier in the day, one of the Korean porters, or 'Gooks' as they were more affectionately known, had washed my underwear for me. It was still damp and frozen stiff when he brought it back to my bunker. My string vest was as rigid as a piece of wire netting and could be picked up by the edge and waved about without bending. To hang it up, all I had to do was bend the narrow shoulder pieces and hang them over a telephone cable somewhere. This was fine until it thawed out but every item was clean again. They only needed to be allowed time to completely dry out in the sun and then be aired by the fire in the bunker.

I learned something important about these freezing temperatures we were getting—almost the hard way. During stand-to that morning, the aerial for the 62 set needed some adjustment. I was about to reach for it when the corporal shouted at me to stop. He came over and told me that if I had gripped that aerial with my bare hand it would have stuck to it because it was so cold.

Eventually my body heat would have helped release them but blisters would have been the result. It was important to have gloves on before attempting to touch anything metallic that had been outside in these below freezing temperatures. I explained that I had lost my gloves when coming ashore at Inchon and the CQMS had not issued me with another pair. Be that as it may, out of curiosity I put out my finger to very gingerly touch the aerial and sure enough, it felt sticky, as if covered with honey but with a dry kind of stickiness. It was interesting to learn that extreme cold could 'burn' just as much as extreme heat. It was a hazard we had not been clearly told about, so it was very fortunate that the corporal had been there when he was. Otherwise it would have been my third mishap.

Later that day I met a chap who hated spaghetti. It so happened that the C7 rations we received about three times a week contained tins and tins of the stuff—spaghetti Bolognaise with ground meat and tomato sauce, plain spaghetti in tomato sauce, or spaghetti with mini frankfurters. Over the past few weeks he had accumulated tins of the stuff and didn't want them. When he learned that I liked spaghetti he gave them all to me. So now there was quite a nice little stock of food in my 'larder' for whenever I felt peckish between meals, or late at night. He also gave me another towel and some new socks that were big enough for my size eleven 'plates of meat'. As it happened the timing was superb because all my existing socks were in a shocking condition. Around the heels and toes there were more darns than original sock.

That night, I stayed up late again to help out another duty signaller who was having difficulty staying awake. Fortunately this was a 'normal' night, or morning, and not too many calls came through. I was able to write some letters while he snatched a couple of hours' shut eye.

There was a new sound around the hills that night, one that produced a very eerie echo. The sky was clear and the air crisp. It was a night when the least sound could carry a long way. A battery of very heavy US artillery lay some miles to our rear. There were four guns there of a much heavier caliber than our 25 pounder field artillery. Someone said they had been christened "The Persuaders". The odd thing about them was that they all seemed to fire their shells at exactly the same moment. The resulting explosion shook the earth for miles around, even where we were several miles away. The explosion also had all the keenness of a gigantic whip-crack that rolled and bounced around from hill to hill with a lingering echo, as when the lower notes of a piano are struck when the loud pedal is depressed. It was eerie, yet fascinating, to see how long the echo could be heard as it rolled away into the distance.

Probably in retaliation for the A company skirmish there was quite a bit of action today. The Chinese dropped many mortar bombs on D company. Telephone lines were severed and it was necessary to resort to wireless communication which kept us wireless operators on the hop. In addition to receiving, writing out and delivering messages, the log book had to be kept up to date. This required that we abbreviate every word longer than three letters which probably took us more time that we saved. It was quite a puzzle to know how to abbreviate words such as 'here', 'they' or 'from'.

The news that the Adjutant would be conducting an inspection that morning panicked us into cleaning up our bunkers. In the end it never took place and this was not the first time this happened. It led us to wonder if the threat of an inspection was all that had been intended. It certainly motivated everyone to clean up their act and their quarters very quickly.

A letter from my mother told me of the death of my Uncle Eddie, my father's next younger brother. There was no indication what he had been ill with but, whatever it may have been, he had been a complete invalid for a long time with no hope of recovery. Truth to tell, it was a blessing both for him and everyone else. He was a strange man, about the same height and build as my father but had never married. After my paternal grandfather died and some years before I was born, Uncle Eddy had chosen to live with Granny. In fact, she was the only one of my grandparents that I ever knew. A strange lady, she always dressed in black Edwardian style clothes. My only real memory of Uncle Eddie was of the day he called round to see my mother and found me sitting and playing on the concrete drive. I was about nine years old but he thought to warn me that if I did that too often I would develop 'piles'. Many years were to pass before I found out he was talking about haemorrhoids.

The sergeant asked me to go with him to the Aussie lines on the other side of the Samichon valley. Four times we crossed animal tracks in the snow that looked remarkably like those of large dogs. The sergeant wondered if they might be tracks of mountain lions that were believed to roam wild in the central Korean mountains. While passing through the barbed wire fence to enter the Aussie position, I slipped and did more damage to my right hand. Fortunately the blisters had healed well but the skin was still pretty tender and ripping it open on the wire made a bit of a mess of it again. Unfortunately, I made no other record of this excursion.

That evening the sergeant asked if I would like to help compile the twice-weekly "NAAFI orders" for members of the BHQ signals platoon. This meant taking individual orders and then compiling the totals for each category or item. They could include anything from Japanese Asahi beer and Australian canned peaches and pears, to tobacco, cigarettes and cigarette papers. The orders were then sent to the battalion RQMS at B echelon for collation and then passed on to the NAAFI. The corporal warned me not to get involved with the actual collection of the money because of the responsibility this would carry. This was the sergeant's job. However, it felt good to do this job and organise everything efficiently. It was almost as if I had gone into business for myself.

We lose one good man and one officer

I drew the worst 'stag' for guard duty—from 03:45 to 04:45. It seemed to presage that this day, 11th January 1952, would be another day of bad, sad news. A patrol went out from C Company during the wee hours of the 10th January to inspect hill 169 and find out what the Chinese were doing on it. Aerial reports had stated that they were continuing to dig themselves in. The tunnels evidently went down over twenty feet or more to bunkers deep inside the hill where they would be quite safe from bombs and shells.

The patrol reached the hill but was ambushed and the officer, Second Lieutenant Burgess, badly wounded in the lower chest and thigh, died. To my utter dismay, my friend Lance Corporal Alec Ahern was killed. Two others, Privates Chard and Kenway also died but I didn't know them as well as I had known Alec.

Alec and I had got to know each other on the *Georgic* and, together with Brian, had explored central Singapore together. He was one of the pleasantest, intelligent, tolerant and gentle natured chaps I had ever met and his death profoundly shocked and saddened me. Given his fine qualities, it was a great and quite senseless loss.

A patrol from D Company went out at first light to collect Lt. Burgess's body, met no opposition and returned safely before lunchtime. I was still experiencing shock about Alec Ahern's death and had trouble believing it until it was finally posted up on 'Part 1 Orders'. Then I knew it was true and had to be accepted. Another chap named Lansdowne was listed as missing since no one saw him get killed. It was assumed that he had been captured, poor sod.

After the night's events the day was completely boring and uneventful in every way. I overslept again, finally climbing out into the day just after ten o'clock. Except for the odd flurry of activity when an attack went out, or a Chinese barrage came in, there had been many times when life up in the front line had seemed no different than it had been when we were on manoeuvres last year, up on the Buckingham Tofts PTA near Thetford Chase in Norfolk. But the events of the last two nights had sadly disabused me of that idea.

Late news

It was to be many years later that Brian told me he had been on the patrol when Second Lieutenant Burgess was killed. I had always thought that his appointment as company clerk soon after we joined the Welch Regiment in Colchester in 1952 would have removed him out of a rifle section into the HQ section of the company. It was on one of the few occasions that we met while in Korea that he disabused me of this.

In a letter written to me on 30th August 2001, almost fifty years later, he told me of his participation in that patrol. What he had to say was very revealing and I quote:

"With regard to the Second Lieutenant Burgess death you mention, I have some recollection of this incident. We [usually] patrolled across the Samichon, over Pheasant [a hill in the 169 area] onto the second hill. Here one section stayed to cover and the other moved onto 169 for a look onto the other side, then we withdrew back to our own lines. I thought that was dodgy enough when I was on the patrol even though we were not required to make contact with the Chinks.

In mid January, the 10th comes to mind, Second Lieutenant Burgess led a standing patrol onto 169 in the time-honoured fashion. However, on this occasion he decided to go with his section further down into the valley below 169 where they were bumped by the Chinese. (It was known before this day that he was 'gong happy' [keen to earn a medal] in competition with his twin brother in the Norfolk's).

As I remember, Ken Kenway, B. Chard, L/c Ahern [?] were killed along with Burgess. Bill Lansdowne was seen to be taken prisoner but was found shot in the back one month later. The last victim, 'Paddy' Moore was wounded in the stomach and pelvis and died about three days later. The whole thing was a sad and unnecessary loss of life caused by someone who wanted to be a hero. To add insult, we were required to attend a hollow square ceremony, where they brought along Burgess's body draped in the Union Jack, his boots sticking out underneath, so that he could receive full Military Honours. The other lads had no such recognition, for we never saw them again."

View SE from Pan Buri across Samichon River to Yong Dong

My letters home recalled these events differently to Brian's account above. Burgess led his patrol on the 11th January while L/c Ahern, Kenway and Chard were killed on the patrol the day before, a fact confirmed on the Welch Regiment Roll of Honour. Somehow I had rolled these two patrols into one, possibly because there was a gap in the record contained in my letters.

In addition to his account of the patrol, Brian also believed that the Welch Regiment was not based on The Hook but on the eastern side of the Samichon valley in an area known as Yong Dong, (Chongdong-Ni on the maps) and that The Hook was occupied by the US Marines.

Brian's account also differs from those of Charlie Haynes who was a machine gunner with the Welch Regiment at the time. Positioned at a forward point passed by the standing patrols mentioned in the above account he knew exactly where we had been, on The Hook. The US Marines had been on the Hook before and would be again, but from December 1951 to March 1952 it was the Welch Regiment that occupied it.

Later I discovered how this error had arisen in Brian's memory. When the Welch arrived in Korea, a month or so before Brian and I arrived out there, they had taken over from the reformed Gloucestershire Regiment who were deployed in the Yong Dong area on the eastern side of the Samichon valley. They would not have been sent straight to a critically important sector in the front because the officers and men needed time to become acclimatised and prepared. Once the hand-over had been completed they were then sent across to The Hook where we joined them. Further evidence comes from my recollection of accompanying the HQ Signals sergeant on a trip across the Samichon to visit the Australian lines there. This would have me agree with Haynes. I have a photograph of Yong Dong on the other side of the river that I took from the western side of the Samichon.

Factual details apart, Brian's recall of the gung ho attitude of Burgess and the common knowledge that he had some kind of competition going with a twin brother, would be correct. Confirmation came later from other sources. However, this kind of detail would not figure in any official report. Such events tend to be prettied up to look good in the official record.

Back to the humdrum

It was "NAAFI orders day" again and as I prepared to start collecting orders someone told me that the sergeant I was supposed to be 'helping' had been moved back to A Echelon to supervise the preparation for delivery of all the orders from the various companies. Unfortunately he had taken with him details of individual orders from our signals section making it impossible for me to know who had ordered what and how much money had to be collected. I began to chase around asking everyone if they could remember what they had ordered, calculate monies due and collect it from them. However, these 'remembered' orders tallied up differently from that which the sergeant had worked out from the original orders and sent up to me. Stuff was left over that I then had to sell off and collect the required money. On top of all this there had been price changes that I had not been told about and this presented another problem when finalizing accounts to settled with the CQMS.

In spite of all this, everything was settled to the CQMS's satisfaction and I found myself holding a 'buckshee' two shillings and sixpence. Not at all prepared to try to work out who had paid too much for what, I decided to accept it as 'expenses' and keep 'mum'.

Around 15:30, while having a 'kip', I was woken by terrible screaming nearby. Quickly getting up, I found one of the Korean porters dancing around with his trousers on fire. It took a few moments to find something with which to smother the flames so that his still smouldering trousers could be removed. It became clear that he was in a bad way with severe burns on the right thigh and buttock. Another chap came up and stayed with him while I went to phone the RAP and get some medical orderlies on the scene as quickly as possible. Fetching something that the poor chap could rest on and a blanket to keep him warm, we waited for the orderlies to arrive.

One of the many Korean porters assigned to BHQ to do the heavy carrying, he had been lugging a full can of petrol up the hill. The clamp on the cap had not been fully depressed and shut securely and petrol had leaked out onto his trousers. Apparently, after delivering the can and not aware what had happened, he had stopped to light a cigarette. Inevitably the petrol vapour had ignited. He had been wearing one of the padded cotton uniforms typical of the clothing North Korean and Chinese soldiers were supplied with. The material was anything but fireproof and burned very quickly. Even when the flames were extinguished the material continued to smoulder like a fuse.

When I had burned my hand with some petrol a few days before, the pain was considerable so this porter must have been suffering agonies while we waited for the orderlies. But all he seemed worried about was his employment permit and Safe Pass to enter the battalion area. Fortunately, they were in a pocket on the side of his trousers that had not caught fire and had escaped the flames. The orderlies arrived at last, gave him an injection of morphine and took him away on a stretcher.

Time for some music

Late that evening, while on exchange duty, everything was unusually quiet and I played around with the 62 set until I found a station on which Malcuzinsky was playing a Chopin ballade. It was good to listen to some agreeable music without the phone ringing to interrupt. Then I managed to tune in to a concert given by the Benny Goodman Carnegie Hall Jazz Band which, at that time, included members who became well known in their own right. Some like Harry James and Gene Krupa later set up their own bands. There were times when the desire to sit down and listen to some good music without being disturbed every thirty seconds could become quite intense. It was one reason to look forward to the end of national service.

This led to thinking of other reasons for getting it over and done with. To be able to wash and keep clean easily, wear clean and comfortable clothes that fitted, have clean sheets on a well sprung bed so that sleeping on the ground would become a memory and, above all, to drink a decent cup of tea were all good reasons for looking forward to demob day. It would also be good to see a film in the comfort of a cinema with soft seats, or go to a dance and meet some girls. Then again, it would be just as good to just stay home and read or listen to records of favourite music.

As it now was here in Korea, personal hygiene was entirely relative depending on the temperature when you woke up. Invariably I slept with my trousers on and only removed my damp socks to avoid getting foot rot. Those new Boucheron boots, although waterproof, made my feet sweat excessively. As for my clothing, it was either too large or too small and keeping it clean would be almost impossible were it not for the Korean porters who did some laundering for us. Sleeping on the ground was, in many respects, an improvement on some army beds I had known but the continual twisting and turning to locate a comfortable position for my hips would only be remedied by a soft sprung mattress. As for tea, the stuff served up at the cookhouse or in the NAAFI had invariably been stewed to the consistency of soup. A nice, freshly brewed pot of Brooke Bond Dividend tea was something often talked about and ardently longed for. In one letter home I even asked that someone send me a packet. It never arrived.

The adjutant loses it

Sometimes unbelievably stupid things could happen here that did nothing to ease these thoughts and feelings. Accidents and senseless deaths on patrol aside, there were other incidents that could have a seriously demoralising effect and fuel real discontent and resentment.

One night, around 23:00, as a couple of us were checking the HQ electricity supply system, we heard a rather loud voice down in the crawl trench below us. This was so unusual that to listen we crept nearer until able to make out the figures of the adjutant and a sergeant standing by one of the bunkers off the crawl trench. The chap on guard was there and one sleepy, tousle haired member of the signals platoon who had just been rudely awakened.

The adjutant was in a real rage and handing out a first class 'rocket' to the sleepy signaller for having smoke coming out of the chimney of his bunker. For a moment we could hardly credit what we were hearing; it was so absurd. Then he fired another 'rocket' at the guard for being away from his post calling him, among other things, a "yellow coward".

That sort of talk sounded hysterical and not good coming from a captain. It was also displaying the lack of a quality that should have been essential in an officer of his rank, the capacity to remain cool under all circumstances. This was not helpful for us ORs. We later learned that the poor fellow on guard who had copped this tirade had merely been doing his duty and making the occasional contact with the chap on guard along the next stretch of crawl trench.

The outcome was that both chaps were put on a 'fizzer'. Fortunately, they came before an officer who possessed both common sense and a sense of humour. After hearing them state their case he had no hesitation in dismissing the charges.

The stupidity of this event became even more apparent in light of the fact that from the time the battalion arrived on The Hook, the CO had ordered that fires were to be lit only at night when the smoke would not be visible to the enemy, even if their patrols might smell it. By the time I arrived on the scene just before Christmas the order had been forgotten and fires were kept going all day and all night. No one seemed to mind whether smoke was visible by day or not. The enemy knew where we were anyway. For the Adjutant to come round and kick up such a hysterical fuss about smoke from a fire during the night seemed illogical and the manner in which he did so uncalled for.

The next evening another chap was put on a 'fizzer' for exactly the same reason, for having smoke coming out of the chimney of his bunker. This was despite the fact that his fire had gone out and was quite cold. He had also been asleep for over four hours which was confirmed by the CSM. The charge was pressed but again, common sense and fairness prevailed and he was acquitted. One was left to wonder what words the CO might have had in his adjutant's shell like ear about these carryings on.

Such incidents, such displays of ill temper and irrationality, could hardly be expected to give us confidence in those in command or assure us that they would be capable of making rational decisions in times of real urgency and emergency. The only excuse that came to mind for the adjutant's weird behaviour was the death of Second Lieutenant Burgess the other night. He was the first officer from The Welch to be killed here. As it turned out, although other officers were wounded, Burgess was the only officer in the battalion who would die here in Korea. However, there was no doubting that the loss of six men in two nights had shaken everyone.

The aftermath of the above incidents was threefold. The signals officer banned all fires in the signals exchange between 17:45 and 07:15 hours, the coldest period of the 24 hour day when temperatures could plummet to 20° C below freezing, even lower. Then the adjutant came into the exchange one evening and saw about half a dozen of us sitting there talking, as much for the combined warmth provided by our body heat in one small area as for company. He didn't care for this saying that if the Chinese were to bombard us and scored a direct hit on the exchange, too many people would be killed or wounded at one time. It was a big 'if' but when compared with his recent irrationality, he had presented a reasonable scenario. However, it also begged a big question. Was it any more reasonable for us to go back to our bunkers and freeze to death or were solitary deaths preferable to group deaths?

Lastly, the adjutant succeeded in infecting the CSM with this idea that when "two or three were gathered together" it presented an unacceptable hazard and was to be avoided. Unfortunately the CSM's ability to apply this rule proved even feebler than the adjutant's. He only had to see a small group of us standing together having a discussion to yell at us to keep moving. On one occasion when the signals corporal was discussing with two of us something about a line that needed to be checked out, the CSM came along and told us to move on. The corporal dearly wanted to thump him for being a 'stupid bastard'.

Yet another ridiculous incident occurred a few days later. One of the signallers had been detailed to find and repair a break in a telephone line. He had washed and shaved, tidied himself up, picked up his rifle and gear and gone off. When he returned he bumped into the Adjutant and was given an inspection on the spot and berated for having dirty hands. When the signals sergeant heard of this he raised the matter with the Adjutant who maintained that he had not criticised the signaller because his hands were dirty but because his shirt had been dirty. We could only wonder if the responsibility of command was causing the poor man to 'lose' it.

There were several other times when we suspected certain officers of being a little the worse for drink. Usually they uncharacteristically became too jovial and chatty with us members of the lower ranks. There were times when, for similar reasons, we also wondered about the Commanding Officer. If he ever went for a wander at night and was challenged by someone on guard, he seldom knew the current password. What would happen if an attack came through our lines while they were in that sort of state? Probably they would sober up damned quick but such thoughts could be very disquieting for us humble squaddies.

When added to the boredom of life here, the endless guard duties and the lack of decent sleep, such incidents contained all the ingredients for trouble. There were those among the lower ranks who were quite capable, without getting caught, of setting up something to go seriously wrong for certain officers. Of course, if such things were to happen, everyone would probably pay a price but that was not the point. Like this war, when seen from the squaddies perspective, none of this was really necessary.

There were more casualties yesterday when the Chinese mortared one of the forward positions. One officer, a sergeant and a private were wounded. The private later died of his wounds. And the emergency uncovered another stupidity. The MO had two ambulance jeeps for use on such occasions. These jeeps carried a special extension at the back that allowed two stretchers to be slid in and carried with relative ease. When this incident occurred neither of them were available. They were miles away back at A Echelon. An ordinary jeep had to be used, which was far from satisfactory. Once again the Adjutant did his nut about it and placed almost all the MO's staff on a charge even though it had really been down to the MO where those jeeps should have been. Sadly, the MO was another 'pipped' idiot and not really much older than we conscripts. Probably fresh out of medical school and about as naive as we were, he was something of a snob which had everyone wondered why he ever deigned to join the army in the first place. He tended to suck up to the other officers, to pay special attention to them at the expense of the ordinary ranks. This obvious immaturity meant he would become quite insensitive at times which could be quite nauseating.

The MO was responsible for initiating another farce whose impact rippled through all ranks of the battalion. It was comparable in some respects to the 'no fires at night' order. Three chaps from a forward company had reported sick with foot rot. This was caused by not having been able to take their boots and socks off for some time because of all the recent activity up at the sharp end. The MO sent a report to the Adjutant recommending that there be daily foot inspections for everyone in the battalion. As a result, at 14:00 each afternoon, everyone had to present bared feet for inspection. This even applied to us at BHQ who, even at a distance of three hundred yards from the front line, could have dared to go to bed in pyjamas if we had them. We had always taken our boots off at night, so the chance of us getting foot rot was much less when compared with the living conditions of chaps at the sharp end.

Until that time, the normal procedure was to have a foot inspection once a week. The frequency could have been increased to twice weekly but to have them once a day seemed excessive. It also required both the RSM and CSM to conduct the inspections and, as we soon found out, they were usually far too busy on more important matters to actually carry them out. We were frequently left hanging about with bare feet for three quarters of an hour, then told that the inspection was postponed until 17:30. Even then, after another long wait with freezing toes, it would invariably be cancelled. Enthusiasm for keeping up this farce fizzled very quickly as it probably had up at the sharp end.

My opinion of the MO didn't improve when I had chance to witness an example of his insensitivity first hand. Ironically, having discovered that a rash had developed overnight between my right little toe and its neighbour, I reported sick and went back to the RAP for treatment. While waiting there the Padré arrived. Immediately, the MO cosied up to him.

"Good morning Padré," he said. "How are you today? Is there anything I can do for you?"

"Oh—good morning," the Padré replied in a rather vague manner. "As a matter of fact I've just called by to see if you have—if there is anyone here—wounded or very sick—who might like a little company for a while; you know—just doin' my job."

The MO wasn't to be put off quite so easily and continued to try and make polite and inconsequential conversation. However, he was not so busy exercising his charm that he failed to overhear a chap come in to the tent and ask the Duty Orderly if he could go Dental Sick.

The MO immediately turned round and snapped at him, "Dental sick days are Mondays and Fridays."

The Padré, on hearing this, asked, "But—wasn't yesterday a dental sick day too?" to which the MO replied, "Yes, but that was for the privileged few."

Getting organised

It was time to collect the section NAAFI orders again, a job I thoroughly enjoyed. I went round taking the orders and money, retired to my bunker to produce the aggregate order, tallied up the monies and then took it all to the CQMS. He checked things out, was happy with the way things had been done and quite content for me to continue doing this job. He even added the comment that it was the first time in ages that it had been properly organised. That left a good feeling.

My attention had also been drawn to another organisational problem that had been getting on everyone's nerves—the guard duty roster. Everyone had to do a stag on guard, except those signallers who were on exchange duty during the night, and the rosters were usually prepared well in advance by the sergeant. However, they were frequently thrown into confusion when someone was posted to another company and no one came in to replace them. Their stag time had to be allocated among those remaining. Over a period of four days, we lost four chaps from our roster and the sergeant responsible for drawing it up. The roster fell apart. When the chaps on exchange duty offered to help out and still do their other duties, this only added to the difficulty. Trying to fit them in when they would not be on exchange duty and not asleep made things just too complex.

Several solutions were proposed but some chaps objected when they found they were doing the same stag in the small hours of the morning for three days on end. This played havoc with their sleep patterns and their nerves and they complained vehemently about it. The roster was drawn up on a more haphazard basis with no settled rotation and this worked for most of us. However, there was one chap, an obstreperous, loud-mouthed and very self-centred bloke who always griped about whatever was proposed. No roster, whether drawn up by the CSM or any of the corporals would suit him. Why anyone paid attention to his griping I never understood. He was only a bloody private after all, like most of us.

Without saying anything to anyone, I decided to give some thought to the problem. Well aware of everything that needed to be factored in I worked at it until I came up with an arrangement that might work. It ensured that chaps who had got the unpopular stags one night were able to catch up on their sleep the next. My idea was passed round and everyone seemed happy with it, even the griper. When submitted to the CSM, much to my amazement he also accepted it. Was there any precedent, I wondered, where a private, despite the presence of several beings of higher rank, wrote out a guard duty roster? To say that I was chuffed would put it mildly but it also said much about how different relations with the NCOs could be under active service conditions. There was usually much more fellow feeling around and few occasions when they pulled rank on us lesser mortals.

After a few days in which nothing of particular interest happened, one night a real doozy of an incident occurred. The roof of the bunker housing the battery charging engine collapsed. A wall had subsided and brought the roof down. The engine, covered in a mess of steel pickets, sticks, straw and earth, had stalled. The direct lighting system failed, the batteries soon gave out and lights went out everywhere. Consequently everyone 'lost it' at the same time, not just the power but their equanimity as well. The CO became indignantly angry, the SO became more urgently and eloquently angry, the Duty Officer became petulantly angry while the CSM flapped around despairingly like an old hen trying to make out he was doing something about it. To make things even more complicated this happened late at night. It may even have been early in the morning but either way it was dark. All their protests as they blundered around in the dark resembled some comical moment in a Whitehall Farce when all the lights go out in mid scene.

Meanwhile, we poor mugs from the signals section were working frantically to clear the mess away, extract the engine and get everything going again with only feeble torch light by which to see what we were doing. I was still disadvantaged by my hands which remained in a quite delicate condition from the burns and that encounter with the barbed wire.

Eventually the engine was dragged clear, taken to another unoccupied bunker, cleaned up, refuelled, checked, all the connections to batteries in VIP bunkers repaired and started. Lights restored, we were all totally exhausted.

A concert party

There was applause for the organisation in this man's army today. At last, in the very middle of this bitter winter weather, we were told to go and draw the rest of our winter kit. This including a second pair of those woollen inner trousers—specially designed to keep the 'old fella' warm as some of the old hands commented. The CQMS also told me that he had a new pair of size 11½ ammunition boots to replace the Boucheron boots that I had been wearing. No more excessively sweaty feet at last.

That afternoon, those not down for an immediate spell on duty were taken to see an American touring concert party. The theme of their show was rivalry between recruiting officers of the various US services, Army,

Navy, Air Force and Marines. They were trying to persuade a dithering civilian that he ought to join their particular branch of the services. The sketches were well written and the acting a little hammy at times but the music, provided by a combo of trumpet, trombone, accordion, piano, bass and drums, was great. When all was said and done, it was an enjoyable show. It certainly made a change to get some live entertainment when all we usually managed was what could be picked up on the 62 set in the exchange.

Of course, there were those among us who pulled it to pieces mostly it seemed, because the whole thing had been so "American", even to the extent of including a sentimental and patriotic American song. Admittedly, they did come across as rather crass but that didn't spoil the laughs we had. A good laugh was always welcomed here whether inspired by English, American, Australian, Canadian, Korean or Japanese comedians. Strangely, it was mostly the genuine Welshmen among us who were most critical. They were probably longing for their Sundays in Chapel.

Late that evening there was a buzz that the Chinese were on the move. The Leicesters over to the east of us had withdrawn from one hill in the face of a stiff attack. Here, Hill 169, which had once been in no-mans-land, now seemed to be more securely in Chinese hands. Orders came for some of our stuff to be moved back to the 'Kansas' reserve line, the one south of the River Imjin and where the Glosters had been when they were wiped out last March. We had everything ready to go by 23:30 that night.

After everything seemed to quieten down again, I played around with the 62 set and picked up the sounds of hot jive, music by Morton Gould and songs sung by Ella Fitzgerald and others. The song titles seemed to say it all. "I can dream can't I?" stirred an immense nostalgia for home and was followed all too appropriately by "My heart cries for you", "Show me the way to go home" and "Thinking of you". How adept those Yanks were with their music at making themselves and everyone else feel homesick. Looking around, all we could see were four dirt walls, a rough tree trunk ceiling, a weak electric light, a few boxes to sit on, a sooty brew can, signals gear everywhere, a pair of earphones at the end of a very long cable and that was 'Home Sweet Home' for us.

Then what did we hear? "Everything I have is yours". For a few moments, Bing Crosby brought some relief with "The Chattanooga Shoeshine Boy" but this jollier mood was short lived with a reprise of "My heart cries for you". It would have been emotionally healthier for us if the only music we could pick up was jazz be it Traditional, Dixie or Progressive. We could then pretend we were having a real rave up.

These smoochie songs made things very difficult, filling the air with ennui. Yet, despite all the longing to be back at home that they engendered, I wouldn't have missed being here for worlds despite the very real possibility of something lethal suddenly happening, despite the boredom, despite the sometimes desperate searching for some little joy here or there, despite the oftentimes utter fatigue and the realisation of how stupid this war was and some of the people who had been put in charge of running it—and us. These were the times when I wanted to meet up with Brian and talk things through as we had on the *Georgic*. I sent him a tin of cigarettes and a letter and would see if I could go up to see him one evening in the Signals Dispatch jeep.

Accident prone?

It was one of those days when nothing went right. At 03:30 the guard I was due to relieve came and woke me. The prize idiot, then went straight off to his bunker and didn't wait for me to actually arrive to relieve him. Of course, I went straight back to sleep again. This resulted in there being no one on guard in that post between 03:30 to 05:30 because I wasn't awake to rouse my relief.

When I finally woke up and realised what had happened, I experienced what was probably the worst torment of my time in the army. Visions of being court-martialled haunted me until around 08:00 when the Lance Corporal in command of last night's guard, realizing how this had happened, told me the whole thing would be dropped. He just warned me to be bloody careful in future for everyone's sake. Both the chap who woke me to relieve him and I would have been in severe trouble, but so would that Corporal because he was supposed to check on the guards, and hadn't.

A number of other irritating little things happened throughout the day but the most significant one occurred that evening when I was sitting in the signals exchange cleaning my rifle. I did something that should never be done. When reassembling moving and moveable parts, the bolt and the magazine, the right procedure was to replace the bolt and close it and then replace the magazine. For some reason I chose to do things the other way round and replaced a loaded magazine first. I then inserted and closed the bolt. I thought it would be quite safe to push the top round down into the magazine with my left forefinger and eased the bolt over it. For some reason it didn't work.

I pushed the bolt home and secured it. This primed the trigger action. I squeezed the trigger to ease it off and there was a god-almighty bang. A round was discharged and the bullet smashed into the wall just to the left of the telephone exchange. The ensuing silence was total. There were four others in the exchange at the time, the signaller on duty sitting in front of the exchange and three others sitting behind me. They were stunned into absolute stillness for quite a few seconds. No one said a word. Not only had I scared the chocolate pudding out of everyone but I was left to contemplate the state of my own pants in absolute silence for a moment or two. The duty signaller slowly turned and looked at me, face as white as the proverbial sheet, and just shook his head in disbelief.

Thankfully no one had come close to being injured but, more significantly for me, no one outside the exchange seemed to have heard the shot and come to investigate. I remained very nervous lest word got out and I was called to account for my stupidity. But nobody ratted on me and in time, I was able to forget that it had happened. However, this incident and the earlier one about guard duty left me feeling very shaken and unsure of myself, fervently hoping that things would improve. As things turned out, that was the only time while I was in Korea, outside a practice firing range, that I would fire my rifle.

My earlier resolve to write something home every day had almost evaporated over the past few weeks for a number of reasons. The most prominent was the difficulty to think of or do anything that was not directly related to surviving amid the circumstances we were living in. It was as if the entire situation used every vestige of physical and mental energy in me. There was little of the latter to devote to writing home. My letters became episodic, a little written everyday as and when I was able to find the time and energy.

The weather had become very uncertain, going in the course of the day from freezing cold to a surprising mildness, from hail and snow to bright warm sunshine. Given all the stories about possible 20 to 40 degrees of frost on the Fahrenheit scale, these mild periods had surprised us. Everything could still freeze up at night but by midday we could find ourselves slipping or sliding in inch thick mud. Snowfalls were never heavy, the snow did not lie around for too long, and we always found overcast days warmer than when the sky was clear.

A letter from home asked about our living conditions. Evidently, there had been an article in one of the national papers that was very critical of the circumstances in which we were living here. I eventually wrote:

"Battalion HQ is very cushy. Food is plentiful—we get three hot meals a day except when C7 boxes are issued. Water comes in jerry cans, four gallons at a time from wells and springs at the bottom of the hill but has to be well boiled or treated with water purification tablets. Korean porters do all the heavy fetching and carrying for us. Those chaps can certainly work hard. So can the enemy. Reports were continually coming in from observers and spotter planes about the extent to which Chinese is constructing connecting trenches, tunnels and bunkers all along their front line. They are like human moles. But our Korean porters are just as tough.

One thing which one cannot seem to determine about the Koreans is their approximate age, unless it is very obvious. Some are seventeen years old while others may be twenty-seven but I'm blessed if you can tell which is which. Their complexion is not yellow but a sallow golden brown and in most cases their skin is beautifully clear. Their clothing consists of oddments of Korean, US and British army uniforms including the boots. The Korean uniforms are thick quilted efforts filled with Kapok or whatever.

They are reversible between white and olive green so that they can be worn one way when snow has fallen or the other way after it has thawed. We have a separate set of thin white smocks and trousers to wear over our everyday gear if we need a snow disguise.

The porters are quite amusing in the way they try to make themselves understood and as one of our chaps said, "If they didn't have hands they would be speechless." Some of the younger Gooks have picked up our language quite quickly, including the bad language, and can thus be very cheeky or insolent on occasion. Still, that must be tolerated for most of them are good workers and we would have to work a lot harder ourselves if they were not here to help us.

To go back to the subject of life here—food is OK and water is pretty plentiful. Sleeping and working quarters are holes about five to six feet deep covered with roofs of logs and dirt to varying depths. If you can get a good source of heat it is possible to dry them out to a great extent and thereby achieve a certain degree of comfort. One can "pinchee pinchee" boxes, as the Gooks would say, from various sources and use them as seats, cupboards or shelves.

Some chaps have erected double bunks inside their bunkers using eight foot long barbed wire fencing pickets and telephone cable but yours truly still lies on the floor because, due to continual moving of personnel, I've never managed to have a partner for long with whom to make that kind of "home". Still, I manage to sleep warmly on the floor.

It is surprising how comfortable one can make a hole in the ground. With a few coats hanging about, papers, books, oddments of kit and a few 'pin ups' a homely atmosphere can be established which is really amazing. Of course there is always the danger of the roof collapsing or the sides caving in but strange to say, one never thinks of them—until the RAOC start blasting out a road at the foot of the hill. Then the whole hill shudders and one gets a collar full of dirt that has trickled from the roof. Still, it's all in a day's "war" so to speak.

We have a pukka little lavatory here, a box with a hole suitably shaped and sanded for comfort and a lid so that the whole thing is portable. As the sergeant has the habit of saying when he wants to make light conversation, "There's nothing I like better than a comfortable shit." This reminds me that, much to my surprise, I haven't been at all constipated so far and hope things stay that way.

So, as you can see, I don't find things so uncomfortable and with your steady supply of letters, don't consider I am doing at all badly. In fact I think I am very lucky."

A brief history lesson

I had an interesting conversation with a couple of our Korean porters doing some washing down by the pond. With a lot of patience and gesticulating, I found out that on the Korean calendar the year was 4285 and not 1952 as on ours. It seemed that this date stemmed from the founding of one of the earliest Kingdoms on the Korean peninsula, the Kingdom of Chosen in our year 2333 BC. I don't think the British Isles were habitable back then. Certainly our history didn't go back that far.

10

The New Year Continues

2nd February-6th March 1952

Five Star Accommodation

I had requested a writing case for a Christmas present. It arrived this morning. Of dark brown grained leather with a zip around three sides, it was ideal for my present circumstances, held a decent sized pad of writing paper but wouldn't take up too much room in my pack. However, my fountain pen had broken and I now had to write in pencil.

The letter that came with the writing case mentioned newspaper reports of snowfalls four feet deep here in Korea but, as far as we were concerned, they had not been where we presently were. In the three blizzards received so far, less than a total of twelve inches had fallen. Those heavier falls must have been somewhere else, perhaps in the mountains further east. I wrote back that during the day temperatures could be mild enough for us to go about in shirts and pullovers unless there was a cold wind blowing from the north. Then we certainly needed our windproof jackets or parkas.

Apart from routine duties on guard or the exchange, the past few days had been spent turning our bunker into five star accommodation. The entrance was altered to open less directly to the crawl trench. A makeshift door had been fitted up and a small skylight fitted in the roof. Using fence pickets and telephone wire we had made bunks to take us off the floor and on three sides sandbags had been hung on the walls to keep things cleaner. Shelves had been made with wood from old packing cases that 'just happened' to come our way and a 12 volt electric light fixed up to run off a wireless battery.

The jerry-can fire had been replaced with an even more efficient arrangement using a 20 pound shell case scrounged from the crew of a Centurion tank. It was roughly two feet long, about five inches across the base and between two and a half to two and three quarters of an inch across the open end where the projectile had once been fixed. Half a dozen holes punched about two inches up round the base would allow air in and an inch of sand was placed in the bottom of the shell case for fuel to drip onto. Another hole was punched approximately half way up the side just big enough to take a thin piece of metal tubing. This tubing was connected to the end of a length of rubber tubing scrounged from a medical orderly and the other end inserted into a can of petrol. A clamp made from two small pieces of wood about three inches long placed across the tube with the ends bound round with rubber bands controlled the petrol flow. It was fiddly to adjust but did the job.

The petrol can was placed in a niche in the wall so that it was higher than the shell case and the flow started by sucking on the metal tube until a syphoning action was started. The tube was placed in the upper hole so that the petrol dripped down inside onto the sand. When this was lit and the petrol drip adjusted, the fire just kept going at a moderate pace. Even if the petrol was allowed to drip about once every two seconds, the shell case would still end up glowing red hot. even on the coldest night the bunker soon become as warm as toast.

It was an amazingly ingenious device, consumed petrol very economically and we considered it a most proper use for old shell cases. It was certainly a damn sight easier to control and infinitely safer than the one Will and I had experimented with back in December. This fire was a work of art and very efficient.

The job of sorting out the NAAFI orders twice a week was still in my care. So far, all had gone very efficiently and there had been no complaints. My right hand was now all but completely recovered from the burns and the barbed wire damage, but I now had a small problem with my left hand that had been gashed open when I slipped on ice and fell on it while going down the hill. Thankfully, it was repairing quickly.

The King is dead—long live the Queen

On Saturday, 8th February 1952, around 21:00 we tuned the 62 set to the Australian Broadcasting Corporation (ABC) and heard of the death of King George VI. He had died in his sleep at Sandringham House. That evening the telephone exchange ran hot as officers discussed the news and the next morning they all appeared wearing black armbands.

The Regimental Flag hung at half-mast and the divisional artillery fired a 101-gun salute. Princess Elizabeth, now Queen Elizabeth, was on holiday in Africa when the news broke.

Later that day came news that was a far greater shock for us squaddies. The body of Private Bill Lansdowne had been found. Missing from a patrol that went out on January 11th, several others on that patrol thought they had seen the Chinese take him off. It had been assumed that he was a prisoner of war. Now, almost a month later, his body bore evidence that he had been shot in the back. We could only suppose that he tried to escape from his captors and they couldn't be bothered to go after him. He was only a poor bloody private anyway and wouldn't have been able to tell their intelligence people much. There was no indication of what condition his body was in after lying out there in no-man's-land in bitter winter weather. He was in my draft at Bulford Camp a year ago last December but I didn't know him very well.

Very early this morning a quite serious incident occurred. The patrol going to reconnoiter Hill 169 was ambushed after it had crossed the stream below out forward positions. It had not got even halfway there. Last year the arrangement had been that our chaps would occupy 169 by night and the Chinese by day. It had become almost routine for the patrol to go out at first light, follow a particular path down through our forward company positions, across the paddies at the foot of the hill and across a small stream. It had ended on 9th February when our patrol was ambushed in thick fog as it began the climb onto 169. Now we just sent out these patrols to have a look around.

Two men were killed, Private Norman Babbage, the wireless operator and Corporal Reginald Greaves a member of a rescue party that went out from 'A' Company. No more regular patrols were sent to 169 after that incident. The Chinese had take possession with every intention of staying there. They had dug a four mile crawl trench around it with bunkers twenty feet down at thirty yard intervals which just showed what we were up against.

I later found this comment in Robert O'Neal's book which has some bearing on those patrols— *"Any form of routine patrolling is dangerous because it invites enemy ambush, it kills initiative, it wearies the men both mentally and physically and it achieves little."* Item(i)4. 1st Comdiv GOC. Personal Memorandum to 3RAR.

We completed the reconstruction of the exchange bunker which had been deepened by another four feet. A stronger, thicker roof was constructed to provide greater protection from enemy mortar fire. There had been much laughter as we hauled great tree trunks up the hill to take the weight of all the soil that would go on top. By the time all the sticks, rice straw and earth had been placed over them, the roof was probably more than three feet thick.

My letters home continued to be written less often. Mental weariness only permitted attention to those things necessary for survival and there was also an increasing physical tiredness from never getting a full night's sleep. When I wasn't on exchange duty or on guard, and if it wasn't a matter of attending to basic necessities such as washing and shaving, eating and drinking and processes of elimination, all I wanted to do was sleep, or just sit around and daydream. A state of mental torpor seemed constant during these off duty periods and it was becoming bloody annoying. I wanted to write home but seemed to lack any will to do so.

A parcel arrived from Uncle Reg. He was a pharmacist at Boots the Chemist in Swanage and had thoughtfully included lemonade crystals, a bottle of Ovaltine tablets, a tin of lanolin for cracked, dry hands and plenty of laxatives. It was all good sensible stuff to have and the laxatives were very timely.

Another item of news from home that intrigued me concerned my mother. She had auditioned for and obtained the position of soloist at the Christian Science Church in Bournemouth. Evidently it was their custom to hire a professional singer to sing the anthem in their morning and evening services each Sunday. All things being equal, I hoped to be home to hear her sing there before her contract ends. (In the end, contrary to normal practice, she remained their soloist for five years)

That evening, before sunset and 'stand to', I sat outside my bunker and considered the landscape again. Geography had been one of my favourite subjects at school and it was clear that the shape of this country had been predominantly fashioned by water although the mountain peaks with their fantastically grotesque profiles would have been affected more by the action of frost and ice. The valley floors were quite flat from decades of being terraced. Even the smallest hill tended to resemble a lump of mud that had just been dropped onto a billiard table. Naturally, the mood of the landscape changed depending on whether the skies were clear or cloudy. Viewed from my elevated vantage point, range after range of hills wandering off into the distance, their colour fading the farther away they were. Looking eastward as the sun began to drop, the normally drab colours of the hills became a range of more dusky shades from brown through to a misty violet that were very beautiful to behold. Where snow still lay on the ground, the lines of crawl trenches were etched onto the scene like spider's webs. Usually it was quiet and deceptively peaceful. But when the artillery let off a salvo, or we got explosions from incoming mortar bombs, the sounds then bounced orchestrally back and forth off the hills and in and out of the valleys.

Night-time would present an altogether different and more disquieting prospect, especially if snow were still lying about. The surrounding spurs and valleys could loom menacingly but when the moon was up picture book scenes of the Holy Land on that first Christmas came to mind, the snow glinting white in the moonlight, the stars so very clear, the coldness and the quietness very intense. I would then started to listen for the singing of angels but the only sounds, if any, would be the whistling of shells as they screamed overhead, whistling angels of death.

A few days had passed since the ambush of the last daytime patrol to 169. Judging by all the activity up front, it was pay-back time. A number of 25 pounders rolled past the foot of the hill to positions nearer our forward sections. A little later, we heard them firing and saw red smoke rising from 169. We knew that ordinary shelling wouldn't affect Chinese positions once they had been allowed to dig in so we guessed something else was afoot. Sure enough, a few minutes later, a flight of bombers passed overhead and we saw bombs dropping onto those positions on 169. They were clearly visible as they fell so must have been some of the largest available. I recall the distinct interval between the moment they impacted and seeing and hearing the explosions. They were huge; the only comparable noise so far was when the Yankee 'Persuaders' all fired together. For those watching from a safe distance, it was an impressive spectacle. For the Chinese on 169, if they weren't dead or buried alive, they would probably have become permanently deaf.

Gunner Charlie Haynes commented later on this attack:

"It was shortly after them [the Chinese] making themselves at home, [on 169] that the Yanks bombed it with heavy bombers. A team with ground to air radio moved into our position and directed the planes onto the target. I can still recall the voice of the operator saying to the flight crews "Observe Red smoke over Target Area" (Three inch smoke bombs from a New Zealand artillery section brought up for the occasion). The Yanks dropped about a dozen delayed fused bombs right on target. The craters were enormous. There must still be signs of them to this day. The USAF was using 500lb bombs dropped by parachute and 'Tarzan', a 2000lb radio guided monster."

Charlie Haynes, machine gunner

Operation Snare

On the 10th February, an exercise called Operation Snare was launched along this section of the front line. For six days we were ordered to lie 'doggo'—no fires, all movement kept to the absolute minimum and C7 rations every day. No patrols went out; the objective was apparently to arouse the curiosity of the Chinese and to lure them into sending out patrols to find out what had happened to us.

Maybe they could be persuaded to launch an offensive during which we would capture some prisoners. This had always been the priority for our patrols anyway. So far it had been our chaps who had been most actively patrolling no-mans-land, getting involved in skirmishes and ambushes and suffering losses but they never returned with prisoners. Operation Snare was designed to turn the tables and capture a few.

It was an operation ordered from 3rd Army Group HQ. Our divisional commander Major General Cassels and his subordinate commanders were of the opinion that Operation Snare would not succeed; it would just give the Chinese time to improve badly damaged positions free from any harassment. When he protested this to his American superior he was overruled. As things turned out, he was correct. The Chinese just sent out a few patrols to check that we were still there then got on with their digging and tunnelling. From what we heard later and as anticipated, little was achieved.

The following extract from an account recorded in the annals of the Welch Regt. casts more light on the results of this operation:

"Between the 10th. and 17th. February 1952, 'Operation Snare' was put into effect along the whole of the U.S. 8th Army and Commonwealth Division Front. The orders required units not to engage the enemy with any form of fire other than from small arms, and only then, in the event of an actual attack. It was hoped that this inactivity would arouse the curiosity of the Chinese and encourage them to intensify patrol activity, thus presenting the U.N. troops with opportunities to capture prisoners for intelligence purposes.

From a Commonwealth Division point of view, the plan was counter productive, for the Chinese, once having established that the positions opposite to them was still occupied, took advantage of the situation to work on strong bunkers on the forward slopes overlooking the Division's lines, and with a minimum of interference. From these vantage points they were able to make daylight patrolling an extremely hazardous occupation, as in places the forward posts were only 600 yards apart. In due course daylight patrols were discontinued, such activities being more certain of success during the hours of darkness."

When those six days were up, the Chinese must have once again wondered if the end of the world was nigh. Sharp on 06:00, every weapon was brought to bear on enemy targets. The racket was enormous. The guns supporting the 28th and 29th Brigades launched a huge barrage on the opposite Chinese positions. The 'Persuaders' (8 inch Howitzers), 25 pounders, Centurion 20 pounders, Bofors guns, Vickers Machine Guns and 4.2 inch and 3 inch mortars opened up and kept the barrage going until midday. The din was incredible.

When everything quietened down once more, it was back to normal with a vengeance. On duty, off duty, eat, dig, dig, dig, eat, on duty, off duty, eat, sleep, wake, shave, on duty, off duty, dig, dig, dig, sleep, wake, shave, on duty, off duty and so on. We could light fires again and the cookhouse started to serve proper meals. My personal larder of other chaps unwanted C7 rations had grown considerably.

Writer's block again

Newspapers that my brother David had started sending to me by sea mail back in November started to arrive. They had taken just over two months to get here. Letters received by many of the chaps mentioned a new social development back home—a growing interest in Square Dancing. In one of her letters, my Mother referred to it as "this square bashing mania" which provided a good laugh. I was sure she knew what square bashing really was and had confused it with Square Dancing.

My writing home remained as spasmodic as ever. Letters from so many people, all needing a reply, had only served to increase my frustration. I wasn't feeling miserable all the time. Far from it in fact. In many ways I was finding much to enjoy but mustering the resolve to sit and write about them just failed to kick in. There were so many times when I would pick up my new writing case, undo it and pick up my pencil only to find that my mind was blank; nothing flowed. In the end I would say, "Hell, this is useless. Bugger it." and pack everything away again.

Another week passed; I added beer to my NAAFI order. Why not? Three bottles of Asahi lager twice a week wouldn't break the bank. It would make a change from water that tasted of purification tablets or over-stewed tea that furred the tongue. I also placed a regular order for canned Australian fruit—peaches, pears or apricots, two large tins with each order. These were luxuries we had only tasted at home on very special occasions. The food rationing during the war was still a very clear memory and little things like this now made life here more pleasurable. I could make a pig of myself by eating a whole tin at one go. Alcohol loomed larger in another respect. We were supposed to be receiving a tot of rum every two or three days—for 'medicinal reasons' the SO reckoned. The warmth that spread around one's insides was very pleasant but we didn't get them as regularly as we had been told.

As a wireless operator, it was usually possible to get out of a lot of things. However, we were now officially excused from having to do guard duty out in the crawl trenches and given permission to sleep during the day if we had been on duty overnight. Someone had at last woken up to what we had been enduring and concluded that, considering the vitally important role we played in maintaining communications, especially here in the sharp end, tired wireless operators might become inefficient and a liability. That would not be a 'good thing'

After we had put the final touches to the rebuilding of the exchange bunker, HQ Company defence platoon began to rebuild the Command Post bunker in much the same way and for the same reasons. To make a special job of it, they lined the walls with filled sandbags but three days later one of the walls started, seriously and dangerously, to cave in. The poor beggars had to take the whole place to pieces and start again. It was just as well that things were quiet on this section of the front. Meanwhile, the truce talks continued to bicker along.

Welcome news was spreading that the battalion will go into reserve in a month's time. This will be the time when we might get five days leave in Tokyo called R&R. This stood for "Rest & Recuperation" but we interpreted it as "Rack & Ruin". A draw was held for the order in which we would go and I drew number twelve. Evidently, we would be flown to Japan for this ('Jay-pan' as the Yanks and Canadians call it, as if it were some oriental design of toilet.) I wondered if there was a chance that Brian might get to go at the same time but considered it highly unlikely.

To my delight, he phoned while I was on duty, the first time we had spoken to each other in a month. He commented on how jealous the other guys in our draft were of my ending up in battalion HQ. Nevertheless, he seemed to be doing OK as unofficial "company clerk". It seemed the Major "couldn't do without him" so he doubted if he would get any R&R. But he jested.

There were signs that winter was at last coming to an end and a more thorough thaw setting in. It had snowed twice during the last three days and each time it quickly turned to slush. The Korean porters told us that this had been a mild winter, even though the ground had frozen to a depth of two feet. I wondered how deeply it froze in a hard winter. And what were summers like? The porters said they were hot with lots of snakes, lizards, beetles, ants and dust. We would probably end up preferring winter to summer since all this native fauna seemed likely to be much bigger than anything we were accustomed to back home.

The CO and RSM decided that it was time to reinstitute proper order and discipline on Command Post hill as if we were in barracks back in England. We wondered if brooms would be issued and orders given to sweep the paths around the hill. Would we have to lay whitewashed stones along the edges so that they were clearly visible at night? Would shattered trees be cut down and surviving bushes pruned for when spring finally came so that they sprouted leaves and flowers in an orderly way? Was the CO going to have the QM order in boxes of daffodil and tulip bulbs to be planted outside the Command Post and the Officers Mess? None of these things came to pass, thank God.

After the exchange had been refurbished, we had an attack of 'inspection blight'. The CO and the Adjutant called by expressing disappointment that everything was so quiet and they were unable to see things functioning at top speed. How moronic! In those times when we were very busy they were too, with their duties! However, they were pleased with what they saw and with the way things had been set up. That made Captain Dyer happy and a happy signals officer meant that everyone else could feel happy. Next day the Colonel of the Royal Rifle Regiment arrived to inspect us and he too went away evidently pleased by what he saw.

St David's Day

On Saturday, 1st March 1952, while still in the frontline, 1 Battalion the Welch Regiment celebrated St. David's Day. There was almost an air of "Bugger the Chinese. Let 'em come, but if they do then they will have to wait till we're done," around the hill. The size and nature of the NAAFI orders that I collected yesterday had greatly surprised me. Orders for Asahi beer had dramatically increased, the total order coming to 103 bottles for the fourteen chaps in the HQ Signals section alone. Now I understood why! St. David's Day was a great occasion for the Taffies among us. Only they were required to attend BHQ Muster Parade this morning. Nevertheless, it proved to be both an amusing and a very moving day for us non-Welsh members of the battalion. Not required to attend any of their national events, when not on duty we stood by and watched.

At one moment in the parade, there was a ceremonial distribution of tender little green leeks to be worn behind cap badges. In addition to the "Wearing of the Leek", any officer celebrating their first St. David's Day with the battalion, any Sergeant who had attained that rank since last year's celebrations and the youngest Welshman present were required to eat a leek before the assembled company. This wearing of the Leek later provided us 'foreigners' with opportunities to gently rib our Taffy mates and ask, "Why have you got a little green thing growing out of your head? Are you a Martian?", "Do you grow grass behind your ears too?", or "Is the potato crop in your socks doing well?"

The sergeant later told me that two thousand leeks had been flown in from Japan for the occasion. Since there were only about three hundred Welshmen in the battalion, I wondered if the other seventeen hundred would be turned into leek and potato soup and served up at each meal for the next week. What strange things our QM had to think about. Did the 'Skins' celebrate St Patrick's Day with the wearing of "The Green" and would the Japanese be able to provide them with sufficient Shamrock?

Everyone in the company was invited to take part in the slap up lunch that the cookhouse produced. Free beer and cigarettes were provided while the Regimental Goat Mascot, Taffy IX, received the UN and Commonwealth Korea Ribbons in a ceremony attended by all the Divisional Brass. After that all the Taffies left for a programme of fun and games that was held somewhere while I was on duty in the exchange. Now I understood why so many Englishmen were in this battalion. Someone was needed to look after the store while they indulged in their national high jinks.

That evening's feast was another amazing occasion like that on Christmas Day. Once again, the food was great and everyone was in a very good mood. Gradually it slipped into sentimentality and the singing began. I knew that Welsh Male Voice Choirs were famous the world over but, while these men at BHQ were no choir, one could be forgiven for thinking otherwise because they certainly sang as if they were, as indeed they had last Christmas. The rich sonorous singing was mostly in perfect unison but when there was any opportunity to harmonise it was out of this world. Their rendering of 'Land of my Fathers' and 'Men of Harlech' was truly inspiring and it was impossible not to join in, even though none of us knew the Welsh words and could only hum the tune. Eventually I did learn that the battalion actually had a choir. They performed at the final farewell parade at the UN cemetery in Pusan.

There had been many occasions when I had heard my mother sing in Gilbert & Sullivan operettas and concert parties for the troops stationed locally during the war. This had given me an appreciation of good singing. That evening I knew that what I was hearing was extremely good. It seemed that every Welshman had been born with perfect pitch and a true ear for harmony. I had a small talent for this myself and joined in with gusto. It was an amazingly moving end to an otherwise strange celebration to have in the front line and a testimony to the spirit of the chaps here.

Brian appeared about mid morning. He had come back on some errand for his CO and took time to find out where I was hiding. We celebrated with a whole tin of pears. It was good to have one of our natters about anything and everything. He told me that a reporter had visited their positions and interviewed him. His photo had been taken and he had been told that a copy of it and the write up would be sent to his mother. It might even be published locally. I made a note to ask my family to watch out for it. Stories circulated that Arthur Helliwell from *The People* newspaper was here somewhere. He had sent in a story from Tokyo and was also expected to visit The Welch Regiment.

More visitors

Several officers from the The Princess Patricia's Canadian Light Infantry (PPCLI) visited us to inspect our positions and were very complimentary. From what we overheard, they considered that we had one of the best set-ups in the whole Division, which didn't say much for the others. Evidently, the 'Pats' would be relieving us when our turn to go into reserve arrived in a week's time.

A small wireless exercise was organised that took me past the Leicestershire Regiment's HQ. I spotted a chap there who had been on the Signals Course at Harwich. We were both surprised to see each other. Another surprise was the arrival of Corporal Ron Church, one of the instructors on that Signals Course to join the Welch yesterday. It was an odd little reunion and good to see him again. We had always got on well together. It could have been him who had commented on my alleged sense of humour to the CO at Dovercourt that he had referred to on the passing out parade. I forgot to ask Ron about that.

The approach of spring initiated a big flap among the officers. There was great emphasis on digging in more securely and reinforcing the barbed wire defences. Evidently, the Chinese had become more active, shooting up and ambushing our patrols and there was a suspicion that they could be working up to some kind of offensive as they had done a year ago. Preparations also began in earnest for the move into Reserve. We will spend four to six weeks there before relieving some other battalion in the division due to go home. We were also eagerly waiting for our five days R&R in Tokyo. Evidently the flight from Kimpo airfield over Korea to Japan was quite spectacular and it was possible to get a good look at this country from a higher, angelic viewpoint—and wonder again why man had ever come to live here.

Apart from a slight rise in the average temperature, spring had not yet shown any signs of approach. The hills were still brown and drear, the occasional snowfall being the only thing to brighten the view with a short-lived coat of white. But the porters told us that very soon the land would all turn green again, as if by magic. That had to be seen to be believed. It was not possible to ignore how devastated this land was with shell craters, blackened villages and the wrecks of tanks and vehicles everywhere. But the most significant signs by far had been the untilled and overgrown paddies and the absence of any old woodland, most of the trees having either been blown apart, taken for fuel, or used as roofing for bunkers. Perhaps the sight that was most significant of how this land had been 'crucified' by this war was the number of hills that had been circled with crawl trenches and barbed wire like so many Crowns of Thorns. And of course, invisible to the eye but there nonetheless, were the minefields. It would probably take years of back breaking and often lethal toil to get this land back in shape again.

The 'space heater' in the exchange was proving so efficient that we often had to go outside to cool off. But that was not a problem, at least, not like that with the electricity generator. It had developed a habit of running out of fuel in the small hours of the morning. When that happened someone had to grope their way in the dark, cursing and blinding every step of the way, to refuel and start it up again. Until then one had to keep operations going by lighting a succession of matches—and trying to avoid burning ones fingers. Strangely, candles had been noticeable by their comparative rarity here. Another problem was the frequency with which our wireless sets kept breaking down. They had to be sent back to workshops well behind the lines for repair and the delay in getting replacements could be very frustrating.

II

In Brigade Reserve

7th March-16th April 1952

Mucky bunkers

The battalion moved into reserve positions two days earlier than expected. Orders were suddenly received to pack up our gear, both personal and military and have everything taken to the assembly areas where trucks would arrive to collect it. Our new accommodations provided many shocks and surprises being in little better state than pigsties, full of rubbish and with crumbling walls all needing major work done on them. The CO of the PPCLI might well have been pleased with the standard of the bunkers his men would take over from us, but if this was where they had been then he should have been ashamed of the state they had been left in for us. However, there was not much else to do here in reserve except sort our accommodation out and wait for our turns to go on R&R, so we got stuck into the job of making ourselves comfortable.

We were now situated on the north bank of the River Imjin where it flowed westward toward the sea. To the south, Gloster Hill stood out miles above all the others and I had an eerie thought that perhaps, when the Glosters were encircled and fighting for their lives, a Chinese commander might have been watching from where I now stood. The sight of the smooth blue water of the river, with the sandy beach on the south side opposite steep dark bluffs was refreshing. The moon rose that night, adding its own enchantment to the scene. It glinted on the water and silhouetted the weird shapes of the still snowbound mountains to the south and southeast. Then, just as I was absorbing all this, there came the flash, pause, crash, blast, reverberation and whistle of the shells passing overhead. The howitzers on the south bank had opened up.

Later that evening, when my turn on duty came, I found a poem that someone had left pinned up on the exchange notice board. Called simply "Korea", I copied it out on a letter form to send home. It was another example of the work of that prolific poet 'Anon', this time in sombre mood:

Korea

There is a place across the ocean that is God's forgotten land
Made of mangrove, swamps and paddies, lofty crags and barren land.
'Twas to this place I journeyed on a misbegotten day
While the sun beat hotly on me—and the Devil led the way.
'Twas a country called Korea—only God, not I, knew why.
Filled with dirty swampy and paddies, lots of filth and mountains high.
It was there they chose to send us, just a sad and lonely few,
To a land that's full of beggars, yellow fever, danger too.
Yes, I saw the Devil beckon and I heard the angels sing.
I heard Gabriel blow his trumpet and say, 'Death, where's thy sting?'
It's a land that God's forgotten, where he spent his seventh day.
It was he who built the framework—then let Satan have his way.

Spring is springing

It had been unseasonably warm for the past few days, almost as if Mother Nature had decided to bypass spring and go straight into summer. Skies were clear, the winds hardly noticeable and the sun warming enough for us to wander around in shirt sleeve order during the day. The nights were also clear, with the moon and stars very bright, but they could still be bitterly cold. We had been waking to quite heavy frosts.

Most of our time was spent getting organised, making our bunkers more shipshape and up to the standard of those we had handed over to the PPCLI. Unfortunately, the adjutant and RSM Richards once more chose to reintroduce their enthusiasm for "bullshit". The Motor Transport (MT) Square in the centre of the camp had been neatly delineated with 'whitewashed' 25-pound shell cases and a row of young pine trees planted just beyond to add a softening touch. Signs had been erected, some merely bearing a set of initials—C.V., C.O., I.O., R.S.M., R.A.P. and C.P., others more explicit—Adjutant, Chaplain, Signals Office and Guard Room. The biggest sign of all stood near the Guard Room and bore the regimental colours, the unit number and the Commonwealth Division sign. It added a spot of colour to an otherwise still drab landscape.

The military police had taken over responsibility for security. Smartly dressed in new combat suits, white belts, gaiters and helmets, they wore two armbands, one bearing the letters MP and the other showing their rank and regimental and divisional flashes. They proceeded to institute a strict regime of guard duties with teams of twelve chaps detailed for duty every night. At any one time, four of them would be on prowler guard in pairs, two hours on and four hours off.

The RSM also smartened up muster parade. We now had to be washed and shaved before breakfast and on parade at 08:30 with boots, combat suit and rifle in spotless condition. Naturally, all this produced a lot of muttering. "Where the hell does he think we are? Back in Colchester? Someone ought to tell him we are in a live war zone!" Secretly however, I believe we were all proud of the results. We felt we were better soldiers for having such standards of discipline restored while in reserve. We might have envied the Yanks their laid-back ways and apparent lack of respect for their officers but we found it difficult to rate them highly as soldiers, certainly not from what we knew of their field craft which we considered too gung-ho. But perhaps we had watched too many of their war films and got the wrong impression.

Having said all that, we signallers, with our irregular duty periods, still needed opportunity to catch up on sleep if we were to remain efficient. Exempted from these muster parades, we were still able to watch the other poor sods on parade and feel sorry for them as they tried, with some semblance of alacrity and smartness, to obey the orders barked out by the RSM. After all, it was over five months since any of us had last been required to jump through these hoops.

Bath time

Twenty chaps were taken to a Canadian support unit where we could have a hot shower. Three large tents had been set up end to end. The first contained a barber and shoe shine facilities so we took off our boots and proceed into the second tent to strip off all our gear. When we moved to the third tent there was a scramble for one of the shower jets of hot water.

It was an absolute joy to have the first really complete wash since arriving here almost four months ago.

The Canadians had also installed a laundry system along with the showers so that on emerging from the shower tent, we received a fresh, clean set of underwear. The whole place was very slickly operated and all twenty of us went through in half an hour emerging sparkling clean and ready to go. It seemed that anyone in the vicinity, or just passing by, could drop in for a shower at any time, even our chaps out on line mending parties. I was never aware of any British army unit like it here, more was the pity.

Of mice, men and things

Here in Korea it was 02:00 and my mother's birthday. For her it was still the day before and she was probably having tea or getting dinner ready. How odd things can become on this planet as it spins on its axis in space.

Stories were circulating that the Chinese had accused the UN of using biological warfare against their troops by dropping infected lice and rodents on their side of the front line. We considered this to be both stupid and untrue, laughable in fact because such a tactic would easily have backfired on us. Neither of those creatures would respect a front line. Besides, disease was an easy enough thing to pick up if one were careless about certain fundamentals of hygiene, personal or otherwise. We believed the accusations against the UN to be a rather crude propaganda ploy.

On the other hand, the Chinese were reputed to be very lax about hygiene and if they were suffering lice and rodent born infections it was probably their own fault. Reports told of Chinese prisoners being in a filthy condition when captured and chaps who had actually seen the conditions they lived in when one of their positions had been overrun said they were squalid and full of filth. The fact that the lines had been pretty static for some time didn't help and only increased the need for greater attention to all aspects of hygiene. If we ever made a drive forward, we would have to be very awake to these matters should we ever take over Chinese positions for ourselves.

Rats were everywhere here, sometimes in plague proportions. We avoided leaving food lying about in the bunkers, leaving packs and bedding rolls undone or just lying around in a heap. Some chaps had found so many rat holes inside bunkers they wished to occupy that they had to use smoke to get them to come out and a grenade to finish them off.

Half a century later I discovered something that seemed more like the truth. When we first heard of this in Korea we thought it ridiculous. It now seems that there was possibly some substance to the story, that the USA did conduct germ warfare as a 'black', or covert, operation known to the US President but not to the UN high command. It is a subject still in contention.

The rules we were given regarding hygiene were strictly enforced and any slackness could warrant getting put on a 'fizzer'. All natural water sources carried infection of some sort, which was why every drop was treated before it could be used. The taste wasn't great which was why so much beer was requested with the NAAFI orders twice a week. And cookhouse tea didn't taste much better than the water. It was stewed stiff enough to stand a spoon in by the time we got it and was probably dosed with bromide anyway to keep 'natural urges' in check.

Sonju fever was another hazard, a deadly disease of the guts caused by a bug carried by Korean mice. A captain at brigade HQ, a young, well built and very fit chap who had once visited our exchange, had evidently contracted Sonju fever and was in a very bad way with it. I had one of the little fellows lodging in my bunker at that time but it never had a chance to get too personal.

I was still greatly enjoying the view across the valley of the River Imjin from our reserve positions. The water, sleekly reflecting the blue of the sky as it swept past that beach, looked very inviting, especially after a couple of sweaty hours slogging away to deepen the crawl trench. It was a continual surprise how, amidst all the desolation of this land and the frequent boredom of our lives here, it was always possible to find natural beauty capable of cheering the soul. Often I would stand outside the exchange bunker, the breeze in my face gazing out over the valley. As I enjoyed the view of the river valley below and the fantastic silhouette of the mountains to the south, all kinds of scents carrying many memories would be borne in that breeze to play in my mind.

Homesick? It was hard not to be from time to time. Sometimes I seemed to smell the sea and would recall days on the beach at Sandbanks or Studland. Sometimes I would smell the open fields of the Purbeck valley between Corfe Castle and Swanage, or the bluebell woods on the cliff tops above Old Harry Rocks, or at Creech. Usually we could joke and laugh, work, read, eat or sleep without caring a damn where we were but often I would imagine that, instead of being 11,000 miles away from home on the other side of the world, we were only 200 miles away on an exercise on the PTA in Norfolk.

Then, focusing once more on that view of the River Imjin, I would be brought back to cold reality. I was indeed 11000 miles from home and this was indeed a live war zone—or supposed to be. Then there would be the realisation that another three and half months had slipped by leaving only another five before we could return home. So time here had the same habit of passing as relentlessly as had the sea miles on the voyage out. The day really would arrive when we would find ourselves leaving Korea for the equally relentless voyage back home. All we had to do was make sure we survived. Only God knew how big a thing that might be to ask. It hadn't succeeded for Alec.

The question when we get back home will be how to survive in civvy street. I had no idea what I wished to do with the rest of my life. Somewhere in my mind lurked the idea that civvy street and I would not get along too well. Perhaps I should have followed up the suggestion made by the CO at Harwich about going for officer training. I couldn't have made a worse job of it than some of our junior officers here.

Later that evening, the weather changed and brought the first big rainfall since we arrived here. It caught everyone on the hop. For the past week we had been trying to bring our bunker up to the same standard as the one we had up on the Hook. We had dismantled and reconstructed the fence picket and telephone cable double bunk-beds because they were too narrow, dug the floor out another two feet and then started to sort the roof out. We had managed to rig up a temporary roof with pickets and pieces of canvas but it was not securely weighted down. Try as we might, we could obtain no sandbags nor was there much earth available to weigh things down. That night, after we had crept into our sleeping bags, the wind picked up and ripped half the roof off. Then it began to sleet and the water poured in. Fortunately I had rigged up my groundsheet over my bunk, which was the top one, and this prevented our sleeping bags from getting wet but it was a messy job to crawl out of them, fumble into some clothes, grope our way outside in this premature 'April shower' and try to sort the roof out. Amid the rain, the mud and in the cold and dark, the results of our efforts were not particularly good. It was like entering a shower when we went back inside and the floor was swimming in water. Nevertheless, we knew one thing for certain: getting the roof fixed properly when it got light would have top priority. Struggling back into our bags, we tried to get back to sleep but the wind and sleet kept us awake all night.

When reveille was finally blown all signs of the storm had disappeared. We emerged to find the mountains to the south sketched out in white from the sleet that had fallen. As a view, it was incredibly beautiful but we had little time to indulge the luxury of contemplating it. We were dragged back to damp and dismal reality by the information that the CO was to inspect all signals platoon bunkers that afternoon. We had our work cut out to dig all the mud out and get things shipshape but finally it was done and we hoped for a half decent nights sleep that night, the first in over thirty-six hours.

A change of company

Last Thursday, 28th March, the signals officer miraculously answered a silent prayer that I had been offering up for many days—that I be posted out of battalion HQ. He sent me off to join the signals section at 'D' Company HQ. Here the company signals exchange was in a tent shared with the stores, which proved to be very useful. This tent had been erected on a terrace half excavated out of the side of a hill and half built up with sand bags and the excavated soil. The sides of the tent on the uphill side had been laid back into a ditch cut out the length of the tent and away at both ends to carry rainwater away. It had also created a shelf along that side inside the tent on which the wireless and telephone exchange was set up along with other gear best kept off the floor.

Officially, our accommodation was a bunker excavated from the hillside nearby. It was about four yards square and contained five bunks but would have been very crowded had we all used it. Unofficially, given the fact that there was plenty of room, we slept in the signals tent. The bunker was cosy and we kept it tidy in case of emergencies. The only problem with the tent was that, except for one box, which was seating for whoever was on duty, there was nothing to sit on except the floor.

There were five of us in this section to handle the telephone exchange and wireless communications. The corporal was a big, craggy Welshman named Jim Maggs who was pretty easy going. The others were lantern-jawed Dave Lewis, lanky Haydn Angell and another craggy looking Welshman whom everyone just called Tommo. I was the only English chap there. Each of us did a stag of about two and a half hours on and ten hours off so that duty periods rotated slowly and were less stressful. Something that I really came to appreciate was that the officers did not bother us. In fact, they were quite affable toward us. They trusted that we knew our jobs and left us to get on with them. We were almost a law unto ourselves.

The temperatures had risen a little over the past few days so we no longer got sleet. The heavens now leaked torrential rain. The only thing that had to be ensured was that the drainage ditch along the uphill side of the tent was kept clear and deep enough to cope not only with rainwater flowing off the tent but any flowing down the hillside. Down below in the valley lay the road to the front line which carried a great deal of traffic, mostly trucks, jeeps and American tanks. Occasionally a medical helicopter would fly over like some mechanical dragonfly.

There were many ways in which being with a rifle company was a great relief after life in BHQ. Not the least improvement was being out of reach of the RSM's "bullshit" with which we were continually being mucked around. After a few days in 'D' Company, I realised just how tired in both mind and body I had become. Maybe the reason for my transfer was my suspicion that I was gaining a reputation for being 'dense'. But it was certainly a move for the better, a deliverance.

The move to D Company cost me my place for R&R leave in Tokyo and left me with no idea when I would get it, if ever. However, it was an opportunity to save more pennies to take with me if and when that time came. Meanwhile there were the occasional trips back to Support Company at F Echelon, where a decent cinema had been set up showing reasonably up to date films like *"Hotel Sahara"* and *"Crosswinds"*. I bought a camera from Dave Lewis which had film in it and I could now take a few photographs of life here to send home.

D company signals tent

The rain clouds cleared, the weather improved and became quite warm again, like a late spring day in England. The thaw proceeded apace with the result that the roads became very slippery and treacherous. Where they had been specially constructed across paddy fields, the soft shoulders could become dangerous. In other places soft patches on the roads had been churned into quagmires. It was quite an experience to ride anywhere along them. However, there were still no early signs of spring's green spreading across the landscape. The brown hills still stretched away for miles in all directions to end up in awesome looking mountain ranges along the horizon. D Company's elevation was higher than that of BHQ and the views of the River Imjin were even more spectacular. It was possible to see the whole sweep of the river and also the confluence with the River Samichon, the area reckoned to be the weakest link in our defences.

Several times it occurred to us to wonder exactly why the Commonwealth Division had been allocated to this part of the line. The American UN command probably had a special regard for the Commonwealth regiments after their achievements the year before at Gloster Hill and Kapyong. For the past few days, some members of 'D' Company had gone back to the Gloster's old positions on the Kansas Line south of the river. This fall-back defence line had to be refurbished, the crawl trenches dug out and the barbed wire defences repaired against the possibility of full-scale warfare being resumed in the near future. However, things were said to be looking up once more at the truce talks so we felt that this possibility had become remote. Every other day a signaller had to go back with them, taking the 31 set to check on communications.

We heard reports that the 'Pats', who took over our old positions on The Hook, were copping far more attention from the Chinese than we had and were being hammered with intense shell and mortar fire and suffering quite a few casualties.

Copies of *The People* were circulating that contained articles written by Arthur Helliwell, one from Japan and one from Korea, the last in the form of a letter to the mother of one of the lads in the front line. He had the story pretty correct in both places, about Tokyo according to those who had already gone on R&R and about Korea according to my own experience. Most people at home who had read his article on Korea would have been shocked to learn about how we lived, unaware of the degree to which we had become used to it. The dirt and lack of ordinary civilised amenities didn't bother us as much as folk back home might have expected. We had come to terms with the situation and turned our attention to finding small ways to enjoy life and make it more comfortable. It was possible to say that spirits were high and a lot of the credit for this had to go to the officers and NCOs who were, in our company at least, easy to get along with.

I had a suspicion that, had any one of us been given a choice between life here and life back in Sobraon Barracks in Colchester, we might just have preferred it here but without having the dangers to to life and limb to contend with. I also had to admit that life in one of the rifle companies was decidedly better than life had been back at BHQ.

A visit to C Company

It was April Fools' Day and I fancied finding out where C Company HQ was and whether it was possible to walk over to see Brian, Alec and some of the other chaps that I had joined up with. I asked our 2IC about this. He pointed out on a map where they were tucked along the reverse side of a small side valley only a ten-minute walk away across the ridge. He gave me permission to go but I was to stick to clearly defined paths.

I hadn't phoned to tell them that I was coming over so my arrival was a surprise. 'C' Company HQ wasn't at all difficult to find because a rather macabre sign confirmed that I had found them. A genuine and much bleached human skull and cross bones, supposedly Chinese, were fixed to the top of a post with a sign for C Company beneath. Brian said the idea had come from one of the officers.

They had been busy making themselves comfortable too. Brian's domain, the company office, was housed in a tent beside the track and part had been set aside as a kind of recreation area. Alec, revealing a hitherto hidden talent, had painted a sign for it. Using a photograph of a pin-up girl stuck to a board as the basis, he had then hung it from a very neatly painted sign that read "The Verge Inn". What else? The letters were in the Welsh colours: red on a green and white background.

Alec Fulcher the sign writer C coy pub sign

Bottles of beer were produced and we sat around talking for a couple of hours. Neither Brian nor Alec had any idea when they would go on R&R and there was no way we could organise to go together. I paid them a visit again on two other occasions, walking over just before dark to spend the evening nattering away over a tin of fruit and a few bottles of beer.

On one of these visits, Brian told me that, from time to time, he felt extremely lonely. In this regard I was perhaps more fortunate and had many opportunities to talk to lots of people, especially when on duty but Brian invariably worked alone and seldom saw anyone to speak to. He received plenty of mail from home but this loneliness was making it more difficult for him to ignore the more disagreeable aspects of life here. He seemed unable to find small beauties to delight his soul. For my part, loneliness was a feeling that didn't bother me too much. Provided there was the occasional chance to sit in the sun for a while on the top of a hill with the breeze on my face, I could imagine being anywhere else that I fancied, doing anything else that I wanted.

Brian—C Coy reserve

During such moments here in Korea, it seemed that I was only playing at being a soldier much as, when nine or ten years old, I had played war games with the other kids up on an old piece of overgrown waste land near my home. There we played 'Cops and robbers', 'Cowboys and Indians', or 'Tommys and Huns'. The only difference here in Korea was that if you were unfortunate enough to 'be killed' it was not a matter of lying down and counting to fifty then getting up and continuing to play. Here the hazards were only too real. But when was life ever safe and not full of hazardous situations, whether imaginary or real? Fourteen men had been killed in action up on The Hook. If they had remained in England, they might have been killed in road accidents or in some other way. Who was to tell?

In the last analysis, deep down nobody really 'liked' this existence but most of us made the best of it all and to some extent managed to get used to it. What may have helped us cope was the knowledge that we were not regular soldiers but conscripts on a very limited engagement. One day soon, our time in this man's army would come to and end, we would be removed from harms way and shipped back home to be demobbed. All we had to do was survive.

Corporal Maggs managed to scrounge some large wooden boxes from the stores. He intended using one as a table but I suggested that, if they were carefully taken apart and the nails saved and straightened out, we could make a proper table and have stuff left over for a bench. And that is what we did. First, a small writing area was constructed in the exchange corner. Then the rest of the wood was used to make a table about three feet square, an armchair and a chaise longue—something to stretch out on off the floor and relax. Such luxury! It was all very flash and I wondered if we would get orders for more. It was certainly possible for many aspects of life here to be made more comfortable with such simple constructions.

D coy signals tent with furniture

The chaise longue had been placed near the shelf with the wireless set and exchange. Later that day, I found the corporal fast asleep on it when he was supposed to be on duty. Taking care not to wake him, I fetched my camera and took a photograph of him in the land of nod. Later, when I told him he had gone to sleep on duty, he denied it most vigorously but I hadn't the heart to tell him that there was as yet undeveloped evidence in my camera to prove it.

Jolly boating weather

Yesterday, we were trucked down to the River Imjin for a session on the loading, launching and handling of assault boats. It was very warm work under the bright, hot sun. There was much wise-cracking that our efforts should have been recorded for a film called "Across the Imjin", much in the style of "The Sands of Iwo Jima" but we couldn't decide who would play John Wayne.

Swimming in River Imjin

After the work part of the day was over, we went for a swim but, by God, that water was cold. It was only about four feet deep in midstream and flowing at about four or five knots according to one 'expert'. But word was that in the rainy season it would rise another forty-five feet or more and flow at treble the speed. It was a good day and although feeling utterly shagged out, I felt very relaxed. Besides, seeing a company of bare white bums and shrivelled dicks frolicking in the river would have been sufficient to make any day memorable.

Spring is sprung at last

At last this devastated countryside began to show signs of life. Little patches of green began to decorate the bare brown hills and paddies. Tender little blades of grass were springing up everywhere and buds were bursting open on the shrubs and the few remaining trees. One shrub produced the most delicate pale mauve flowers even before leaves had a chance to appear. Yet another bore what looked like little mushrooms of small yellow flowers, once again before leaves had appeared. What looked to be a relative of the Pussy Willow bore catkins with small red knobs all over them that ripened, burst and then turned black. I asked one of our Korean porters for the names of these flowering shrubs but unfortunately made no record of them.

The weather continued to warm up, the ground to dry out and the brown landscape turn green. Before long dust would be the problem. Word went round to be ready to move back into the front line in a week's time, much earlier than we had been led to expect. Apparently, we were to relieve the King's Shropshire Light Infantry who, from reports, had been occupying a section of the front that the Chinese liked to use for target practice. My first real taste of life right up at the sharp end was approaching, a time to keep one ear permanently open for the sound of Death's whistle.

The subject of R&R came up and numbers were placed in a tin hat and drawn to determine the order in which we would go. I drew number 3 and would probably go as soon as we had moved back into the front line. Two £3 Postal Orders came in the mail from home to top up the funds I would be able to take with me.

12

Back to the sharp end

16th April-18th April 1952

Moving Up

We moved up into positions on Hill 355, also known as Little Gibraltar. We had expected to relieve the Shropshires (KSLI) but instead it was the Borderers (KOSB) about whom there is more to say later. One of the platoon officers told us that we were now on the eastern end of the Commonwealth Division section of the front, so our neighbours to the right would be Korean or American.

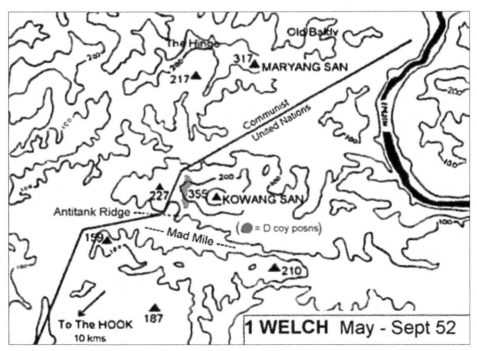

D Company, 1 Welch position on Hill 355 summer 195

They, being the main movers behind the UN resistance to the Communist North Korean invasion in 1950, were the natural targets for North Korean and Chinese animosity, which was a hundred times more intense than toward us. Our rather casual animosity toward the Yanks was a love affair by comparison.

D Company was positioned along two spurs, one running southwest and the other northwest from high up on the western flank of Hill 355, a number derived from its height in metres above sea level. It was also known as 'Little Gibraltar' because of its profile from a certain direction. One platoon was on the northwest ridge where it started to slope down to a saddle connecting 355 to the Chinese outpost on Hill 227 variously known as 'John' or 'Fanny Hill' depending on who you talked to. The latter name derived from the fact that there was a huge crater on the summit surrounded by bushes. The other platoons were along the southwest ridge which continued below us out into the valley where it became Anti-tank Ridge. This was covered with a few battered pine trees. How they had managed to survive was anyone's guess.

JF, Dave Lewis, Cpl Jim Maggs & Tommo - 'D' Coy Signals 355 June 1952

Members of D coy signals

A company of 1 Battalion, Royal Australian Regiment (1RAR) held Anti-tank Ridge while their other companies were on the line of hills from Hill 210 to 159 across the valley below. This valley was popularly known to us as "Mad Mile" because it was so straight, but the Canadians, when they were here, called it the "Cannonball Run".

View across mad Mile—Antitank Ridge at bottom right

The road back along Mad Mile led to our battalion HQ. In the other direction it led straight to the Chinese positions. One story told of an American artillery Forward Observation Officer (FOO) who was given a map reference on Mad Mile where he was to set up his observation post. When halted by the sentry on the road at Antitank Ridge and told that this was the beginning of no-mans land, he replied that they had a map ref to go to and continued on. The map reference he was aiming for was the target area for their guns rather than the observation point. His driver duly delivered both them and the jeep into the hands of the Chinese.

2 Mad Mile from 355 looking across to Hill 159

View of Mad Mile past flank of Hill 227 on right

The Chinese gunners had a very clear view up Mad Mile and any traffic using it. They sporadically dropped shells up that valley. Although the road was seldom hit, our telephone lines laid alongside were frequently cut. This would require two signallers to go out to find and repair the break, not a pleasant prospect if the shelling was continuing. Knees would quickly turn to jelly if a tell tale whistle was heard overhead while out on such a job.

Hill 227 was only a few hundred yards away from our perimeter. Strategically, its significance for the Chinese was akin to that of Hill 169 in relation to The Hook in that it put a kink in the frontline. Down below and in the shadow of 227, a standing patrol or forward listening post was dug into a small knoll and held by a section of three or four chaps connected to company HQ by telephone and a small portable radio as carried by section leaders when on patrol. It worked to the 31 set back in the exchange bunker. Right in the middle of our HQ position a Centurion tank had been dug into the ridge so that only the turret was visible. It had a good angle of fire for its 20 pound gun from the north-east round to what I reckoned to be west-northwest.

A Centurion tank dug in to the crest of a ridge

The view northwest was across a broad valley to a low line of hills where the main Chinese troop positions lay. To the far right of that line of hills but hidden from our view by the mass of 355, was Hill 317 and other features such as The Hinge and Old Baldy, scenes of hard fighting only a few months ago. Later, when I was able to examine contour maps of the area, I could understand why 317 and 227 had been so difficult to hold on to. Had the UN tried to retake them the war would have been a lot hotter in our part of the line than it turned out to be.

The exchange bunker, with its field telephone exchange, the 62 set for internal battalion communications and the 31 set used for internal company wireless communications, was built off the crawl trench on the reverse side of the southwestern ridge and only a few yards from the Centurion tank. Personal bunkers were similarly built all round the crawl trenches for the men in the rifle sections and there were a few others further down the reverse slope of the ridge that HQ personel used.

Welsh humour

That afternoon, Captain Dyer, the signals officer, paid us a visit to see if everything was OK. He was personally checking that everything to do with the communications network was in place and in good order following the move up to the front. I was on exchange duty while he was with us and answered a call from a couple of linesmen who were out from BHQ looking for a line break somewhere along Mad Mile. I knew both of them quite well from my time at BHQ. They had evidently found the break and were just making sure they could get through to both my exchange and that at BHQ before repairing it. They knew that the SO was with us since they had seen him pass in his jeep earlier on.

Evans was a short, dark haired Welshman with an impish sense of humour while his mate Williams was a lanky guy who always struck me as being a few trees short of a forest for some reason. After I had chatted to Evans for a moment, he asked me if he could speak to the signals officer. Since the captain was standing behind me I turned and said,

"Evans wants a word with you, sir." The SO took the handset and said,

"Hello, Signals Officer here. What do you want, Evans?"

"Not me, sir," said Evans. "It's Williams 'oos wantin' a word with you, sir." There was a pause. Evans had evidently handed the phone to Williams telling him that the SO wanted a word.

"Williams yer, sir," we heard him say in his broad Welsh voice.

"What do you want Williams?" the SO asked and I heard Williams splutter

" Me, sir? I dunno, sir. I don't want nuthin', sir. I don't want to speak to you, sir. Evans said it was you wanted a word with me, sir, and just gave me the phone." You could feel the poor guy's total confusion at this point.

"Put Evans back on the line," snapped the SO.

"Yes, sir, you want to speak to me," came the sound of Evans' voice, all innocent-like.

"Evans?" he hissed, "If you ever pull another stunt like that I will come down there, stick both ends of the line into your cock and generate until your eyeballs light up. Do you understand me?"

"Yessir, yessir." he replied. And quickly hung up.

Those who overheard this little exchange were bursting with laughter. Looking at the SO, I saw that he was laughing too, a very good sign. We all considered him to be a good officer, one who knew his job and knew his men and how to get the best out them, which was not by being on their backs all the time.

Brian's company was up on the top of Hill 355 and we were now nearer to each other than at any time since we had been in the front line. One afternoon, I managed to get away to pay him a visit. It was only a matter of minutes to walk up a crawl trench on the reverse side of the ridge to get to his HQ platoon position. He had been to see the barber and his fuzzy hair style had been reduced to a one inch crop. Strangely, he was quite bashful about letting me see it. He then told me that he had found a way to cope with the loneliness he had complained of by having six pen friends back in the UK. They were all girls, three in Cardiff and three in Bristol. This was really extraordinary because he had always given me the impression that he didn't like writing letters very much.

We had no rain for a fortnight. Then, last night, two hours in advance, we were told that a gale was imminent. And what a wind that was. Someone mentioned the figure 50mph (80kph) but I reckoned it was more like 60 mph (100kph) It nearly blew us and everything else away. We were told to expect plenty of rain but, thank goodness, it never came. It probably got blown away before it could reach the ground. Even if it had landed, we were prepared for it. Although our bunker roof would leak like a sieve we had taken precautions to ensure that our beds were not dripped on and that our kit stayed above water level.

13

TOKYO INTERLUDE

19th April-27th April 1952

Tokyo Beckons

Very early this morning, just before stand to, the company 2i/c, came by and told me to get my gear packed. I was going back to A Echelon. When I asked why, what had happened, a big grin lit his face and he told me that I was going for five days R&R in Tokyo. I would be away longer than the five days because of the time it would take to get me there and back. First, I had would go by jeep to A Echelon where I would spend the night and leave most of my kit. My back pack would be sufficient for everything I needed to take while on leave, all basic clothes and personal stuff. Then, after a long truck journey to Seoul and the next night, I would go to Kimpo airbase for the flight to Japan. There I would have five clear days at the Commonwealth Division Rest Centre before returning.

With no time to waste, I quickly collected and packed my gear, putting what I would need to take to Tokyo in my back pack and then went outside to watch for the jeep to come down Mad Mile. At last I was off to experience "Rack & Ruin" as the jokers among us had named it.

Everyone else was on stand to, the sun not yet risen when I spotted the jeep as it came down Mad Mile, more by the dust it was kicking up than anything else. The driver should have known better because Chinese observers could see right up that valley and clouds of dust were a dead give-away that there was a target for them. Thankfully the enemy guns remained silent. The driver came as far up the back of the ridge as he could and I clambered my way down to him with all my gear hanging round my neck. Then we were off, the driver making good time to get out of that valley and out of sight of those Chinese observers.

At A Echelon, I was shown to a tent and chose a camp bed where I would sleep that night. It was suggested that I go and have some breakfast then check gear that was not going with me into the stores tent. After that, my time was my own to wander around, read, or sleep as I pleased. But the first things I really wanted to do were to have a good lazy wash and shave. As the morning passed, other Tokyo bound chaps arrived to claim beds in the tent but there was no one among them that I knew.

Next morning, after another leisurely wash, shave and breakfast, we were mustered, instructed to be on our best behaviour and put aboard a huge US truck for the journey to Seoul. It had a canvas cover, presumably to keep excessive draughts off and bench seating down both sides. Unable to grab a seat near the tail, my view was limited to what I could see looking straight out through the back. We crossed the Pintail Bridge over the River Imjin, a new steel bridge built across a gorge sometime in 1952 by US engineers. It was designed to withstand the forty-five feet rise in the water level during the summer rains and subsequent floods but on this day, the river flowed lazily along some fifty feet below.

As we progressed further south the road surface improved and we were not thrown around quite so much. They were still treacherously slippery and twice we had to get out while the driver winched his truck onto the road after taking a bend too quickly. Eventually we arrived at the Forward Marshalling Area (FMA) in Seoul where we spent a very cold night and were finally woken by the yelling of Korean kids down in the back yard asking for tidbits.

The truck to Kimpo Airfield left at 08:30 so we needed to be up early to wash, shave, pack and go for breakfast. The half hour journey westward out of the city took us back across the Han River. At the airfield Base Club, many others were waiting to go on R&R, most of them Americans. By the size and spaciousness of the interior it must have previously been a hangar.

Making our way to the cafeteria/bar area we sat down to consider what we wanted to eat or drink. Several airmen were leaning against the bar drinking coffee and eating ring doughnuts. Mostly they wore huge dark blue padded flight jackets that made them look like body builders. They all carried automatic pistols slung low on their thighs which made a strange impression on us because we had seen similar sights in Western cowboy films. The whole experience was quite awesome, quite surreal. However, it was real enough, as were the coffee and doughnuts we were given by the counter staff. They were free, just as well because we only had BAFs with us which could not be used here. With no idea what time our flight would leave, we sat around chatting or playing cards until it was well past midday. Meanwhile, other groups from the Commonwealth Division arrived to swell our numbers.

Eventually, at 13:00, we were called outside, told to climb aboard some open trucks and taken out onto the airfield. The weather had turned cloudy and dull. In all directions we could see US aircraft—jet fighters, spotter planes, bombers and transports. We drew up beside a four engine Douglas Skymaster transport and climbed aboard. The seating consisted of metal framed canvas seats down each side secured to the fuselage. I took one on the starboard side by a window. This was to be my very first flight so I wanted to look down on the country we would be flying over.

The crew who came on board were dressed like the guys we had seen in the club. They told us to fasten our safety belts, pulled up the door and went forward to the cockpit. When the engines started up, one at a time, the whole plane vibrated incredibly as we taxied out to the runway, even more so as the engines were revved up for take-off. This was all very exciting because, apart from an uncle who had been in the RAF in India during the war, nobody else in my family had ever flown before. There was a subtle change in the vibration in the plane as the wheels lost contact with the ground and we were all leaned more noticeably sideways toward the tail as the nose came up.

Finally, having reached cruising height, we could take our safety belts off. We hit a patch of turbulence that made me feel slightly nauseous but things smoothed out again and it wore off. I turned to look out of the window. Way below lay Korea, a wrinkled, dull brown and khaki green landscape of fearsome mountain ranges and valleys but little else. It was like looking at a page in a topographical atlas with a 3D effect added but no visible contour lines or printed names. So this was the land the war had raged back and forth over since I was on that farming holiday in Pembrokeshire, South Wales, in June 1950.

The view became monotonous so I examined the interior of the aircraft. Everything was very utilitarian and painted a dull olive green or sienna brown. The seats could fold back to increase the space for cargo storage and everywhere there were devices by which it could be secured. Over our heads were rails to which ripcords for opening parachutes could be attached if paratroops were being carried. Notices indicated where life jackets were stored, stated that that smoking was prohibited but there was little else of interest. I took out a book to read but the printed words blurred with the droning sound and the vibration of the engines. I nodded off.

Korean landscape from the air

Awoken by someone shouting that we were flying over water, I looked out of the window. Monotonous khaki mountains had given way to an equally monotonous grey blue sea which meant we were well on our way to Tokyo. After that, it seemed no time at all before I sensed the nose dip slightly, that the plane was starting to descend. Outside, the weather had closed in and we were flying through cloud. Over the PA system, we were instructed to fasten safety belts and secure our belongings. As we descended below cloud level, the Japanese countryside appeared below looking as neat and tidy as Korea was ramshackle.

It was dusk and raining so the view was not clear until we got much lower. Buildings stretched as far as we could see and the street and city lights had come on. The engines began to roar and there was a shudder as the wing flaps were extended to reduce air speed. The nose rose and finally, with a bump, we were once more on the ground and cruising along a runway. After the plane had taxied to a halt near a hangar, one of the crew opened the door. Steps were driven up and without any more ceremony we were told to go and get aboard some busses that were waiting. Scuttling through the rain, we clambered aboard and were soon under way again. It was quite a long drive through the suburbs of Tokyo but eventually we turned through some rather grand gates and pulled up outside the main entrance to large building several stories high.

Once the Ebisu Hotel, it had been commandeered as the Commonwealth Division Rest Centre in Tokyo. We entered and waited in the huge reception hall until an officer arrived to tell us about the facilities at the centre. I was shown to a small double room which I was to share with a corporal in the RAMC. He did nothing to invite conversation so I had no idea where he was based in Korea.

We had been told to have a shower then report to the Quartermaster's Stores. There we were issued with clean battledresses, berets, belts, underwear and socks. The battledress blouse bore no insignia of any kind, no regimental or divisional flashes and no emblems of rank. It felt very strange, and in a way, naked to have no form of unit identification. Back in Korea, the articles of military clothing that even the Korean porters had scrounged bore flashes of some kind. Here we were to remain quite incognito it seemed. We were asked to get changed and bring all our old clothing back to the stores.

After dinner, in the Rest Centre Club, I bumped into a Canadian I had met during the 'cruise' on the *Empire Longford*. We were both surprised to see each other. Unfortunately he was too drunk to make much sense other than to tell me that this was his last night in Tokyo. Anyway, I was so utterly tired that I didn't want to spend any time with him and headed for my bed. It was just unfortunate that having become so used to sleeping rough, a well sprung mattress with cool, clean sheets did not help me sleep at all well that night.

The next morning, finding a seat at a table in the dining hall, I was waited on by an extremely beautiful Japanese girl. There were many others, equally lovely, waiting on other tables. Inexplicably, I suddenly felt very shy and awkward in her presence but eventually got past it to enjoy an excellent breakfast.

Going outside I found a group of Canadians and got into conversation with them. It turned out that they were from the PPCLI, the battalion that had taken over from us on The Hook when we went into brigade reserve. Naturally I asked what they thought of the positions they had taken over from the Welch and they made very complimentary noises, as indeed they should. Their regimental base was in Alberta but when I asked where they were individually from, it seemed that they came from all over Canada. As we talked, my musical ear led me to unconsciously mimic their drawling accent. I only realised just how much I had picked up on it when one of them turned and asked, "Which part of Canada are you from?" I smiled and replied, "Ah cum frum liddle ol' Poole in Doorset, Ennglund," and we all laughed.

Looking back now, those few days spent in Tokyo passed in a blur. I made no notes and no attempt to write home. All that remained were a series of snapshots of places and experiences drawn from memory. Sadly, many details are lacking. Far too much was new and strange to be remembered without making notes. One small detail I did remember was the rate of exchange—1008 yen for £1 but they could disappear faster than water down a drain.

Along with a couple of other chaps, we set off to find the suburban electric train station for Ebisu and go into central Tokyo. An enormous crowd was waiting for the train. When it pulled in and had discharged passengers wanting to get off, there was a great rush by those waiting to get aboard. Station officials got behind those at the back of the crowd and pushed so that we ended as tightly packed as proverbial sardines. It made the 'mating calls' of our English bus conductors such as "Pass right down the bus, PLEASE." followed by "Hold on tight, PLEASE," seem like politeness incarnate compared to this rugby scrum. No need for strap-hanging here in Japan. No one could move, let alone fall over whenever the train jerked forward or came to a sudden stop. Eventually, arriving at a station serving central Tokyo, the press of bodies eased as the human tide flooded out of the compartment on its way to places of work.

This was my first time in such a large city, Singapore excepted. I had never visited London or any other large English city so I felt very much like a country bumpkin in town for the first time. The buildings were higher than any I had seen before and completely covered with neon signs and boards from just above head height to high above the roofs. Their complexity and colours were amazing. We just wandered around gawping at the shops, the signs, the traffic and the people. Everything seemed to have been Americanised. The shops were full of bright and lovely goods of every description, all of them looking far too expensive for us. The crowds were also incredible and it was interesting to observe that, while girls and younger women had taken to wearing western style clothing, a few of the older women still wore the extremely elaborate traditional dress, looking like so many Madame Butterflies.

Ginza, Tokyo at 1114 hours

I was also fascinated by the many business men walking around, all dressed alike in black, high-buttoned, single-breasted suits, carrying rolled black umbrellas, black brief cases and wearing black bowler hats. It looked so old-fashioned and very reminiscent of scenes in the City of London where, although still the traditional dress, it was on the way out. I observed how, if a group of them had been standing in conversation and the time had come to part, they would all step back and bow to each other before moving on.

While walking on Ginza, the main shopping street, I had an embarrassing encounter with such a group. Approaching a crossroads, I turned my head to look to my right to see what traffic was approaching at the precise moment that a quartet of these little bowler hatted men standing on the corner decided to perform their little parting ceremony. One of them stepped back neatly into my path and we collided. We were both very surprised but recovered quickly to look at each other, nod apologies and move on.

The traffic was continuous and there were many small, tinny looking cars, much like sardine cans on wheels, that made a noise as if the big ends or the exhaust had broken. They all seemed to be of the same make—Datsuns. Undoubtedly Japanese, it appeared that their car industry was up and running once more as part of Japan's post-war recovery.

Returning to Ebisu around mid-afternoon, I had dinner and then joined another couple of chaps who were going back into central Tokyo central to see the night life. So back we went once more to the station, boarded the electric train and returned once more into that neon lit jungle. Nightclubs had been declared out of bounds for us so we went to a cinema to see Abbott and Costello *In The Foreign Legion*. Fortunately it was in English with Japanese subtitles. Outside again we were continually accosted by pimps who seemed able to offer us anything with two legs and the necessary facilities, irrespective of age or sex. There were many very beautiful girls about too but, by 22:30 we finally had enough of this pointless pavement-bashing, made our way back to the station, took the train back to Ebisu and went to bed.

Manhood at last

The only other thing I recalled of interest, or significance, was the manner in which I finally lost my virginity. In the all-male society of the battalion and the front line, the talk was often of women and of sexual experiences with them. Some were quite lascivious, especially from those who had already been on R&R. The authorities knew about all this and we had all received what was euphemistically called a "short arm inspection" by the MO at Ebisu, together with a description of the first symptoms of several forms of VD and what we should do if we contracted any of them. But I had no thought of going out to find a woman to have sex with. What eventually happened though—well, it just happened.

On the way into the city one afternoon I met Dan at the station who was also on his own. Wandering aimlessly around we passed one of the pachinko parlours that had sprung up everywhere. Their walls were lined with vertical pinball machines. In the middle of the room was a small kiosk-cum-cash desk at which one could buy cigarettes or sweets or, more significantly, the ball-bearings required to play the machines.

More out of curiosity than anything else, except boredom perhaps, we entered one of these parlours, bought a supply of ball-bearings, found unoccupied machines and started to play. A ball dropped into a cup would roll to a position from where, by depressing and releasing a small lever, it could be projected to fly up and around the face of the machine until it dropped into one of the many small cups that projected from it. If you were lucky and the ball dropped into certain cups, more ball-bearings would be released. If you were unlucky the machine would just swallow up that ball-bearing and you would be one ball the poorer so to speak. If, having tired of the game, you wanted to leave you could cash in any ball bearings you had left, or perhaps had accumulated, for cigarettes, or a lighter, or sweets or some other item.

For a while I did quite well, winning many extra ball-bearings but this was followed by a long losing streak until I had no ball-bearings left. About to turn away, a girl at the next machine tugged my sleeve and gave me half a dozen of her ball bearings. I smiled, thanked her and started playing again, won a few more and then lost them all. I looked at her and smiled. She looked at me, smiled, and asked in her singsong English if I was hungry and would I like to come back to her home for a meal? I told her I was with a friend to which she replied that she was too. I called Dan over and told him we had been invited to this girl's home for a meal. Being as bored as I was and having never been inside a Japanese house either, he was quite happy with this idea so off we went.

We were led to a house in a road a little way behind the street in which the pachinko parlour had been located. I recall being asked at the entrance to remove my shoes and put on some felt slippers but I couldn't find any big enough for me. We entered a hall where the walls were wooden screens covered with what looked like a textured parchment paper or tracing paper, a pale creamy white in colour. A partition was slid back to reveal a small room quite bare of furnishings except for a broad, low, highly polished wooden table in the middle of the floor. The floor was also of highly polished wood covered with a rice straw mat. One of the girls ushered us in and invited us to sit on small cushions.

Meanwhile the other girl had disappeared to the back of the house. When she returned they both knelt down and sat on their heels, at the same time appearing to shrink in size compared to us Englishmen. I felt as large as a whale and equally uncomfortable trying to imitate them. An old woman appeared and placed some dishes on the table. They contained rice and some egg noodle dish. She laid four sets of chopsticks on the table then left and returned with eight bowls, four of which contained tea. I watched as the girls scooped some rice and egg noodles into two of the bowls and handed them to us inviting us to eat.

Using chopsticks for the first time proved very difficult. My hands, like my feet, were quite large and I was completely ham fisted trying to manipulate these simple, delicate instruments. I spilt rice and egg noodles all over the table and my lap and decided that it would be better to use my fingers if the girls couldn't find a fork for me. Dan seemed to be doing much better than me. I noticed that the girls picked up their bowls, held them close to their chins and scooped rice and noodles into their mouths. I tried this method but still made a complete mess of things. Seeing my difficulty, one of the girls started to feed me morsels of rice and noodles. Not having been fed by anyone since I was about one year old, this was most enjoyable.

It now became excruciatingly uncomfortable for me to kneel on the floor. This position had me towering over the low table and that probably contributed to my clumsiness with the chopsticks. I was also getting cramp in my calves and urgently needed to change my position. Easing sideways off my heels to sit on the left side of my behind, I stretched my legs out to my right. There was a tearing noise as one of my size elevens disappeared through the wall. This was deeply embarrassing. I was filled with dismay and apologised. However, the girl indicated that it would be no problem to repair the damage and returned to feeding me. The dimensions of the entire experience only served to increase my feeling of being a stranded whale.

After we had finished eating and drunk our tea, they asked us if we would like to stay the night. It was then that my naivety vanished. We had actually been 'picked up' but with extraordinary subtlety and charm. Furthermore, despite my inability to feed myself decently and the physical discomfort that led to me sticking my foot through the wall, it had thus far all been delightful. Set against the background of the past six months in Korea there was no way either Dan or I wished to go back out into the night to try to find our way back to the Rest Centre. There was a fantasy quality about this situation which we could not, and did not want to struggle with. So, looking at each other, we nodded and accepted the invitation.

The girls then showed us to another, larger room at the back of the house. The ceiling was higher, up into the rafters in fact but, apart from a circular well-like construction in one corner, it was empty. Then one of the girls opened a cupboard in the far left hand corner and pulled out a rolled up mattress. After unrolling it on the floor she returned to pull out another. This too was unrolled. Quilts were laid over these and small sausage shaped cushions placed at one end. Then they left.

We looked at each other, wondering what would happen next. At the time, I recall looking round and being very impressed by the economic use of space. At home most people were accustomed to having special rooms permanently fitted out solely for the purpose of sleeping. Here it seemed that an ordinary living space could be quickly converted into a sleeping area and equally quickly be restored for normal daytime use just by rolling and storing away the mattress and bedding. It was like having an extra room in the house.

The girls returned but dressed only in very simple, sleeveless, white shifts that just covered them. We were invited to undress and then to lie on the mattresses. They lay beside us and pulled the quilts over. Things then became even more dreamlike. No one had ever touched me before where and in the way that Japanese girl then began to touch me. As I responded to the flood of extraordinarily pleasurable sensations that began to course through my body, my mind slipped into neutral. Nothing existed outside that quilt and the warmth of her embrace.

But I was as much a newcomer to love-making as I had been in the use of chop sticks. Quick to realise this, with extraordinary skill she began to gently guide me through the part I had to play. Finally the act achieved its ultimate blinding consummation for me.

We separated and I lay back, utterly relaxed and profoundly content. After a while, aware of other noises in the room, I rolled over to find Dan occupied with his girl as I had been with mine. But I was too far away in a Nirvana of sensual and sexual bliss to really be interested in watching him.

An hour must have passed before my girl started to touch me again. I thought of the times I had heard chaps talking about this sort of thing up in the front line and had believed them to be exaggerating. But they hadn't been exaggerating in the least. I had experienced self manipulated orgasms since I was twelve years old but to experience them with the intimate and tender help of this girl was unbelievably beautiful. And she seemed unbothered by the fact that I had not used a condom.

This time I was more active and at one point, raised my head and found Dan was watching me, a big grin all over his face. What the hell, I thought and got to it again. After climaxing again it was my turn to watch him in action. Strangely, it did not feel in the least a perverted thing to do. We then all went to sleep.

When my girl woke me it was beginning to get light. She invited me to get up and come with her, leading me over to the well that I had observed in a corner of the room. It was filled with hot water and she indicated that I should lower myself into it. It was odd to find myself standing up to my chest in hot water but she insisted I duck right down into it, my head as well.

She then proceeded to wash my hair, my face, shoulders and arms, rinsed the soap off and told me to climb out. She then proceeded to wash the rest of me—every little bit of me. What more ways could she possibly find to tease me, to please me? She had fed me, taken my virginity in the most wonderful way and now she was washing me—all over! Her gentleness and the intimate caressing movements of her soapy hands soon prompted a quick rinse off, a very quick drying off and a return to the mattress for another journey to Nirvana.

Afterwards I again climbed back into the well to rinse off and the girl once more proceeded to dry me all over with particular attention to the 'all' part and aroused me once more. This was getting to be too much of an extremely good thing and when she noticed, we did indeed retire under the quilt again while Dan was treated to the same delightful scrub down that I had just received. Later, while lying back under the quilt, we were each brought a bowl of tea to drink. While we were getting dressed the quilts and mattresses were rolled up and put away in the cupboards and the room became quite bare again.

I can only assume that we paid the girls something for their services. I honestly cannot remember, nor how much. Both of us were still too overcome by the whole experience to really care but we both agreed that we could not have lost our virginity in a more delightful way. We were left to wonder if anything like that would ever happen to us again. As the years passed, I came to realise that this experience had, in one sense, forever spoiled all future sexual experience for me.

I remember little of our return to Ebisu or anything else that happened during the rest of my days on R&R. I probably felt a few qualms lest I had picked up some form of VD and for the next few months I kept a careful watch for any signs. But none appeared and I knew I could still remember the experience she had given me with absolute joy for the rest of my days.

Back to the front

It was pouring with rain again on the last morning of our leave. We were issued with fresh kit and told that the clothes we were leaving in would be collected when we got back to the battalion. After breakfast we collected our gear and boarded the buses waiting to take us to the airfield for the return flight to Kimpo. Once more we wound our way back through the Tokyo suburbs. The weather was overcast and I thought the chance of seeing Mount Fujiyama when we took off would not be possible. That would be most disappointing. At the airfield, no sooner had we climbed aboard, taken our seats and belted up than the plane taxied to the end of the runway, took off into driving rain and began to climb. Then suddenly the cabin was flooded with sunlight. We had climbed above the clouds and I rushed to look out of the nearest window. There, projecting majestically above the level upper surface of the clouds, was the perfectly symmetrical cone of Fujiyama wearing its mantle of snow just as I had seen in so many pictures. It was the perfect sight with which to end this visit to Japan.

The rest of the flight was unremarkable except that while flying over the mountains up the centre of the Korean peninsula we hit considerable turbulence. The plane began to jerk up and down and from side to side and the captain asked us to return to our seats and put on our safety belts.

The tossing about grew stronger. One moment the plane was dropping very quickly and I felt as though I had suddenly lost weight. Then, just as rapidly, I felt very heavy when the plane rose as swiftly as it had fallen. The captain announced that we were encountering air pockets, that there were vomit bags tucked under the seats if we needed one! The turbulence and air pockets continued to throw the aircraft about for about half an hour then the flight became smooth for the rest of the way

Douglas Skymaster—to and from Tokyo

to Kimpo. When we landed we went to the Base Club for a coffee and the ubiquitous donut before boarding trucks to take us straight back 'home'.

Nobody seemed in a mood to take any notice of anything. Our heads were too full of those five days and all that we had seen—and done. It would never be repeated, of that much we were quite certain.

14

BACK TO FRONT

28th April to 7th July 1952

Birds, Frogs and Showers

If that was R&R then I had had it. I returned to the front line and developed a heavy cold, probably from exposure to the crowds we had mingled with on Ginza and all the dampness and rain during those days in Tokyo. It took a while to settle back into life at the sharp end. The first few days were a real struggle; my cold left me unusually tired. Every scrap of energy was devoted to my job. Other time was spent reading whatever was to hand or sleeping. The weather had also turned quite hot by day and the countryside become very dusty. Many chaps had been sunbathing and acquired good tans but this was not for me.

Night shifts on the exchange were long and most of the daylight hours were spent outside repairing telephone lines broken by Chinese mortar or shellfire. For the last few days they had been specifically targeting the top of 355 and our telephone lines along Mad Mile. This had everyone, at every level of authority, flapping like crazy. The 62 set network was also put to very good use while line repair parties were out.

The most pleasant times of the day were early mornings around dawn and 'stand to' time and the evenings before 'stand-to'. Then the war seemed far away, happening somewhere else. The whole countryside would be still and quiet except, amazingly, for the twitter of small birds and more amazingly, the croak of frogs. Spring had transformed the hills and valleys with lush greenery and for once one could see how this land might be habitable after all.

It was Friday, 18th May and over two weeks since my last letter home. There were only another six and a half months of national service to go. Given that it would take a month to sail home, we would probably be pulled out sometime in late October or early in November to leave Korea in time to get us home by early December. There were rumours that the whole battalion would be withdrawn around then and sent to Hong Kong.

An ingenious cold shower had been erected down the reverse slope of our positions. Water from a natural, free flowing stream had been directed along a few lengths of fencing pickets for about ten yards, supported where necessary by piles of sandbags, or bizarre frameworks of sticks. At the end, where it was about seven feet (two metres) off the ground, water fell into an old C7 tin, the base perforated to make a shower rose. The water was very cold but with the high daytime temperatures we were now getting, a shower was very refreshing and the best way to wash the dust out of one's hair.

Ablutions beneath Hill 355

The invitation

A letter arrived on the 21st May from Mr Cullingford, my history teacher at Poole Grammar School. It was an invitation to write an article for the school magazine about life on active service in Korea. I was surprised and felt very flattered but had a feeling that this would be the straw to break the camel's back where writing was concerned. It was already a problem putting pen to paper to write home. The wish to oblige Cully was there but the mental energy to produce something worthy was extremely low. Yet despite this monstrous lethargy and lack of confidence, I agreed to write something for him.

The Chinese ambush one another

In the early hours of the next morning there was a fair amount of activity. My turn on duty at the exchange coincided with a fighting patrol going out from one of our platoons to investigate some Chinese diggings on 227. While they were prowling around, they heard sounds and almost ran into six Chinese soldiers also out on the prowl. They set up an ambush and lay low, waiting. When the enemy was about four or five yards away, our chaps let rip. It was quite a change for one of our patrols to ambush a Chinese patrol. All too often it had been the other way around.

Later, after recommencing their patrol, they came under fire themselves. In seeking cover L/cpl Bourne ducked so smartly into a ditch that he knocked himself out. The rest of the patrol didn't realise this and reported him dead when they returned. The major blew his top and sent out a small recovery patrol to bring his body in but the corporal had regained consciousness and started to make his way back to the company position. At one time he had to lie low to let another patrol pass by but eventually made it back to the perimeter of the platoon position, gave the password and was allowed back through the wire. The major was greatly relieved to know of his safe return. The second patrol had a good look round, couldn't find his body and returned. They also had to take steps to evade another patrol of around twenty men. No-mans-land seemed to be crawling with Chinese patrols that morning.

Sometime after our chaps had safely returned, the sounds of a firefight were heard down in the valley below us. There was the crackle of rifle and sub-machine gunfire then the crumps as mortar bombs exploded. The major checked with other company commanders to see if they had any patrols out down there. No one had. He reported back to BHQ that there was some curious enemy activity out in no-man's-land in front of our positions and asked that an artillery stonk be brought down on the area. And what a racket that brought as artillery, mortars and machine gun fire opened up. Fire rained down on the area in which that last enemy patrol had been spotted on the slopes below our position and the area from which the sounds of that mysterious gunfire had come.

This morning, with the coming of daylight an air strike was called in. Sabre jets roared low up the valley in front of our positions firing their

Mike Churchill, Porchester
before going on patrol

cannons and releasing their bomb loads. Soon after they had climbed away we heard the crump as those bombs exploded and saw huge clouds of black smoke rise up in the air. God help anyone who was caught when one of those napalm bombs went off. However, from where we stood watching, it was all quite spectacular, like something out of an American war film, except that it was really happening out there in front of us.

As for L/Cpl Bourne, he survived with nothing worse than a headache for his experience. There was one casualty among our chaps though that caused me some sadness. Just before stand-to that evening, Mike Churchill from Porchester, and who was in my draft, had come by the exchange.

He was a stretcher bearer and on his way, complete with his stretcher and face daubed with mud, to join that patrol. He stood in the crawl trench holding his stretcher to attention beside him while I took his photograph. Four hours later his patrol got into that fire fight with the second Chinese patrol and the enemy lobbed some mortar bombs into the fray. Mike took a piece of shrapnel up his backside and was brought back on his own stretcher. He was sent to hospital in Kure, Japan. The fortunes of war are so very unpredictable that it was incidents like this that continued to make me fervently glad that I was a signaller and not a humble rifleman.

Where angels fear to tread?

On the evening of 22nd May, I did the weirdest and maddest thing ever. In retrospect it far surpassed the time when I fired off a round in the signals exchange back at BHQ. It was almost the end of my stag on exchange duty and coming up to stand-to time. I was doing the routine check of all the company phone lines to make sure they were working properly. To my dismay, there was no reply from the little forward listening post down below in no-mans-land toward Hill 227. If their line was broken this was bad news both for us and the chaps down there. Turning to one of the other signallers, I asked him to take over while I went to find and mend the break.

Grabbing a large pair of pliers and a roll of insulation tape, I followed the line across to the forward crawl trench and to the point where the barbed wire could be moved aside to let our patrols go out and return. I scrambled through and continued to follow the line down the hill. So concerned was I with the need to get that phone connection working again that I was totally oblivious to the fact that I could be seen by any Chinese lookout on Hill 227.

I found no break anywhere along that line all the way into the outpost. The chaps there were very surprised to see me as I walked into their observation bunker.

"Hello, Johnno. What you doin' here?' the section leader asked.

"Your bloody phone isn't working so I've came down to find out what was wrong," I replied

"Nuthin' wrong with the phone, is there boys?

"Then why didn't someone answer when I was doing the line check just now? And there is no break in the line that I could find."

I turned to check the phone and found their end of the line dangling in space. Turning back to them I shouted,

"You bloody idiots! You haven't even connected it."

"Oh, haven't we now? 'Ow could that 'ave 'appened?" said the corporal.

"You might bloody well ask!" I retorted, "You've brought me down here on a bloody wild goose chase! Now I've got to find my way back in the dark when everyone will be on stand-to."

I connected the phone, checked back to the exchange that it was now working, told those guys exactly what I thought of them once more and left to make my way back up the hill as quickly as I could. It had now grown quite dark and I knew that the whole company would be on stand-to. I deliberately made some noise as I approached.

Finally the perimeter barbed wire fencing loomed ahead. Somewhere in the darkness ahead of me on the other side of the wire, made even darker by the shadows of the pine trees, I knew that someone would be on stand-to. They would be wondering what the hell was going on out beyond the wire.

"Halt. Who goes there?" A shaky voice rang out from the shadows.

"It's me, Milnthorpe. Let me in."

"What the bloody hell are you doing out there? What have you been doing?"

"Repairing the bloody phone line to the outpost. I thought the line was broken but the bastards down there hadn't connected the handset."

"What's the password?" the voice asked as an afterthought.

"I don't know. No one told me before I went out."

"Oh, OK. Come on through."

Scrambling through the barbed wire as best as I could in the dark, I stood on the edge of the crawl trench and was about to jump down when the corporal in charge of that section appeared.

"Who's that," he demanded.

"It's Milnthorpe, Corp. He's been out mending a line to the outpost."

"Where's your bloody rifle, Milnthorpe?" the Corporal asked.

"Back in the exchange," I replied.

"That's bloody clever of you, isn't it?" he commented.

"Well, it was an emergency and I forgot about it," I said.

And I had been in a hurry. Anyway, what use would a rifle have been to me if I had come under fire or met a Chinky patrol? It would just have been an encumbrance I could have done without. Now if I had been issued with a Sten Gun . . . . .

"Milnthorpe!"

A quiet, cultivated but very firm voice had spoken out of the darkness behind the corporal. It was the platoon officer, fortunately one with whom I got on quite well.

"Yessir?" I quickly replied.

"In future you will always take your rifle with you wherever you go, won't you?" he said, stressing the last two words.

"Yessir." I replied and jumped down in to the crawl trench.

Muttering "Yes, sir, yes, sir, three bags full, sir," under my breath, I quickly made my way back to the exchange to check that line to the outpost again. Neither the corporal nor the officer had been in the least concerned that I had been needlessly put in harms way by those idiots in the outpost. Their only concern was that I had gone out there unencumbered by the mandatory rifle.

Anyway, it would be my only venture into no-mans-land on one of the most problematic sections of the front line. Right under the noses of the Chinese, armed only with a ten-inch pair of pliers and a roll of insulation tape, I had advanced alone to within a few yards of their forward positions and returned safely to tell the tale.

But I was damned sure I would never do it again. It really showed how impossible it could sometimes become to take seriously the fact that we really were involved in a live war, a war in which people actually got killed or wounded by real bullets. There would always be part of me that would never quite shake this sense of the unreality of it all. Had that not been so, I might have had the sense when I reconnected the phone and rang the exchange to ask someone to tell that platoon officer that I was out there.

[To avoid any confusion in the reader's mind, until my late forties I was known as John Milnthorpe. Then, for personal reasons, I made a statutory declaration and took the name Hatchard, my mother's maiden name.]

The visitor

On May 26th a most unexpected visitor approached our position, the last we would ever have imagined having. That afternoon a Chinese soldier had emerged out of hiding below our perimeter wire and advanced with his hands in the air to surrender. Naturally, everyone was on the alert though there was little chance of an attack in broad daylight. The Chinese were not that stupid. He was carefully watched as he approached and when the officer on that section was satisfied that he posed no threat he was allowed through. He was escorted round to the exchange and kept there while battalion HQ was informed of his arrival and arrangements made for the Military Police to collect him. In the meantime he just stood quietly outside the exchange. He wasn't much over five feet tall and dressed in the usual drab, khaki cotton uniform that wouldn't have done much for him in colder conditions.

Me outside signals bunker

One of our chaps took out a packet of cigarettes and offered him one. He flinched and backed away in such a manner that we wondered what on earth he had been told about us to make him so wary of such a simple human gesture? After some urging, he eventually accepted it and the light to go with it. Half an hour later two MPs drove down the valley road, parked, climbed up and took him away back to Intelligence HQ for questioning.

I never heard any more about him until, many years later, Charlie Haynes wrote this account to me:

"A commissioned officer of the Chinese Division across the valley walked across no-man's-land scaled the forward slope of 355 (unchallenged) and surrendered to the first sentry he met [D Company positions]. Some days prior to this, we witnessed, at a position half way between the enemy positions and ourselves, a lengthy small arms and grenade encounter between two patrolling parties. Radio contacts at the time established that no UN forces had patrols in the vicinity. We learned some weeks after the event, that the Intelligence debriefing of the officer revealed that he was, in fact, the leader of one of the patrols involved in the fire-fight and that they were both Chinese units, each assuming the other was the enemy, resulting in some loss of life. As the story goes, his superiors had placed the responsibility for the error on this officer and had offered him the option of a court martial, or his volunteering to lead a daylight patrol to attack the 355 positions, both options suicidal. He chose to risk the walk across and surrender. He was questioned by Intelligence and gave the location of a concentration of Chinese infantry, living in a honeycomb of tunnels, in a minor feature [Hill 227], some 2 hundred yards forward of their main positions, presumably in preparation for an assault on 355. An air strike was then called down on this position."

Another nut case?

The next night, on 27th May, another fighting patrol went out from our company and walked straight into an ambush. It was during my stag on wireless control duty and I was in contact with the signaller on the patrol when this happened. The lieutenant and the five men with him encountered fire from three machine guns and only one chap had completely escaped injury. The lieutenant ordered his men to withdraw and the signaller with the patrol conveyed to me the gist of what was going on.

Unfortunately, our major arrived at the exchange and was standing behind me. He heard this communication, went totally nuts, grabbed the mike and shouted angrily into it, "Attack! Attack! Attack!" I was stunned both by his order and the manner in which he gave it. So was the signaller at the other end. We heard no more from them until they finally returned back through the wire.

That signaller was Evans, the same chap who had played the joke on his mate with the Signals Officer some weeks ago. He later revealed that he had been so disgusted by the major's order that, after he informed his officer, he unclipped his wireless set and threw it as far away from him as he could. It turned out that both the lieutenant and the section corporal were badly injured and it required a courageous and very determined effort by the rest of the men to bring them safely back behind our lines.

We thought there should be a couple of citations for bravery out of this action, but were also of the opinion that the major ought to be ordered to lead the next patrol personally. It was a shame about that lieutenant too. He was a very pleasant chap who always had a smile and an encouraging word for us whenever he came round, the complete opposite of the hysterical major.

Evans later explained the loss of the wireless set to the major by saying that it was hit by enemy fire. Since it was useless and only got in his way he took it off and threw it away. He also took the opportunity to inform the major that the wireless set had also probably saved him from being seriously injured. What a smart piece of thinking that was!

Given that truce talks were being held, we had some difficulty understanding why it was still thought necessary to go looking for trouble like that. All those casualties seemed so unnecessary and I was still feeling badly about the death of Alec Ahern. All it would take for this war to simply go phut would be for both sides to stop sending out provocative patrols and cease all the noisy harassing fire they put down. It was all just a matter of keeping face, like a couple of tough guys flexing their muscles as they weighed each other up looked for an opening to land a punch without opening themselves to receive one back.

Another time I overheard a couple of officers talking excitedly about someone having spotted five Chinese soldiers about five miles away. They immediately called down fire on them from our Centurion tank and then persuaded the 25 pounders and mortars to send a contribution over. It seemed idiotic and over the top.

While talking of official idiocies, two new orders had come through. The first was to hand in the American pattern steel helmets that we had been issued with. Not that we wore them very much but they made excellent wash basins and would be greatly missed. The second order was to wear our black berets at all times and keep our badges well polished. From the start that order was destined to be honoured more in the breach than in the observance. If we wore anything it was our cap-comforters. No one was going to walk around advertising themselves by wearing a 'mirror' on their head that could send light signals to the Chinese. Our chaps could often be clearly seen wandering about on Little Gibraltar but surprisingly, they didn't attract that much fire from the Chinese. What did occasionally draw fire was the Welch Battle Flag on top of 355. They liked to use it for target practice.

Surprise, surprise!

This morning everyone received a food parcel from Australia. They were neatly packed in wooden boxes and contained:

1 tin of fruit (1lb), 1 tin cream (4ozs), 1 packet biscuits, 1 tin sweet condensed milk, 4 bars chocolate, 2 packets sweets, 1 plum pudding (Xmas type), 3 packets chewing gum, 2 razor blades, 1 large airmail writing pad, 1 packet envelopes, 1 pencil, 1 candle (12 inch), 1 packet playing cards.

Not bad at all. A letter inside stated that this was a gift from the Patriotic Fund of Queensland. Mind you, it raised a few grumbles amongst the lads.

"If a nation of barely eight million souls could do this for every soldier in the British Commonwealth Division, why couldn't a nation of fifty million do something like this too?" But I was just grateful and very pleased to have it all. The wooden boxes were going to be useful too.

Back in business again

Today the sergeant asked if I would like to pick up my old job of collecting the twice-weekly NAAFI orders for D Company HQ personnel. He had heard from his mate at BHQ that I had made a pretty good job of it back there. I jumped at it. This was something I knew I could do well. He asked what I kept by way of commission and didn't believe me when told that I did it for love of the job and to prevent anyone else from screwing it up as had happened once at BHQ. It was also a relief to have something practical to do when not on duty.

It also took my mind off that blessed article for the school magazine which was causing me a heap of grief but no more than I had anticipated when the invitation came. Half a signals record book had already been filled with attempt after attempt to start writing something that I felt worthy of publication. Perhaps I was just being overly self—critical but the deadline was fast approaching for me to finish it and get it in the post.

Bunkers and tank (top R) on reverse slope - 1952

My 'new' bunker below 355

A door opens

The month of May ended with a vengeance. Last night strong winds and torrential rain set in and our living conditions suffered as a result. Bunker roofs leaked, miniature earth slides occurred all along the crawl trenches which had to be cleared away and there was mud everywhere.

Whether it was coincidental or deliberate we didn't know but that night the Chinese decided to shell us and they were landing them ever closer to our positions as dawn was breaking.

In the wee hours of the morning the wall of my bunker showed ominous signs of collapse. I told the sergeant and later he showed me another into which I could move. It was outside the crawl trench and lower down the reverse slope below the signals exchange bunker. On inspecting it, I found a whole heap of rubbish at the far end and cleared it out. Among this rubbish was a book. It had no covers and was damp right through so I placed it on the roof of the bunker to dry out in the sun thinking to look at it later. Then I set about moving my gear in.

From the entrance, the view extended out over Mad Mile toward Hill 210. Below and further to the right was the pine tree covered Antitank Ridge which concealed the route up to our position. To the south west, ridge after ridge of hills stretched away into the distance.

That evening, as the sun began to set, I sat on the roof of my new bunker and drank the whole scene in. It was a warm, late spring evening. Here and there, cherry trees were in full bloom, splashes of rich pink dotted over the hillsides. The ridges displayed a sequence of increasingly misty colours from green through blue to dusky mauve. For once it was an incredibly peaceful and very beautiful evening up here in the front line. No shells or mortar bombs were flying overhead in either direction, no machine gun fire, no aircraft nor any other noise of war. It was one of those moments when the thought of being so far from home did not weigh heavily on the heart. The atmosphere carried such a sweet stillness and beauty that one could only be grateful for the ability to experience it, more so because its special quality and the special joy it brought was happening here in Korea.

Remembering the coverless book on the roof behind me, I picked it up. It had dried out very well. The thought crossed my mind that this might not be a good time to start reading something possibly at variance with the spirit of this moment but all the same I decided to have a look at it. Turning over the first fly leaf I read the title—"The Eyes of the World," an interesting enough title to be sure. The author, Harold Bell Wright, was unknown to me but the reviews included in this edition were quite positive. Next came an illustration of a young woman in a white dress smelling some red roses as she caressed the head of a red setter dog. Opposite this came the full title page and overleaf was the date of publication in 1914 when it had sold for a mere $1. Opposite this was a dedication to "Benjamin H. Pearson—Student, Artist, Gentleman".

The next page bore two passages of blank verse which I read—

"I have learned
To look on Nature not as in the hour
Of thoughtless youth; but hearing oftentimes
The sad, still music of humanity,
Not harsh or grating, though of ample power
To chasten and subdue. And I have felt,
A presence that disturbs me with the joy
of elevated thoughts; a sense sublime
Of something far more deeply interfused,
Whose dwelling is in the lights of setting suns,
And the round ocean and the living air,
And the blue sky and in the mind of man.
A motion and a spirit that impels
All thinking things, all objects of all thoughts,
And rolls through all things.
Therefore am I still
A lover of the meadows and the woods
And mountains . . . .
. . . . And this prayer I make,
Knowing that Nature never did betray
The heart that loved her. 'Tis her privilege
Through all the years of this one life, to lead
From joy to joy; for she can so inform
The mind that is within us—so impress
With quietness and beauty and so feed
With lofty thoughts—that neither evil tongues,
Rash judgments, nor the sneers of selfish men,
Nor greetings where no kindness is, nor all
The dreary intercourse of daily life,
Shall e'er prevail against us, or disturb
Our cheerful faith."

William Wordsworth

I finished reading, let the book rest in my lap and just sat there, not moving. The quietness and beauty of those words and of the evening combined and soaked through every part of my being. The same extraordinary emotion and realisation experienced in St Andrew's Cathedral, Singapore, flooded over me once more. The crude reality of where I was and why was totally eclipsed by something transcendent and timeless.

Wordsworth's beautifully crafted words had completely echoed my mood and the general nature of my thoughts a moment or two before. Time in the usual sense of the word did not exist. Those words that had expressed the thoughts and realizations of a man who, generations before me, had lived the best years of his life in the peaceful hills and dales of the Lake District, had now become mine.

Here, thousands of miles away from home and anything remotely familiar, in a land that was usually anything but peaceful, some mysterious working of the universe had placed before me words that matched the thoughts and feelings that had been aroused by a similar sensitivity to natural beauty. I only knew that something very special had occurred to and for me at this time and in this place with the reading of those few lines. But it was also an experience whose true significance might only be fully revealed much later.

The moment passed and I started to read the a story about a painter and a musician, man and woman whose sole purpose was to make through their art as true an expression as possible of who they were as human beings. In the process they had to resist varied enticements to prostitute their art and themselves to the whim of degenerate art sponsors.

Even if the style was a bit old fashioned and the theme clearly moralistic, it was beautifully written and my attention was completely absorbed. The state that had been engendered in me by those lines of Wordsworth was such that, when I finished the last page and put the book down, it took me a few moments to realise exactly where I was and why but I knew that a door had opened for me, most certainly into the world of poetry. The prejudice toward it from the manner in which this subject had been presented to me in school had utterly vanished.

There was no indication which of Wordsworth's poems those lines had come from in the book but it was now important for me to get hold of a copy of his poems as soon as possible and track it down.

On returning home I obtained a copy of Wordsworth's poems. Those passages had been taken from a piece entitled "Lines written a few miles above Tintern Abbey on revisiting the banks of the Wye during a tour. July 13th, 1798." Words written almost one hundred and fifty years ago had found a target in my heart and soul. Up to that point, my only connection with Wordsworth's work had been the line, "I wandered lonely as a cloud . . ." Something to do with daffodils!

A disturbed night

In the early hours of the morning of June 18th, the relatively quiet spell we had been enjoying was broken when the Chinese sent out a patrol to poke around our forward listening post, the same one I had sauntered down to armed only with a pair of pliers. They dislodged our chaps and chased them back to our main lines. A chap named Horton was killed covering the withdrawal of the others. Evidently, he just stood up and waded into about twenty Chinese soldiers firing his Bren gun from the hip. That was the last anyone saw of him until another patrol went to find his body and bring it back. The sad thing about his death was that he was almost due to return home. Those who got back safely were only slightly wounded.

The Chinese backed up this move with a lot of machine gun fire and a quite heavy mortar bombardment of our position. But they received as good as they gave. It was a very hectic and utterly sleepless night for all of us. My stag on duty had come along just before the whole action became nasty and very noisy; it was frenetic work attending to all the calls being made by telephone and over the air while trying to keep an accurate log of them all.

Everyone in company HQ remained in very good spirits throughout the whole time and emerged from the experience quite intact despite the mortar bombs that rained down. The major came round to specially commend everyone for the way they had stood up to the onslaught and praise also came from the battalion CO. The signals section was especially commended which pleased us greatly.

Operation Maindy—23rd June

The days have been hot and dusty and my writing block has not abated. Everything I did write was full of apologies and you can imagine my annoyance when I found that the last letter home had not even been posted.

Early this morning, long before stand to would have been called, our artillery started to lay down a stonk on Hill 227, the Chinese stronghold just a few hundred metres away from our positions. A little later came the intermittent sounds of small arms fire and the explosions of grenades. It appeared that a major attack was going in on 227 staged from Antitank Ridge down below us, a position held by 1RAR. At the time, I thought it had been their operation but later I learned that it was B Company from our battalion that had gone out through the Australian lines.

Everything available was being slung at 227 from mortars, machine guns and from the 20 pound gun of our Centurion tank. Every time the tank fired our hill shook and the walls of the exchange bunker threatened to slide in on us. The noise was deafening and the operation lasted just under two hours. We wondered if this was a reprisal for the Chinese attack on our outpost a week ago and if this was to be the start of a series of tit-for-tat affairs every week.

Many years were to pass before I learned that this operation, codenamed "Maindy", was mounted because of intelligence gained from the Chinese officer who surrendered to us back on the 26th May. He told of a build-up of men in the tunnels on 227 and our own patrols had confirmed that the Chinese had honeycombed it with tunnels. Operation Maindy was designed to take the hill for long enough to let sappers through to demolish those tunnels and any bunkers they could get to. Unfortunately the Forward Field Officer (FOO) of the Royal Artillery was killed quite early on in the action which greatly impeded the course of events and its successful outcome. Our company lost two killed, Private Grears and Corporal Meech, and sustained over twenty wounded who had to be carried from the field of battle.

This was a high price for one company to pay for a limited operation like this and required a lot of ambulance activity along the Mad Mile to get them away quickly for medical aid. Their escape route came increasingly into full view of the Chinese artillery observers as dawn broke.

Research: The official story

In the regimental magazine "Men of Harlech" No. 93/52 there appeared an article entitled 'Company Attack'. It concerned a raid against an enemy occupied hill on June 23rd 1952 by a company of 1 Welch and codenamed 'Operation Maindy' (presumably after the barracks in Cardiff!). The account of the action was written by their Company Commander.

He first described how the top of Hill 227 was covered with shell craters, collapsed bunkers, old slit trenches and patches of barbed wire. On the side of this hill that faced our lines the Chinese just dug well camouflaged foxholes from which to fight but on the reverse slope they dug their main communication trench and many deep bunkers connected to a subterranean passage.

B Company had been selected to make this operation. They were already holding a forward position on Hill 355 so this required that they first be brought out into reserve on June 20th for rehearsal. The operation was planned for June 23rd, and they had to be in start positions by 04:15 hours.

The company moved out from its reserve position to an assembly area among a company of 1 Battalion, Royal Australian Regiment holding a position to the west on the lower slopes of Hill 355 [Antitank Ridge]. The move completed by 21:30 hours, June 22nd, they rested until the time came to move forward to the start line. To cheer their spirits they were given hot tea and an issue of rum before moving off.

At 02:20 hours the minefield gap through which the Company would pass to their start line was secured by a section from 1RAR. By 04:05 hours everyone was in position waiting for the order to move forward. The plan for the attack was to have 4 Platoon on the left, 5 Platoon on the right and 6 Platoon minus one section in reserve. Company HQ and the artillery F.O.O. moved behind 5 Platoon. A sapper demolition party, the stretcher bearers and the section from 6 platoon were behind Company HQ.

The attack on Hill 227 began at 04:15 hours. In the move out the sappers, stretcher bearers were dropped off some way from the hill. Within ten minutes both 4 and 5 Platoons were actively engaged with the enemy but reached their objectives. 4 Platoon attacked bunkers on the left, silenced them and were ordered to help 5 Platoon attacking bunkers on the right.

They first cleared three small bunkers then, after some difficulty, cleared the deep bunkers along the main communications trench. By the time they had all been silenced, 4 and 5 platoon commanders, their platoon Sergeants and one other man were all wounded and two others had been killed. The Company Commander then assumed command of both Platoons. Shortly after this he was told that the F.O.O. had been killed and his wireless operator wounded.

The Chinese had initially been taken completely by surprise but now began to bring down heavy shelling, mortars and machine gun fire. Casualties increased and the Company Commander requested permission to withdraw which was granted. The report concluded,

An orderly withdrawal took place with all the dead and wounded coming out first. In the F.D.L's the wounded were all well cared for by the Battalion Medical Officer and his staff. Some were flown out by helicopter and others evacuated by Ambulance Jeep.

"It was with stout hearts because a good job had been done that Company marched back to their own positions, singing as they went. The total of casualties were 3 killed and 23 wounded."

A postscript to Operation Maindy

"In war, truth is the first casualty." Aeschylus

Many years later, after I started to write these memoirs', I made contact with a retired officer from 55 Engineer Squadron, 28th Engineer Regiment, Commonwealth Division. We exchanged notes about our time and experiences in Korea and when the subject of Hill 227 came up he revealed that he had been attached to B Company 1 Welch for Operation Maindy. His mission was to destroy the Chinese bunkers on 227 once they were captured. In one of his emails he wrote,

"A company of the Welch Regiment made an attack on Hill 227 [Operation Maindy, 23rd June 1952] occupied by the N Korean forces. The aim was to blow up the bunkers and the plan was that after they had been secured by the company attack, the engineer support would blow up the bunkers. The Sappers were carrying explosives and bird table like platforms with extendable legs that could be used to jam the explosive against the roof of the bunker from inside. In the event, the bunkers were not captured and the Sappers were not called forward.

The infantry attack was not a complete success and sadly there were a large number of casualties [about 20 plus] including the platoon commanders and platoon sergeants. An important casualty was the RA F.O.O. who was killed early in the attack and as a consequence support fire was less than effective as there was no one to direct the supporting artillery.

This very difficult situation led to the Company Commander pretending to recce the situation and then requesting permission to withdraw. This was given and he then moved out leaving his platoons without leaders. I was the RE officer who was supposed to destroy the bunkers when they were captured but now I had the more important task of bringing the company back to safety. There were no officers or senior NCOs fit to command the company of the Welch Regiment so I took command and guided the platoons back through the minefield and eventually to their camp.

I was angry but due to what I now realise was the silly school boy tradition of "not telling", I did not disclose the cowardly behaviour of the company commander. As a result the company commander was awarded the DSO and his brave and wounded platoon commanders nothing. The RE officer who saved his bacon and fulfilled the wording of his citation was ignored. This situation requires to be rectified."

Can truth ever be told?

The contrasting reports on Operation Maindy, which took place on Saturday 23rd June 1952, make uncomfortable reading. Do they really describe how embarrassing or unpleasant details get glossed over? Where does the truth lie? In the report written by the CO of that company, his description of the conclusion of the operation does not remotely correspond to the observations made by the Engineers officer who was there to lead a team of sappers. His role getting the men back out as safely as possible is not given a mention, an omission guaranteed to intensely annoy him. But he could hardly write about it if he was not present to observe?

Another example came my way later of how regimental pride could subvert a desire for accuracy and honesty. It came to me directly from Major John Gerke, CO of C Company 3RAR. During Operation Commando late in 1951 the KOSB had the task of taking Hill 355. They met strong resistance which threatened to delay achieving the objectives of the operation. Major Gerke was asked by his battalion CO to go and give them a hand.

He led his company across two miles of exposed country, took two small hills east of 355, stormed 355 itself, chased the Chinese off and waited for the first KOSB men to arrive an hour later. When I first dared to write and publish this account in an English veteran's journal it was passionately refuted by one KOSB veteran as a slur on their regiments' honour. But a full account of Major Gerke and his C Company's achievements on that and the subsequent night during Operation Commando as recorded in Robert O'Neill's book, "Australia in the Korean War", was personally confirmed to me when I met him in Perth, Western Australia, two years before he died.

It is an inspiring story. It turns out that the night after taking Hill 355 Major Gerke's company took Hill 317 (map page 200) from the Chinese. Later, he was ordered to hand it over to the KOSB. When the Chinese mounted a ferocious counter attack KOSB were unable to hold onto it. This was when Speakman won his VC. Major Gerke's opinion of the KOSB and their commander, offered to me the last time I met him, were not complimentary. "The Chinese would not have retaken it if we had stayed there."

Fright number one

For some reason, I was feeling great when I awoke today, in top form and not at all downhearted about anything—until I picked up a pen and letter form to write home. I felt like some sort of Jekyll and Hyde character who only needed to think of writing home to change from one character to quite another. It was as much as I could do to acknowledge letters and postal orders received.

At lunchtime, I had an extremely scary experience. While on exchange duty I found that the phone line to our platoon positions out on the northwest ridge was not working. When my relief turned up I mentioned this and set off to find and remedy the problem. The line ran from the exchange bunker over the top of our southwest ridge and into a crawl trench that ran out to the platoon position. It was not a very deep trench, barely up to my waist at its deepest and ran more or less along the crest of the ridge. It only got deeper as I approached the hill where the platoon was dug in.

While moving along the trench and focussing on checking the telephone line, I was vaguely aware of a succession of pops away in the distance to the north but took no particular notice. A few seconds later a chorus of whistles grew increasingly louder. Mortar bombs—and heading my way! There was an explosion some yards ahead of me round a bend in the crawl trench. I flung myself flat on the ground, my mind in a total whirl as I waited and wondered what the outcome of this situation would be. Four more times the whistle of the remaining bombs grew louder until they exploded somewhere near me. Each time, I screwed my eyes tight, flinched all over, dug my fingers into the ground and tried to pretend I wasn't really there.

Happily, none of them landed where they could do me damage and I cautiously got up and walked on, continuing to follow the telephone line. As I neared the entrance to the bunker where the platoon telephone and 31 set had been kept, I found that one bomb had exploded right in the entrance. Since that had been my destination I thanked God I had not reached it sooner.

Even more, I thanked God that it was not a C7s day. If it had been, the whole platoon would still have been around their position eating out of cans. Instead, they were all back at the cookhouse at company HQ getting their lunch. I was too shaken to enter that signals bunker and find out what had happened to the equipment in there and took great pains to keep very low as I returned to the HQ exchange area.

Thinking about it all afterwards, I reckoned it had just been my bad luck to be spotted by some Chinese fellow with a pair

C7s for lunch

of binoculars who happened to be focusing on that part of 355. Maybe he had spotted members of the platoon wandering along that shallow stretch of crawl trench on their way to get their lunch and then seen me as I walked in the opposite direction. Maybe he thought the chaps had all returned and ordered the mortars to fire. On the other hand, it had been my great good luck that they had all failed to find the spot where I had been desperately hugging Mother Earth. For a few moments I had been as scared as I never wish to be again.

In the evening I climbed up to the top of Little Gibraltar in the moonlight to see Brian for the first time in weeks and tell him what had happened. We were content to keep each other quiet company over a bottle of beer on the top of the hill in the moonlight. He then told me of an extremely unpleasant experience his company recently had as the warmer weather set in. Evidently, during the battles on Hill 355 in November 1951, the Chinese had suffered very severe casualties. The bodies had been hastily buried around the hill and the severe cold of the Korean winter had kept them in cold storage as it were. However, come the spring and warmer weather, the stench from the bodies had become pretty intolerable. A sergeant from the Australian Medical Corps came to deal with the situation and 'recruited' the men of 'C' Company to disinter the bodies and give most of them a decent burial. Brian's comment was, "We came here to fight not act as blooming undertakers."

Operation Blaze—5th July and fright number two

Today another attack was staged on Hill 227 by the Aussie company on Anti-tank Ridge. Once again all hell broke loose as our artillery put down a softening-up barrage. However, what stunned us most was the fact that the attack went out in broad daylight. From our vantage point we were able to watch as the Aussie platoons advanced toward 227. It was long after stand-down had ended and to our minds it seemed the very worst time to launch such an attack.

We had always believed that the best time was before it began to get light. Men would be deployed up to a start line under cover of darkness and then, while the light was still uncertain, move forward to their objectives. This was how things had been organised nine days before with operation

"Maindy". To go in when it was broad daylight seemed to us to be the height of stupidity. This time the Chinese were able to respond very quickly with shells and mortar bombs.

Fortunately for us in D Company, the Chinese directed their fire onto the Aussie positions and we were once more in the spectator galleries. However, our battalion did not escape scot-free. Four chaps from our HQ signals section were on line repair duties down along Mad Mile. When the Aussie attack went in they started climbing up the reverse slope behind Anti-tank Ridge to reach the shelter of D Company positions. As soon as the Chinese stonk started they spread out and broke into a trot to reach us as quickly as they could. At the time, I was standing in the entrance to my bunker watching the mayhem below on the ridge.

There was a very clear view down through the trees where the undergrowth was low and I watched those four chaps as they came belting up the hill. There were only about a hundred yards left to cover when I heard the whistle of a mortar bomb. It landed right among them. When the dust cleared three bodies lay on the ground while there was no sign of the fourth chap.

The shout "stretcher bearers" rang out and the next moment our medical orderlies were racing down the hill to where those signallers lay. As for me, I was stunned, utterly paralysed, rigid with shock from what I had just witnessed. I couldn't have moved even to scratch myself let alone go down to see if I could help. Fear? Shock? I couldn't really tell but it was the second time in four days that I had known such an extreme moment. All I could do was watch as three bodies were slowly brought back up the hill. Two were dead, Privates Harris and Rowe, while the other was badly injured.

The fourth chap was found lying in some bushes where the blast had blown him. He was physically uninjured and, helped by one of the orderlies, was able to walk up under his own steam. All the while the sounds of the battle around Hill 227 raged on.

This incident again brought the theme of Thornton Wilder's *"The Bridge of San Luis Rey"* to mind. What was going on in the lives of those four men that brought them together at that precise place and time so that a single mortar should kill two, injure a third and allow the fourth to go free of physical injury?

My paralysis eventually left me and I went up to the exchange, passing the bodies of the two chaps who had been killed. They were lying side by side on stretchers and covered with blankets. The wounded chap had been taken to the medical bunker. He had evidently been side on to the blast and sustained wounds principally across the belly and back. The chap who had escaped injury was in deep shock and just stood in the crawl trench outside the exchange staring with a fixed but empty, uncomprehending look on his face. It was all he could do to hear the offer and accept a cigarette. I later heard that he was returned home as unfit for further service.

To lose four signallers like that because some commander had made what we considered a tactical error to attack a heavily defended Chinese position two hours after sun up was a disgrace. I had to believe that communication between adjacent battalions was better than that. Our CO and his senior staff, including the SO, must have known this attack was to take place.

All of us in D Company HQ remained absolutely dumbfounded by the timing of that attack and wondered what the outcome would be for those who had been in charge. Later we watched as ambulance jeeps marked clearly with red crosses came down the road and took the dead and wounded away. During Operation Blaze three members of 1 RAR were killed and thirty-four were wounded including the FOO—again!

Later that afternoon, when the NAAFI orders had arrived and been distributed, many of us congregated under the rear of the Centurion tank to bask in the sun, discuss the implications of that morning's attack and get mildly drunk on Asahi lager. Rumours abounded that we were to move back into reserve again. Several of our chaps had already gone back, deemed unfit for further service up front because of experiences while out on patrol.

At pay parade, the company clerk informed me that I was now classed as a four star soldier and would be on regular's pay. It appeared that this promotion was mainly due to my being a signaler. But all us national servicemen should have been on regular's pay as soon as we arrived here. We were facing exactly the same risks as the regulars who had volunteered to join the army. To send national servicemen on active service to meet international commitments smacked of doing things on the cheap and not a policy I would have thought a socialist government would have endorsed.

15

In Company Reserve

10th July to 21st July 1952

Holes in the Ground

At last it was our turn to go into company reserve. Three months in the front line, staring across no-mans-land at the Chinese positions on Hill 227 and being the company in closest proximity to them was enough for one go. I managed to get up the hill to see Brian before we pulled out and took some photographs only to find out later that the camera was faulty, the film loose and nothing came out.

Our move back was later than we had been told but we were very pleased with the accommodation this time. The exchange bunker was large and contained some decently constructed bunks so that if there was someone else around to share the duty we could sleep there when things were slack. Constructed from the customary barbed wire pickets and telephone cable, these bunks had empty machine gun ammunition belts incorporated into them which was a new feature to us. Another chap found that the bed in his bunker hung from a beam in the roof and could be swung gently to and fro. Such ingenuity, especially when we were living in mere holes in the ground.

The roof of the exchange was our only worry since it was comparatively flimsy compared with those we had constructed in the past. But the front line was pretty static and we were now at some remove from being involved should serious action of any kind commence. We hoped to have more time to relax, play about with the 62 set and start getting some good music, something I had missed during those weeks up front.

A schoolboy writes a letter

"Dear soldiers of the UN Forces." This was the opening line of a letter written to the UN soldiers by a Korean schoolboy. I have no idea how it came into my possession or how I came to retain it for so long. It was only when going through the propaganda leaflets I had collected that I discovered it again. Written in pencil on a piece of yellowing paper of little better quality than newspaper, it was not very easy to read.

Letter from Korean schoolboy to UN soldiers

Below is a transcript of the letter. Ch'ongju is halfway between Seoul and Taegu. I made some effort in 2002, through a Korean church in Perth, Western Australia, to find the writer but nothing came of it.

"*Dear soldiers of the UN forces. I thank you soldiers of the UN forces who came here to Korea to fight for the cause of freedom and peace your holy mission in Korea is to achieve national unification of Korea and bring world peace which will last forever I thank you heartily and heap glory on you.* "*Dear soldiers of the UN forces we believe you have the only army which and [sic] destroy the communists. I think I can see vividly the heroic pictures the [sic] of you UN forces who are fighting against the snowy hills and frozen rivers you kill the enemy by thousands and capture him by bunsands [sic—perhaps 'thousands'] my dear so of god*

you have come here to destroy the invading forces of the communists who
have disturbed the peace of the world I imagine the glorious return of you
heroic soldiers of the UN to you peaceful home I am sure your brave deeds
in Korea shall add a glorious page to the history of mankind may god be
with you wherever you
    February [1952] Lee Kim dok Kyong,
    2nd year class, Ch'ongju Technical High School, [South Korea]"

The weather continued hot and muggy. This was preferable to rain given that the roofs of our bunkers were not waterproof. Until now, I never thought it possible to sweat so much. During the day my shirt was almost continuously wringing wet and the heat was energy sapping. Then at night came the mosquitoes. The only consolation was the thought that we could have been sent to Malaya where the mosquitoes would have been much worse and there would have been other matters like malaria to take into account. The weather there would also have been hotter and stickier, and the jungle terrain in which we would have campaigned would have been hellish. We would never really know where the enemy was. So, in terms both of the weather and the kind of action we have been involved in, we have been much better off here in Korea.

We heard that the Black Watch had moved up to relieve the Australian boys next to us and the 'local rag' carried a report of a visit to them by General Van Fleet. He was alleged to have commented how pleased he was to have a "reputation" out in the front line, not his own presumably but that of the Black Watch. A pretty compliment from a Yank.

However, it was a fact that the name of a Regiment no longer told you anything about where its personnel came from. Just as the Welch Regiment was almost fifty percent from the south and west of England—places such as Shaftesbury, Salisbury, Bridport, Weymouth, Poole, Bournemouth, Beaulieu, Portsmouth and Gosport—so the Black Watch contained large numbers of men from Wales, Norfolk and Leicestershire. Bill Speakman was a Liverpudlian in the Black Watch before his transfer to the KOSB.

Sweet harmony

The company had been given a welfare radio set and the Major asked me to set it up somewhere. He did not want it in the officer's mess; he didn't think they were capable of tuning it in to the 'right' sort of music—whatever that might have been. He did not want it in the sergeant's mess; he did not trust them to treat it properly. When he asked me where I thought it should go I naturally suggested the signals exchange bunker.

The exchange was at the top of quite a steep hill and the cookhouse, the dining tent and our bunkers were all at the bottom. It was a bugger of a climb either way. I ran a phone line from the wireless down the hill to an amplifier and speaker so that we could listen to whatever station the chap on duty had tuned in to. In time, it took little effort to extend the line from the dining tent to our bunkers so that we could lie on our beds and listen in through earphones borrowed from combat radios. We were having a very cushy life indeed.

It was possible to tune in to the Commonwealth Division Radio Services, Radio Australia, Radio Ceylon, the BBC Far Eastern Service and the American Forces Radio Service (AFRS). The AFRS had five relay stations spread across Southern Korea—Vagabond, Kilroy, Troubador, Gypsy and Homesteader. None of them were commercial and the only feature that identified them as being military was their broadcasting of various notices directed to military personnel. These could range from reminders that they were abroad and should mind their behaviour to details of times and locations of church services for various denominations. Strangest of all were the reminders about renewal of private vehicle registration. That was presumably intended for those who had left cars back home in the States.

Advice was also provided for soldiers who wished to vote in the upcoming US Presidential election. We heard a programme on AFRS that came from the Republican Party Convention in Chicago when Eisenhower defeated Taft to win his party's nomination. The racket kicked up by the delegates was as appalling as the monotonous, boring, droning voice of the commentator describing the scene, telling us who the various speechmakers were and how the voting was going.

As I write this account half a century later, I find it interesting that the Olympic Games began in Helsinki, Finland on 19th July 1952 but nobody here seemed to be aware of this and we heard nothing about them over any radio station either

Nobody was really expecting to spend much more time in the front line again. The whole battalion would pull back into brigade reserve in three weeks' time to start getting ready for a move to Hong Kong. The story going around was that the Welch will be relieved by the Duke of Wellington's Regiment (the 'Dukes') at the end of November. By that time I hoped to be at least halfway home.

At last the trauma of trying to write that article for the school magazine was beginning to ease and my mental energy to pick up. I started to reply to all the letters awaiting a response. Life in company reserve was very idle. Even though we had to get up when reveille was blown at 05:00, provided we had not been on stag in the exchange, the rest of the day was spent sleeping or reading. In a letter to my brother I tallied up the losses D company had sustained during the three months up at the sharp end. Out of ninety of us who went up, two had been killed and eight wounded, including one officer.

Mucking about with the wireless again

It was generally agreed that Vagabond was the AFRS station that offered the best listening. Its all-night music programmes were the best for whiling away the hours on stag at the exchange. They presented all kinds of music, classical, swing, country and western, romantic songs, popular songs—everything. The most popular songs and singers were "When Your Lover is Gone" by Jo Stafford, "Tenderly" by Rosemary Clooney and Doris Day's renditions of "Lullaby of Broadway" and "Tea For Two". However, the variety and gag shows mostly made us do just that—gag. They were so corny.

I personally became excited whenever Stan Kenton and his band came on. His was probably my favourite of all the big bands. One evening they played a piece that was new to me—"Mambo Rhapsody" and I made a note to tell my brother to look out for it. While I found Kenton's style exciting, not many other chaps seemed to know about the 'Kenton sound' or, if they did, were not very interested in it.

Early one morning while on stag in the exchange, I fiddled with the welfare radio and found a station broadcasting a performance of Tchaikovsky's 4th symphony. Having been unable to listen to any classical music like this for quite a few months, it was great to be able to do so undisturbed—until my relief came at 03:00 hours. Then I took a pair of earphones to my bunk and continued to listen until I dropped off to sleep. It was surprising how pleasant life could be here sometimes.

Being in the Signals section had other benefits. We occasionally had access to information denied most of the others through having to listen to conversations and make brief notes of what they were about for the record. Any talk about troop movements, especially those concerning drafts due to return home, were given special attention. As a result, it became possible to estimate that our draft would probably be pulled out some time toward the end of October to catch the first ship home in November. This would get us home early in December. Since rumour had it that the demob process only took about forty-eight hours, we should be out of uniform soon after. With a leave bounty with pay of a day for every month served in Korea, this should take us up to the end of the year before we needed to pay attention to what we were going to do once back in civvy street.

A package arrived for me from MGM Studios in Hollywood. It was ages since I had written to them asking for some photographs and I had forgotten all about it. They sent me six beautiful, autographed, colour photos of Kathryn Grayson, Lana Turner, June Allyson, Jane Powell, Greer Garson and Leslie Caron. I made makeshift frames for all of them from corrugated cardboard and hung them up in the exchange. We were the envy of the whole company.

The article is finished!

Between stags on duty and sleeping, the last three weeks had been spent working on the article for the School Magazine. Although the request had arrived on 21st May, the date when I really started to write it was June 3rd. It was finally in the post today, the 15th July. It had taken me over six weeks to complete and send off. My misgivings had now intensified with wondering how it would be received. The whole exercise had been traumatic. The very thought of trying to write anything about anything could still fill me with despair. Perhaps I was too much a perfectionist, over critical and reluctant about submitting something that I believed was not up to a generally acceptable standard.

Singing in the rain

On Monday, 21st July, torrential monsoon rains arrived during the early part of the day. If the usual pattern were to be followed these rains would continue until the end of August. With temperatures still high, the least effort made me sweat as if my personal plumbing system had broken down. Fortunately the exchange bunker had two entrances which allowed a refreshing current of air to blow through. By mid afternoon and for an hour or so before a storm broke, the air became very still, black rain clouds built up and it became uncomfortably clammy.

When the heavens finally opened the cracks of lightning, the background rolls of thunder and the hiss of the rain made amazing tympanic music. The display of lightning over the mountains was particularly spectacular and awesome. The storms usually lasted until mid evening with hardly any let-up and the heavy rain began to seriously affect the foundations of some of the battalion bunkers. The walls and roof of one bunker caved in trapping and killing the chap inside.

There was one big problem with trying to cope with these conditions. Since our ponchos, our groundsheets-cum-capes, had been spread over the roofs of our bunkers to keep everything inside dry, whenever we had to move around outside in this rain, at mealtimes for example, we inevitably got soaking wet. Not that it bothered us very much. The temperatures were high, the rain warm. Since we were only wearing shirts and combat trousers they dried easily enough overnight, or next morning at the latest when the sun was up.

There were two quite amusing moments caused by all the rain. One afternoon, after the usual downpour had started, I was hanging around in the exchange when a message came through for our company 2IC. The chap on duty asked if I would take it along to him in his bunker. I sloshed along the crawl trench whistling quite happily to myself. On the way I passed the CSM. He gave me a very queer look as if he thought I was nuts to be whistling in all the rain and mud.

Arriving at the captain's bunker, I gave him the message and waited to see if there was any reply he wished to send. His bunker was quite large and it would have needed three or four ponchos on the roof to keep it dry inside. Looking around, I saw that he had hung his poncho over his bed to stop water dripping onto it. The problem was that the groundsheet had collected water very competently and retained it. There was no way to drain it away. As a result it hung ominously low over his bed like a cow's udder with no teat. Every other corner of his bunker had become pretty soggy.

I was about to ask him how he was going to deal with all the water when the major arrived, took one look at the swollen, suspended groundsheet, grinned like an idiot and gave it a casual but quite substantial poke. Inevitably, the water rippled around and quite a lot sloshed over the edge and dripped straight onto the captain's bed.

I looked at the captain, saw the expression on his face and left his bunker very smartly. His shout of dismay followed me down the crawl trench. It would have been interesting to stay within earshot and hear exactly what he said to the major. I'd have bet good money it was neither polite nor respectful to a superior officer.

The other event occurred that same evening. Someone had organised a film show just for D Company and we all went along to see the *"The Light Touch"*. It starred Stewart Granger, Pier Angeli, George Sanders and Mike Mazurki. A romantic gangster film set in Italy, it was not really a very good film but the music and some of the scenes were quite moving. Anyway, not having seen a film of any description for over three months, this was a real treat. For the first hour all went well. The rain eased and we soaked up some of the sights on the screen that we missed most—houses, cars, civilian clothes, beautiful women, good food and all the other trimmings of civilisation as we might have known it. Then the heavens opened again and it started to bucket down.

Groundsheets had been hung over the screen to protect it from the drips and they, like the one in the captain's bunker, had begun to collect water, sagging ever lower down in front of the screen. Finally water began to spill over the edge and cast shadows on the screen. Then water started to drip everywhere through the tent roof, first drop by drop but increasing until they were little streams. Chaps were covering up left, right and centre to get out of the way of the drips and drops while still trying to watch the film. I ended up huddled under a table for shelter from the water with my head stuck poking out the side to continue watching.

Everyone was wet through. The naked torsos of those who had come without shirts gleamed in the light reflected from the screen as they dashed about attempting to find some drier spot to stand or sit. It was complete chaos. Probably the most bizarre aspect of the whole evening was that, despite the rain pouring in everywhere, the projector never stopped running. The film still rolled and we stayed and watched to the end, by which time the rain had stopped. Sliding, slithering and crashing into each other and every immovable object around, we struggled to leave the cinema-cum-shower tent and clawed our way along slippery paths to our bunkers.

R&R at Inchon

In August, I was given three days leave at the Divisional Rest Centre at Inchon. Transport was laid on to get me back to B Echelon. From there the ride was as hairy as it had been when we arrived last December but this time, when we crossed the Pintail Bridge, the river was in full flood. It had risen to barely one metre beneath the road span and was putting extreme pressure on the supporting piers.

Since only one truck was allowed to cross at a time, we joined a queue on the northern side to wait our turn. There was much road work going on and groups of Korean labourers were standing around, leaning on their shovels like good labourers everywhere when they can find half an excuse.

We inched our way forward until at last it was our turn to cross. Our driver had to maintain a speed of ten mph and we crawled across watching the water tearing past just a few feet beneath us. Someone said that the Chinese were sending huge tree trunks down on the flood water to crash into and destroy the bridges and that tanks were positioned up-stream to blow these out of the water before they could do any damage.

Approach to Pintail Bridge over Imjin April 1952

Pintail bridge April

Eventually we were safely across and off to join the main highway south through Tokchon and Uijongbu. Eventually, we arrived in what was left of the northern suburbs of Seoul. It was still in ruins but there were many signs that the mess was being cleared and some reconstruction going on.

We crossed a pontoon bridge over the Han River and set off west on the road to Inchon. We made one stop long enough to "take a leek". Being in the Welch Regiment made this a very appropriate euphemism for a toilet break. A horde of Korean kids came round clamouring to clean our boots but, probably thinking we were rich US soldiers and made of money, they asked too much.

We pulled in to the Rest Centre later that afternoon and were billeted in wooden huts. As at Ebisu, the beds were very comfortable with good thick mattresses, clean sheets and pillows with pillow cases. We would get three meals a day but would otherwise be left to our own devices.

The camp was situated among trees back from the edge of a wide lagoon—a saltwater lagoon as I later found out. To the left, a small jetty ran out into the lagoon. A couple of small boats were moored further out. Outside the camp limits, the trees continued for a while between the shore of the lagoon and the base of the same low, scrub covered hills so familiar to us further north.

Across the lagoon to our right some rocks projected above the water and on the far side a small hill dominated the skyline. It was made all the more interesting by the handful of straggly, wind-blown pines that decorated the summit and reminded me of ceramics decorated with the blue Chinese Willow Pattern design.

"Willow Tree" hill

The next day I met a chap named Ben Cox who came from Reading and we set off to explore the area. Walking off to the right along the edge of the lagoon we came to a group of small tents erected on either side of a road that ran up from the beach into the hills. Clearly, these belonged to families who had lost their homes in this war. Further on we came to a row of houses, evidently a fishing village since there were no paddy fields around to indicate farming of any kind. Three of them seemed to have survived any military activity that had gone through the area quite well. Their roofs were still well thatched even though they showed signs of ad

Korean houses by lagoon

hoc repairs. But the last house was quite different. It had a pitched roof of wood and tin and the walls were patched up with old cardboard ration boxes that had probably been salvaged from the Rest Centre.

Later, we met a very old man carrying an immense bundle of sticks for firewood on his back. It was three times his size, towered over his head and presented an extraordinary sight. I was sure that I could never find strength to do what he was doing. When he saw me pull out my camera he very obligingly stopped and let me take his picture. He even contributed a very toothless grin for good measure.

We walked on until we could get a view of the Rest Camp. In the distance behind it rose a formidable looking mountain. It must have been every bit as tricky a place to attack as Hill 355 had been, one that must have proved a headache for the troops who went ashore during the amphibious invasion.

We passed beneath the 'Willow Pattern' hill to a point where I could take a picture that would show those wind-bent pines at their best. We then returned to camp, had a meal and lazed around. Later in the afternoon we went down to the jetty for a swim in the lagoon—my only swim in the briny that year.

Next day we wandered off the way we had gone yesterday but this time we walked out on the seaward side of the 'Willow Pattern' hill. There were quite a number of houses at the back of the beach looking in fairly good repair. There were also several Koreans around.

Korean shellfish gatherers near Inchon

One group of men, women and children were squatting on some flat rocks by the edge of the sea. Some of them had what looked like string bags attached to wooden frames that they carried on their backs. Lying on the rocks near them were wooden A-frames some four or five feet in length with a piece of steel strap lashed to the legs of the frame. I went over and pointing to one of the frames, asked what these were for. No one spoke any English but I got the idea that it was a device for raking the mud and sand to expose shell fish that others would then collect. Seeing that the tide was out a long way, exposing acres of mud flats, it was possible they were getting ready to set off to work.

It was pleasant to walk aimlessly along a beach again with nothing particular to do. Ben wasn't particularly talkative so most of our conversation was restricted to pointing out things of possible interest to each other. Eventually we wandered back to the Rest Centre and lazed about waiting for dinner to be served.

That evening I drank a little more beer than I was accustomed to and got drunk for the first time in my life. I felt a little weak at the knees, under the illusion that my mind was still working sensibly and ridiculously happy. There was word that women in one of the houses nearby were available for anyone feeling a particular need for sex but, having seen the houses and some of the women, this held no interest for me.

The final day was spent in utter laziness sleeping, eating and drinking. There was little else to do and that was just as well. It was a rest. The return trip was a mirror image of the outward journey in most respects. The Imjin was, if anything, flowing even higher and this time we had to wear life jackets as we crossed the Pintail Bridge. A lot of use they would have been if anything disastrous did happen. That river was flowing so fast and so deep that we would have been whirled down and away in seconds. Still, it was nice to know someone cared.

16

AT B ECHELON

17th September to 20th October 1952

B Echelon and Taffy

Three days ago, I was sent back to B Echelon, the part of the battalion furthest from the sharp end. Everything and almost everyone who entered or left the battalion passed through B Echelon This was certainly true with regard to supplies and equipment since the QM resided here. However, when my draft arrived at the battalion we had been taken straight to A Echelon, as most likely did all the others.

My move came as a surprise. I had been with D Company for the almost five months and knew everyone pretty well. Maybe the Signals Officer had adopted a policy of moving those whose names had come up on the current Return to Home Establishment (RHE) list to safer billets and well out of any danger in the front line again. At least, I liked to think that. Anyway, this was probably the cushiest billet that any signaller could have; I had no immediate 'boss' and no one to share duties with. These consisted of switching on the B Echelon 62 set twice a day when the battalion was at stand to and checking in—just in case.

The QM had obligingly housed the set in a trailer so that both it and I would be well protected from the elements. It had also been parked out of the way in a corner of B Echelon where it almost guaranteed that I would not be disturbed. The trailer was equipped with a table and drawers and I was now able to sit comfortably to read or write. Not that writing had been such a big thing lately. Writer's block had set in again for the past fortnight.

I slept on a camp bed in one of the tents with the other personnel; they were easy to get along with. Reveille was at 06:15 and breakfast at 07:30

followed by an absolute mockery of a muster parade and arms inspection. When that was over I could get on with my duties as I thought best. The only other thing I had to do was maintain the generator that charged the batteries for the 62 set.

The food at B Echelon was generally good which reminded me again that, almost as soon as we arrived in Korea, the number of times chicken popped up on the menu had been one of the great surprises. It was safe to say that I ate more chicken here in one month than I had ever eaten at home in the past twenty years. What had once been a very rare treat at Christmas time had now become a very commonplace food item. The Yanks had obviously found a way to produce them cheaply and in vast numbers. But no one complained that it was boring.

A view of B Echelon

When I left D Company they were up in the Kansas Line positions south of the River Imjin where the trenches, bunkers and barbed wire entanglements of this main fall back line of defence were still being refurbished. Occasionally I had to take an 88 type wireless set up there to exchange for one that had broken down. This involved a strenuous climb up the crest of a ridge rising straight out of the paddy fields. The summit seemed higher than Little Gibraltar even though it was not.

The view from the top was magnificent and stretched northwards across the valley of the Imjin to the mountains where it was just possible to plot where the current front line lay. (Map: Page 131) The panorama of interlocking ridges and valleys that spread out on either side of the main valley presented an image of formidable territory in which to conduct infantry warfare. The 45 degree slopes were covered with the dense scrub oak that we now knew so well. We could also look across to Gloster Hill, the site of the battle. It was difficult to imagine waves of Chinese soldiers swarming over those hillsides as if they were not there, as happened on that night of the full moon in April 1951.

View of Imjin from Kansas Line

One or two of the Korean porters with D Company had been with the Glosters on that occasion and were able to point out the valley along which a small party of them had managed to escape. One, a middle aged chap who had adopted the name Fred even claimed to be the porter who guided them out. I had got to know him quite well up in the front line.

B Echelon was the domain of the battalion Quarter Master, the only officer in residence, supported by a Regimental Quarter Master Sergeant. To me, the QM was a living caricature of an army officer, a Colonel Blimp type, plump, with a round red face, a clipped manner of speaking but very good-natured. The RQMS was OK but always seemed to think that it was his duty to find something to bitch about just to maintain his reputation.

B Echelon was also home to Taffy IX, the regimental mascot, a white Kashmiri goat who had his own quarters just along from my wireless wagon. He was treated as if he were a human member of the battalion, perhaps even more so in some respects given the fact that, although he spent most of his time in his quarters, he received a daily ration of cigarettes. He ate them with great relish.

Taffy IX - 1st Bn. The Welch Regiment mascot at B Echelon - Korea Sept 1952

The regimental mascot's billet

He was awarded the UN and Commonwealth Division Korea Service medals last St David's Day. Later I found out that, in the battalion records, he was regarded as an enlisted soldier with the rank of lance corporal.

The first of his line had been taken to the Crimean War to provide fresh food for the troops, at least for the small group who were assigned to take care of him. However, he had earned a reprieve by warning them of the approach of a group of enemy soldiers. As a result he was not slaughtered but kept as a mascot and later adopted by the Regiment itself.

Life in B Echelon was very leisurely. I felt pretty secure in the knowledge that I would never return to the sharp end again and it had now become much clearer when we would leave Korea. My name had at last been posted among those on the RHE list. We were to sail on the *Empire Pride*, a typical troopship, due to leave sometime between the 20th and 30th of October. I understood it would dock in Southampton.

This meant that all the chaps in my draft who were still alive and well would leave their positions in the battalion between the 10th and 20th of October. In thirty days' time at the most, we would be taken to the rail-head at Tokchon and put on a train for Pusan going via Seoul, Taejon and Taegu. There, we would hand in our old kit, draw new stuff and board the *Empire Pride* for the voyage home. On arrival at Southampton we would presumably be trucked or trained to Maindy Barracks in Cardiff for final demob and should be home by around December 7th.

It's a good life

It was turning out to be the most Sunday-like Sunday I could remember in ages. The day was warm, sunny and very quiet. The only busy noise was the putter of the charging engine but this was not enough to disturb the peace. However, we were well into September now and the summer was coming to an end. The daytime temperatures could still get high but nights were getting chilly and four blankets were now needed to keep warm enough to sleep.

The few other permanent personnel at B Echelon were easy-going chaps which was not really surprising. They had not faced the stress of the sharp end and life here at the blunt end was not exactly full of parade ground bullshit. They numbered no more than thirty men: storemen,

clerks, drivers and various craftsmen skilled in working with wood and metal.

The Drums and Bugles of the Regiment were also in residence here since this was where their kit and instruments were normally kept. For a while each day, the camp would be filled with the sound of their practice sessions. They were all pretty versatile musicians and often called to play non-martial music at social events so at times these practice sessions could be very entertaining. They enjoyed letting their hair down and jazzing things up a little from time to time.

At mv signals trailer B Echelon

During the morning, smiles broke out all round when the advance party of the Duke of Wellington's Regiment arrived. This was a sure sign that our battalion's tour of duty here in Korea was drawing to a close. The 'Dukes' were to relieve the Welch in 29 Brigade of the Commonwealth Division. This also meant that the staff at B Echelon would soon be very busy getting ready to pack things up as an advance party of the Welch prepared to leave for Hong Kong.

The following Sunday another signaller named Ray arrived in B Echelon to share duties with me. We could now take it in turn to go back to the cinema at Div.HQ while the other stayed around to "guard" the phone and the wireless set. But time was beginning to hang badly. There really was very little to do to pass the hours. It was so peaceful and the living so easy-going that it was beginning to become boring. B Echelon really needed its own cinema.

Meanwhile, both the QM and RQMS were trying to provoke us out of our somnolence by being real kill-joys. Beer consumption had been restricted to one bottle per person per evening. On reflection it was just as well. It would have been only too easy to cope with the boredom by getting drunk each evening and hoping that life would thereby become more interesting. As it was, I invariably gave my bottle to someone else.

Live entertainment had been pretty good over the past few weeks. Two live shows had visited here. The first to arrive was the "Hy Hazel Show". Hy Hazel was a very luscious looking, energetic entertainer as one would expect from an artiste of her class. There was another very attractive woman in the party who sang beautifully and played the violin equally well. They were supported by a comedian named Alec Monroe and an excellent pianist-singer.

The other show that arrived was billed around Carole Carr. In some respects I did not think it quite as good as Hy Hazel's show but it was certainly a much slicker presentation. While Carole was in excellent voice, another performer named Peter Snaith had a cold and could only groan as he accompanied himself on the piano or the accordion. An excellent Aussie comedian was also on the bill.

Both shows were very enjoyable, the only criticism being that they were held in a dead flat paddy field so that we didn't have a brilliant view of the stage. If the stage could have been erected at the base of a hill facing uphill, we could have had good positions from which to watch the performers. God only knew there were enough hills here.

A number of outdoor cinemas had been established around the valley showing the latest films— "Room For One", "Golden Girl", "Scandal Sheet", "My Six Convicts" and many more. But ultimately all they did for us was increase our longing to get home where we could go to a decent and familiar cinema once more and watch a film in comfort, with no rain dripping through the roof.

Church Parade

The one thing that my posting to B Echelon had removed was the chance to spend any time with Brian before we got on that train to Pusan. I caught a glimpse of him on a special church parade that the CO had ordered. And that took place on Sunday, September 28th.

Someone in a Royal Artillery unit had presented to the battalion a cross and two candlesticks. They had been fashioned by Samuel Lee of Seoul from brass 25 pounder shell cases from 14th Field Regiment that had been fired in support of 1st Welch whilst holding Hill 355.

The parade and service were held to dedicate them and the whole battalion had to attend. Only an essential skeleton staff on duty at BHQ were exempt. After being trucked to the place where the parade was to be held, it felt very strange to line up and march off in columns of three again. Being inches taller than most of the others, it brought a revival of my old nickname—'Lofty'.

For the service, the six companies of the battalion formed three sides of a hollow square, six men deep, with the sanctuary area on the fourth side. A table stood in front of a screen made up of camouflage netting with green and brown hessian camouflage strips woven into it. It had been very well done. A Union Jack served as an altar cloth. On the altar stood the cross and candlesticks with a vase of blue Michaelmas daisies on either side, a wild flower that was growing abundantly here at this time of year. The regimental drums had been made into a pyramid before the altar.

When everyone was in position, the CO, the 2IC, the brigadier commanding 29 Infantry Brigade and Taffy IX led by the Goat Major took their places in the centre of the square and the service commenced. For me it was the usual lack-lustre affair, the order of service derived from the Church of England Prayer Book and conducted by the Rev W.W. Rhys, another Welshman who was the Senior Chaplain of the 1st Commonwealth Division. He was assisted by our own Chaplain who, like the battalion CO, was an Irishman but more quietly spoken. The CO read the lesson.

The occasion did nothing to endear church parades to me, or church, or religion come to that. Despite being nominally an Anglican, such rituals and doctrines had become increasingly unenlightening so having to attend and listen to them was disagreeable to say the least. My usual thing on such occasions was to contemplate more personal spiritual issues but, with restless apathy the dominant feeling among those around me, this was hardly a helpful situation in which to contemplate anything.

The elevated Welsh ecclesiastic droned on about the symbolism of the chalice, the cross, the candlesticks and what they represented in terms of the Last Supper, the crucifixion and the joy of the Resurrection. I couldn't quite see the significance of candlesticks in all this, so it seemed that I did listen to him after all—some of the time. If only he had said something about the Michaelmas "Lilies of the Field" daisies that were on the altar and what they represented. That might have been more uplifting. But he didn't.

And wasn't there much more that could have been said about a cross being presented to a military unit actually engaged in a theatre of war? After all, it was a symbol of the sacrifice of a life and Alec Ahern had sacrificed his life here along with many others. And for what exactly? We would have been very interested had this opportunity been taken to tell us.

So, for part of the time I amused myself contemplating the coincidence of being in a regiment whose badge consisted of the Three Feathers insignia of the Prince of Wales (page 22) and his motto "Ich Dien" (pronounced 'ick deen') and a commanding officer with the name of H.H. Deane, Lt.Col. As far as I was aware, he was a very competent commander, not overly pally with the men.

The Service over, we were smartly marched off the field back to where the "Home James and don't spare the horses" trucks had been parked. On the way back to B Echelon, our driver was actually pulled over by an MP and ticked off for speeding. He was only expressing how we all felt. We couldn't get away from that parade ground fast enough.

Winter closing in

The film at Div.HQ that night was *"With a Song in my Heart"* starring Susan Hayward as the American singer Jane Froman. It was a much more elevating experience than that service. The credits revealed that Jane had actually done the singing with Susan miming the words and actions. It was cleverly done and her beautiful contralto voice was a total joy. It was the best film I had seen that year.

The only problem with going to cinemas in a tent at this time of year was that the nights were getting very cold. The only way to keep warm and watch the film in comfort was to huddle under four or five blankets. Yet by day it was still getting warm enough to wander around stripped to the waist.

But winter was slowly and surely creeping up on us. Consignments of battledress uniforms had started to arrive at B Echelon to be prepared for issue before the battalion left for Hong Kong. Arrangements were made for every man in the battalion to try on a uniform, have the arm and leg lengths marked and then leave them so that alterations could be made. The RQMS, in a more relaxed and chatty moment, told me there was quite a flap on to get them all fitted in time. Eight Korean tailors and four sewing machines had been rustled up to cope with the workload this had created.

The B echelon staff were also very busy getting ready for the hand-over to the 'Dukes'. Inventories had to be checked, broken kit dispatched for repair or dumped and all the accounts tidied up. Carpenters were working flat out fabricating boxes of various shapes and sizes in which to pack articles of gear and kit for transit to Hong Kong.

In a way it was a pity we couldn't have stayed with the battalion for a month or so when they finally went there. HK had been fascinating to wander round on our way out and we would have been able to make a better acquaintance with it. By the same token, all the places we had visited had been interesting and our time in them far too short. Another rumour was circulating that, because the situation in Egypt was still very tense, Algiers would now be a port of call for troopships. That could also be an interesting place to visit—if the rumour were to prove true.

At last—a map to look at.

Wandering into the QM's office today, I saw that there was a very large map of Korea on the wall of the tent. No one took any notice of me as I stopped to examine it. Eventually I worked out that B Echelon was just a matter of a hundred yards or so south of the 38th parallel.

For future reference, I noted that the best way to locate our position was to find where 127°E crossed the 38th parallel just on a bend in the River Imjin. The area just to the north and west of that intersecting point was roughly the area that we had operated in for the past few months. It was interesting to have that clear in my mind at last. I had often wished we had access to maps of the area we were in.

Rumblings to the north

There was great activity around Little Gibraltar again last night. The Chinese shelled it heavily and there was much activity over the wireless network. Perhaps they had been stirred into action because the red dragon was no longer flying from the top! Since there was a full moon the COs were discussing whether this was the start of a major push by the Chinese into which we would inevitably be drawn. It caused a big flap among our officers and a state of high alert was maintained for several hours.

If the regiments presently along the front line were to be pushed back it would be up to the Welch to mount a counter attack. Every artillery unit around us opened up in reply and all night long trucks rumbled past carrying ammunition and troops to forward positions.

Here at B Echelon, although we were well back from the main activity in the battalion, I now had to open up the 62 set every hour on the hour to keep the QM informed with what was going on. There was a strong current of excitement and foreboding in the air. My mind was exercised by all sorts of considerations, mostly concern for the chaps up in the rifle companies who were so near to going home, or to Hong Kong.

They would all be standing to in case anything serious developed. It was strange to realise that this time last year the King's Own Scottish Borderers were fighting over Little Gibraltar and other prominent hills to the north east of our sector of the front. It was such a strategically important position, along with all the others with famous names—The Hinge, Old Baldy, The Hook, Siberia, Capitol Hill, Kelly and many more equally idiosyncratic.

What bliss iss thiss!

We have been plagued by clouds of a small flying insect, much smaller than a gnat, more like a midge. It was called 'bliss', as far as I could manage the Korean name. It seemed an utterly inappropriate name for such a nuisance. I was very glad that the window to my wireless trailer had a fine mesh over it to keep the damned things out. They were black, extremely tiny and totally frenetic in the way they moved. It was impossible to walk anywhere in the camp and be free from them.

A time to wait . . .

I felt an increasing tension as the date of our departure for Pusan drew nearer. It was strongest in the evening when there wasn't much to do. It wasn't possible to see a film every evening and interesting books were hard to come by. However, I had found an amusing one called *"Ol' Man Adam an' His Chillun"* by Roark Bradford. They were retellings of stories from the Old Testament as Uncle Remus might have told them, or some other old negro with a loose grip on the story and a great sense of humour. There was more noise from the artillery that evening. We all hoped it wouldn't be a repetition of last night's shindig.

I was now getting good pay of £3/10/00 a week and all found. A third of that was going home for my mother to bank for me, two shillings and eight pence were taken for National Insurance and nine pence was deducted for Income Tax. This provoked an interesting thought as to why we should contribute to the cost of our being here in Korea when we had been placed involuntarily in a position which could actually cost us our lives. Be that as it may, although I could actually draw roughly £2 every week, I invariably only drew £1, the rest building up as credit to be drawn any time after demob.

Notification came yesterday of the Territorial Army (TA) unit with which I would serve once demobbed from full time national service. The notice told me to report to 4 Battalion, The Dorsetshire Regiment in Dorchester on the 4th December 1952 between 14:00 and 17:00. I had forgotten that in addition to two years full time service, national service included three years part-time in the TA, a reserve force to be called up in a time of great emergency. And I wasn't on my way home yet!

Writer's block eases

At long last, and not before time, the letter writing block had eased. There were things that had happened in those long intervals between my letters back in the summer that should have been recorded and sent to the folk back home to supplement what they were reading in the papers.

The battalion moved back up front today and took over positions from The Royal Fusiliers. This seemed to be a very curious move considering it would soon have to pull back out once more when their tour of duty was over and time came to leave for Hong Kong. Perhaps the Chinese shelling the other night had caused a lot of casualties so that our chaps were needed to keep up the strength of the line. Fortunately for the QM, who was well into the preparations to move right out of Korea, B Echelon was staying put. This also suited me very nicely.

Very welcome news

In her last letter my mother sent the pages from the School Magazine with my article in it. It was strange to see it in print and even stranger to find that Mr Cullingford had made very few changes. My mother mentioned that many people had paid some pretty compliments about it. She had also told me that 'Sammy' Stevens, my old Junior School headmaster and good friend of my mother's, had read my contribution to the School Magazine and praised it. Now that was a real turn-up for the books. But I still believed it to be a poor effort, that it could have been much better.

The next day, when Brian turned up at B Echelon on some errand, I had an opportunity to show it to him. He liked it very much and commented that he didn't know I had it in me. Neither had I for that matter. So that was that. Having seen it in print I no longer beat myself for my poor grasp of written English.

Barbershop comedy, scene 1

Somehow I had rubbed the barber up the wrong way and he was making any excuse not to cut my hair. Consequently, it had grown quite thick but not so long as to attract the attention of the RQMS—yet! However, it resulted in a modification of my nickname from 'Lofty' to 'Longfellow', a double reference to my height and the increasingly bohemian appearance my hair was lending me. Chaps kept calling out, "Written any good poems to read to us, Longfellow?" to which I would reply, "Why do you ask? You wouldn't listen to them if I had." Then I was told that the carpenter had been asked to knock up a violin for me. "I knew Longfellow wrote poetry. Did he also play the violin?" I asked?

RQMS Evans and Butch, one of the storemen

At this rate, it would not be too long before either the QM or the RQMS joined the party and demand that I allow the barber use his shears on me. Since his 'shop' was outdoors this would doubtless bring cheers and jeers from anyone who witnessed the operation. A curse on all outdoor barbers!

The weather continued warm enough for sunbathing during the day but nights became so cold that if we were on guard duty we had to wear our winter kit. When the time arrived for us to leave, the days would be even colder, much as it might be back in England. But between now and reaching home we would spend two weeks passing through the sweltering tropics again, an experience that would confirm that we were no longer in harm's way, unless there were some tragedy while at sea. As yet however, no definite date had been posted for when the *Empire Pride* will sail.

Barbershop comedy, scene 2

It was two days later and I had still not been told to see the regimental barber. Then this morning I literally bumped into the RQMS as I walked round the corner of a tent. He stopped and gave me a long hard look. "You lettin' your hair grow so as to get some job you wants back in civvy street, boyo?' he asked in his strong Welsh accent. Certain that he had heard about the 'violin' story and supposing his mood to be amiable, I replied, "Yes, Sarge. I was thinking to become a street musician."

A smile fleetingly crossed his features but a moment later he suddenly barked at me, "See the barber tomorrow". It had all the impact of a car backfiring behind me. It also provoked much laughter among those standing near who had witnessed this little exchange. I had the feeling that the back of my neck, now red hot from sudden embarrassment, was going to feel quite cold in the morning.

Waiting time blues

Battledress fitting was still going on in the tailors' department. Those eight Koreans were really kept hard at work altering trouser and sleeve lengths, sewing on flashes, ribbons, stripes and all the other things that were required for each person to be properly dressed on parade according to rank. Someone told me that the uniforms would not be issued until the battalion had arrived in Hong Kong. Once ready, they had to be labelled with each soldier's name and go to the store for packing and sealing in boxes. But I had also heard that before leaving Korea the battalion would hold a Memorial Parade at the UN War Cemetery at Pusan. Doubtless those uniforms would be needed for that.

As the count-down to our departure continued, it became very evident that autumn was firmly with us. The weather continued fine by day and bitterly cold at night. B Echelon, being in a valley, was usually swamped with mist or fog by 21:00 or 22:00 and this made both the nights and early mornings bitingly cold. The last two mornings we woke to find that a heavy frost had settled on everything during the night. Sometimes, even five blankets were not sufficient to keep the damp chill out.

It was strange to remember how, soon after we arrived last winter and had moved into bunkers, we could get quite snug in them at night and not need extra blankets. Some chaps had never unpacked their bedding rolls. If you had been able to construct some sort of a fire in your bunker the earth seem to absorb and give back the heat all night.

At the moment, we were still in summer kit, whereas other battalions had been issued with winter combat suits and all the other special winter kit that had eventually been issued to us. But this 'oversight' was only felt at night while on guard when it was necessary to wear two or three jumpers and two pairs of trousers to keep even half-warm enough.

The countryside was becoming dressed in familiar autumn colours. Every imaginable tint and shade of brown, yellow and red appeared just as in an English autumn. Recently the surprising discovery was made of some sweet chestnut trees nearby that had produced some very edible nuts. Since then there had been much crunching and munching; they tasted very good especially when baked on the fire.

For the past few days, I had found and tuned the 62 set to another programme of classical music. I had been able to enjoy such favourites as Beethoven's Pastoral symphony, Tchaikovsky's violin concerto and Smetana's tone poem 'Vltava'. Another piece, Beethoven's second symphony was less familiar to me.

On Tuesday, 14th October 1952 the CO ordered all men due to return home on the *Empire Pride* to report to A Echelon and stay there. They would not be sent back up to the front again. That meant that Brian, and many others we had joined up with and who had so far avoided injury or death, would be safe to depart. Quite a number of chaps who had come out with the draft after ours were also going home. The rumour mill had been busy again with a story that the *Empire Pride* was not going to sail between the dates that had been posted but we all blew raspberries at this story. Meanwhile I remained at B Echelon.

Departure time is posted

Today, our departure date from the battalion was posted. We would leave for the railhead at Tokchon on the 20th of the month—only another ten days to go. I immediately wrote this information to my family telling them to address letters to the troopship *Empire Pride* from now on. I also suggested that if they wanted to come and meet the ship they should keep an eye on the shipping arrivals due at Southampton during the first week of December.

The last letter from my mother had contained prints of some of the photographs I had taken. Rather than risk the ruination of the films by having them processed locally I had sent them home. They were not too bad but would have been quite meaningless to my family without my being there to explain what they were about.

I was beginning to feel excited about getting home again and had told my mother that I would like her to take me to a service at the Christian Science Church in Bournemouth. She was the professional soloist there singing sacred anthems at their Sunday services. I would also like to take her to a concert at the Bournemouth Winter Gardens.

17

RETURN TO PUSAN

20th October to 28th October 1952

A time to go . . .

Things began to happen quickly. Reveille was blown at the usual time and after breakfast we went on muster parade and were told to get ready to move. Trucks arrived bringing chaps in from A Echelon and other companies who were due to go home or who were part of the advance party to Hong Kong. I managed to find Brian and from then on we stayed pretty close. The CO came to bid us farewell but I could not remember whether or not he thanked us for our contribution to the war effort. My attention was elsewhere.

At 10:15 we climbed aboard the waiting trucks and were off. We had our last view of the Imjin as we crossed Pintail Bridge; the water level had dropped considerably since that trip to Inchon for R&R. We learned later that it was the first bridge built across the Imjin ever to withstand the monsoon rains. Our route continued partly up the Gloster valley where we caught our last glimpse of that famous hill. Had it not been for the intercession of our CO in Plymouth in February 1951, many of us might have found ourselves on that hill a year ago last April, dead or wounded and prisoners.

The road wound over the mountain range south of the river, the hillsides quite beautiful in their autumn clothing. The scrub oak, such a dreary brown when we arrived, was now even more glorious than it had been in spring when it burst into fresh leaf. The still lingering rich reds and deep greens clung tenaciously to the grey rocky buttresses occasionally broken by ribs of yellow sand washed down in the rains. The scene along that valley was one of quite unexpected beauty and enough to send one's senses reeling. Brian and I seemed the only ones who wanted to remain quiet and take in this beauty. The rest were chattering like sparrows, excited by the fact that they were at last on their way home.

The trucks raced along dusty roads up valleys, over mountain passes and down valleys again. Everyone that we passed provoked some kind of comment from us. Australians and Canadians were cheered enthusiastically but Americans got catcalls and requests to "Move along there". One might well have wondered how they felt about these remarks from this convoy of homeward bound British troops. It was strange, this 'no love lost' relationship on our part toward the Americans; they didn't return our animosity. Whether this was from good nature, good manners, or some unvoiced sense of superiority one couldn't tell. I suspected that ignorance and not a little jealousy lay at the root of our attitude. After all, had it not been for them, we would have had a much harder time here had our kit been standard British army issue. And our rations had been infinitely better for being supplied by the US.

Soon we passed beyond the areas most heavily populated by the military and all that was forgotten. We were now passing between paddies that were under cultivation once more and where the rice had started to ripen. In some places it had already been harvested. The sight of people out working in the fields and paddies would become familiar throughout the rest of the journey down through the Korean peninsula. This was the first crop they had been able to sow and reap for two years and, as usual, it was the women who were bringing in the harvest.

It took two hours to reach the railhead at Tokchon. The trucks pulled into the rail yard and stopped alongside a train fifteen cars long. I counted them. We hauled our kit aboard and stowed it onto racks. The coaches were fitted with wood-slatted, bench seating, not very comfortable for a long journey, but we had been living for a year where the only things to sit on were boxes or bunks so these were a luxury. Climbing out again, we walked over to where tea, biscuits and sweets were being served by a team from the local NAAFI.

We really had to compliment the NAAFI for the way they had organised themselves here behind the lines. In order to 'fleece' us more efficiently of our pay, they had taken over various Korean buildings well behind the front lines and turned them into English style pubs with outdoor tables and brightly coloured umbrellas. This had only been possible because of the relatively static situation along the front line, a result of the ongoing Truce Talks. These establishments had names such as "The Ship Inn" or the "Crown Inn", none nearly as inventive or suggestive as Alec's "Verge Inn".

Southbound

The train finally pulled out around 13:00 but progress was slow and it took an hour to cover the eight or ten miles to Uijongbu. It took even longer to cover the remaining twenty miles to Seoul and we arrived just as dusk began to fall around 17:00. Four hours to cover thirty miles! Hopefully the train would make better time once Seoul was left behind.

En route to Seoul with cultivated paddy fields

After a makeshift meal from cans, we continued the journey southwards. Before it became too dark, I went out onto the little platform at the end of the car and climbed down onto the step no more than a couple of feet above the tracks. From there I could look up and down the length of the train. It was a great feeling to know that we were at last on the way home and I watched the dim outline of the hills and mountains to the northwest slowly sink below the horizon. Then the cold pierced through my dreaming and I returned to the compartment.

It proved extremely difficult to sort ourselves out so that we could get some sleep. Over the past ten months we had all become accustomed to sleeping on the ground or on improvised bunk beds where we could at least stretch out. Sometimes we even slept where we stood or sat in our bunkers but those wooden seats were just impossible to get comfortable on. It was impossible to find a position in which to relax and not until sometime between 01:30 and 02:00, soon after we had passed through Taejon, did many of us finally succeeded in dozing off, more through sheer exhaustion from the trying than anything else.

When dawn broke we were passing Taegu which meant that most of the journey had been made in the dark. In some respects this was a pity but there was sufficient mileage ahead to allow us to have a good look at a more peaceful and cultivated Korea.

Every time and wherever we stopped, crowds of children appeared; all shapes, sizes and conditions of them milled about in their attempts to sell us apples, or simply begging for anything we had to give away. Even when we were moving past villages they ran across the paddies to stand inches away from the cars as they passed, scrabbling for the sweets and biscuits thrown down to them. Out in the country the kids appeared to be quite clean. Those we saw later when we finally arrived in Pusan were another matter altogether.

Seaforth Camp again

The train pulled into the rail terminus at around 10:00 hours. We hauled our kit off, climbed aboard a fleet of trucks waiting nearby and were taken back to the Commonwealth Division Transit camp where we had stayed on arrival last December. Tremendous changes had occurred there during the past ten months. The whole place had been tidied up and a huge NAAFI building erected. Of all the NAAFIs I ever visited, this was probably the most comfortable.

Our sleeping accommodation was in the same wooden-framed tents as before but the roads around the camp had been smartened up and more signs erected to direct newcomers to the various offices and facilities. It was almost as comfortable as the Inchon Rest Centre had been.

Next day we were instructed to get ready for a kit check, not an inspection as such but a check of what might be missing after which we reported to the stores to make up any deficiencies found. Later, ordered to report to the stores again, we exchanged our summer uniforms for regulation battledress. These were such a disgrace that we could only laugh, the joke being that they were of the old style dating back to "18 ought splash" as one wit put it. The blouse buttoned right up to the neck so that a shirt and tie were not required.

They were the same as those issued to the Home Guard or the Land Volunteers during the war, had they been fortunate to get any uniform at all. Threadbare and obviously second, third, fourth or even '99'th hand, it was the uniform we would have for the next three years while serving in the Territorial Army. Exactly what time commitment would be involved had yet to be learned.

Like the uniform I wore while on R&R in Tokyo, they bore no Regimental, Divisional or badge patches of any kind to indicate that we were in any kind of army. At Ebisu this had been understandable. They had been a temporary issue for the duration of our stay. Now we had been made to feel as if we had just joined up, a lot of 'nig-nogs' again. The only distinguishing thing about these uniforms would be the two campaign ribbons to which our service in Korea entitled us, the United Nations Ribbon and the British Commonwealth Division ribbon which, incidentally, would take another six years to arrive.

For the next few days our time was pretty much our own. Reveille went at 06:15 hours but we usually ignored it and stayed put until 07:30, leaving ourselves just enough time to get to the cookhouse for breakfast before they shut up shop. We were given 'work' of sorts filling up various forms. We also had to present for an FFI inspection at the MO's block. In fact, all the tasks we were given proved to be long-winded, time-consuming processes with endless waiting in line or for our names to be called. Not that anyone really minded. We were on our way home at last.

A walk in Pusan

One morning, after all the administrative rigmarole had been completed, Brian and I took a walk into Pusan. We found it to be a grimy, black, stinking, smoky junk yard.

Street scene in Pusan—October 1952

In that sort of environment what could ever be expected of or for the children? The stench was worse than that in Singapore's Chinatown; the dust was worse than at Aden; the filth even more appalling than we had glimpsed at Port Said; the crowded confusion and poverty greater than seen in Hong Kong.

As Corporal "'Tiger'" Davies had written all those months ago, may his eloquence continue to bloom, Pusan did indeed seem like the "asshole of the world" and for ten months, we had indeed been five hundred miles up it. It was, without doubt, the most obnoxious city we had visited.

Finding our way to the UN Military Cemetery outside Pusan, its neatness and peacefulness was a great contrast to the filth and noise of the city. From the entrance between two massive stone pillars, a well maintained road rose gently for about half a mile up the side of a hill above paddies where a new crop was already growing. The road was lined on either side with white posts between which a thick rope had been slung to make a nominal barrier. We walked to the top of the road where, on a level area, there stood a small 'plantation' of white flag poles and an area big enough for parades to be held.

UN War Cemetery, 1952, Bill Lansdowne's grave front left

From there we looked out over an extensive area that had been levelled and laid with grass. Regiments of white crosses marked the graves of those who had died here in Korea. The number, rank and name of the person together with the name of their regiment, was painted neatly on the horizontal piece. Lower down were the letters "RIP". Sadly, as we looked around there was still plenty of room for others who might yet die here.

We wandered among the British graves looking for Alec Ahern's grave but didn't find it. However we did find that of Pte W.E. Lansdowne of D Company, 1 Welch, who had been captured then killed while on patrol from The Hook back in January. We quietly paid our respects to all of them, those we had known and those we had not, then walked back to Seaforth Camp. We did not ventured outside again.

There was little to do to while away the time except read, go for a drink in the NAAFI, go to the cinema, play cards, eat, or go to bed. For others who were lusting for more intimate action, there were such attractions to be found in that midden heap called Pusan, but my adventure in Tokyo could never be equalled there. One brief stroll through Pusan had been enough to satisfy any curiosity on that score.

UN War Cemetery, 2004
Alec Ahern's grave

An item in the camp newspaper reported that the night before we left B Echelon for the train, Little Gibraltar, now held by the Canadians, had again been heavily shelled and attacked. It now seemed very strange to remember that I had spent three months about one hundred yards in front of it and another month just behind it.

We had been led to believe that "Empire" troopships sailed out of and back to Southampton. Now we learned that the *Empire Pride* would not dock in Southampton but in Liverpool. I needed to write home very quickly and give my folk this information.

The countdown to embarkation day passed unremarkably. The one souvenir I bought for myself from the NAAFI shop was a very substantial photograph album. It had solid, wooden, black lacquered covers, the front bearing a red map of the whole of Korea, north and south, on a background of a mountain, a temple rising above pine trees and a washer woman bashing hell out of clothing by a stream. It had ample room to take all the photographs I had managed to "scrounge, pinch, purchase, borrow or honestly snap".

18

HOMEWARD BOUND

29th October to 4th December 1952

Injustice

Movement orders were posted yesterday afternoon. By 08:30 this morning, we had washed, shaved, disposed of breakfast, taken our bedding to the stores, finished packing, attended a roll call and were on open trucks bound for the docks. It was, as when we arrived, a hard ride. Some chaps yelled insults at every American we passed or taunted the Koreans.

At one point, we came up to a Korean woman walking along the side of the road carrying a pot on her head. A chap who hailed from Salisbury, a short little bloke with a round baby face, spotted her, stuck his rifle out, and knocked that pot off her head. It fell onto the road, broke and spilled its contents—beans, into the dust. The look of absolute bewilderment and dismay on the woman's face would be etched in my memory for ever. For a moment a rare anger welled up inside and I had a strong impulse to give that silly little shit a shove and topple him out of the truck. I didn't, but as he turned round with a grin on his little baby face as if to say how clever he was, he must have seen the anger and disgust at his action written on my face. He turned away. Only later would I understand how it was possible for anyone to do silly things when they became over excited about something and that silly people did the silliest things.

We arrived at the docks just after 09:00 and drew up alongside our ship home, a beautiful sight for Korea-tired eyes. We had also arrived at the docks in time to watch a detachment of smart, fresh, Canadian reinforcements march off to waiting trucks as we had once done. To judge by the news we had been getting from the sharp end, if they are going to the battalion holding Little Gibraltar they would need all the good fortune they could get.

Not as big as the *Georgic*, the *HMT Empire Pride* was painted white, the standard for British troopships. Today was also one day short of twelve months since we had sailed out of Liverpool. This time however, we were a motley bunch of dusty, scruffy individuals dressed in threadbare TA battledress. The *Empire Pride* was clearly not going to provide as luxurious a trip home as we had on the way out. Not that it had to be; it was really a floating barracks, not a floating hotel. From the dockside she looked OK but after we boarded at around 09:45 we discovered that all three hundred and forty of us would be accommodated in one huge area: Troopdeck 2 Lower. In this space, equivalent to a medium-sized dance hall, we would eat, play and sleep.

HMT Empire Pride

The only furnishings were tables and bench seats at which we would take our meals, sit and play cards, or do whatever else required a table. Each table was called a 'Mess' and Brian and I found places on Mess 57. As for sleeping arrangements, there would be hammocks, not beds. We were shown where these were stored and how to sling them. This was something we were totally unprepared for.

Ship's Orders stated that reveille would be at 06:00. There would be no set times for meals; we would be called when they were ready. Cleaning duties would be assigned but they too would be at odd hours. Attention was also drawn to where our boat stations were. The journey home was clearly going to be one big crush, as different from the journey out as chalk from cheese. There would be little privacy, little chance of peace and quiet and my chances of writing many letters quickly disappeared. Another problem would be the security of personal possessions in these living conditions. We would probably be entering the mouth of the River Mersey before we even started to get used to them.

The 56th US Army Band marched along the dockside to bid us a musical farewell, a little touch that seemed to neatly round off our time here. They had welcomed us when we disembarked from the *Georgic*. At 1100 we were ordered to boat stations. Hawsers were released, pulled on board and we edged out into the harbour, under way at last.

Farewell to Pusan and Korea

As the ship picked up speed toward the harbour mouth we all stood looking back at the smoky cloud that lay over Pusan squatting beneath its craggy mountains. We continued to watch as it slowly subsided out of sight into the waters of the harbour. When we passed that lighthouse on its decapitated rocky crag we knew we were finally going home; our time in Korea was now history. It felt indescribably good to feel the gentle rolling of the deck underfoot once more, a moment to savour in silence. Everyone else seemed to feel much the same.

First stop Hong Kong

The experience of sleeping in a hammock for the first time was, to say the least, novel. Unfortunately, it was not very restful for someone of my height. Much of the night was spent "effing and blinding" as I twisted and turned trying to find a good position in which to relax and get to sleep. I had slept many times in beds that sagged badly in the middle but at least I had been able to curl up in a ball in the hollow. That was impossible in a hammock. Another factor was that they only came in one standard length much too short to accommodate my length. My feet continually tangled in the ropes at the end.

Reveille finally brought relief. Brian also had much trouble getting comfortable even though he was shorter than me. As he fell out of his hammock he commented, "Now I know what it is like to be the inside of a banana." I don't think there were many of us who had a better night's sleep than we had. Reveille brought another problem. Everyone was so glad to clamber out of their hammocks that they did so at the same time. We all got hopelessly in each other's way as we endeavoured to un-sling and stow them away.

Eventually some order was restored and we queued up at the canteen for a very welcome cup of tea. Thankfully they had opened for service at 06:15. Neither Brian nor I had seen our names posted for any particular fatigues so we concluded we were free to spend our time as we pleased, exceptions being during the Ship's Master's inspection at 10:00, or when boat station drill was announced.

We were up on deck when the sun rose off the port side, a beautiful sight, reminiscent of such times a year ago but this time witnessed in a more contented frame of mind. The relentless throbbing of the engines was not so oppressive. As the sun rose further it became quite warm and reflected off the water with blinding ferocity. We spent much of the day lounging in a shaded corner playing cards; there was little else to do. The food was not too bad but we all admitted to feeling like Oliver Twist; we could have done with a little more. However, it was better than the food had been at the Transit Camp so we could stand it for another four weeks.

We managed to sleep more comfortably than last night but the atmosphere on the troopdeck became extremely muggy. The ventilation was totally inadequate and I was wet with perspiration by the time I had cleared my hammock away. In addition, the weather had turned cloudy and humid and it was trying hard to rain. Thankfully, by lunch time it became less oppressive and around 16:00 the sky was clear again.

The light from a full moon danced very prettily on the sea that night, but full moons would long be associated with a more ominous thought, that of the Chinese predilection for mounting attacks on such nights. I wondered how the Canadians were faring back on Little Gibraltar. It was strange how far away all that now seemed. It hadn't taken long to put it behind.

We passed a few small islands which might have been part of Formosa. But apart from looking forward to reaching Hong Kong the next morning and thinking about having some shore leave before departing again on Sunday evening, it was a pretty boring day. The only excitement was when the "tote" winner was announced. This was based on the distance the ship travelled in 24 hours. Yesterday we tallied 381 miles. While not as fast as the *Georgic* which averaged around 440 miles a day, it was still a fair old speed.

The next morning started with a mad rush because, no sooner had hammocks been stowed than the NCOs started making out Shore Leave passes. They also handled questions concerning currency. We expected to dock in Kowloon by lunchtime and be able to go ashore soon after.

Hong Kong waterfront from Kowloon in 1952

Land was sighted on the starboard side quite early on in the morning and we passed several huge junks lumbering over the swell. They still looked very top-heavy to me, with their low bow, high poop deck and tall, straggly sails. By 11:00 we had rounded the headland and entered the approach into Hong Kong harbour; we slowed to pick up the pilot. The view was very hazy and not at all good for photography.

No time was wasted once the ship was securely berthed. The Welch advance party debarked and we crowded the rails to cheer them off. They were the last we would see of the regiment. Brian and I had already changed into clean uniforms so, collecting passes and £6 in pay, we went ashore and took the ferry across to Victoria Island. We were content to walk around renewing our acquaintance with diverse sights, sounds and smells, all the while continually accosted by small wiry Chinese men inviting us to visit this souvenir shop or that clothes emporium.

Finally we agreed to be led through a maze of small, crowded alleyways of shops that mostly sold books or clothing and arrived at a small shop whose walls were lined with rows of ready-to-wear suits in all kinds of material and colours. Six or seven assistants, or tailors, greeted us and invited us to examine their stock. Perhaps they were all partners in the business.

A single-breasted blue gabardine suit took Brian's fancy. He tried it on and decided to have it. The tailors bustled around him pinning the adjustments that they would have to make so that it would fit him perfectly. I tried on a double-breasted blue-grey worsted suit whose fit was quite good for an off-the-peg job and would need little alteration. It felt great to wear civvies again but my army boots spoiled the experience.

I decided to take the suit and haggled over price, finally agreeing on £3 and an extra £1 for a shirt and tie to go with it. Brian got the same deal but was also able to buy some socks, something I missed out on because of my big feet. We waited in the shop while the alterations were made. They must have worked like greased lightening because it seemed no time at all before we were walking out of that shop with our purchases. Our guide led us back to the main street again.

We met up with several other chaps from our draft and decided to see a film about the US Marines winning the war—again! It may have been *"The Sands of Iwo Jima"*, *"The Battle of Midway"* or *"The Halls of Montezuma"*. The title was not important. Whichever it was, it opened with a celestial chorus singing the Battle Hymn of the US Marine Corps.

We were sitting in the front row of the balcony and all through the film rude comments flew thick and fast among us about various scenes and incidents. By the end we were all hyped up with ridiculing the film and the fact that we were homeward bound.

When the credits finally rolled, they were accompanied by a reprise of that Marine Corps Battle Hymn. We sang along but with our own lyrics:

From the halls of Monte Carlo to the shores of New Orleans
There's a shower of Yankee bastards who call themselves marines.
With a bottle of Coca Cola and a bloody great tub of ice cream
They think they're good kiddies asho-o-ore
But they are buggered when they get to sea.

When the lights went up we found ourselves surrounded by American servicemen. For a moment there was some apprehension as to how they would take our blaspheming the US Marine Corps' Battle Hymn but then we noticed that they were mostly from the USAAF and not at all concerned. Perhaps they shared our sentiments.

HMT Empire Pride in Kowloon

Back on board ship, almost everyone had bought civilian clothes and put them on again as if to stage a fashion parade. A more extraordinary collection would be hard to imagine. Gabardine was the material of choice but it came in every imaginable colour. Shirts too were in all possible shades and patterns. Everyone was excited because the value for money had been so extraordinary. But everyone was now stony broke.

We had a couple of hours ashore this morning. I wandered around Kowloon taking a few photographs of street scenes, the ferry terminal and the sampans clustered around our ship. There were not as many as we had seen last year but there was no obvious reason for this.

Back on board, several local traders had been allowed on to peddle their wares, mostly clothes and some chaps bought more civvies. When one of them tried their new clothes on almost everyone else had to do the same. Then they all strutted around, examining and comparing and paying compliments to each other. It was all understandable because no one had seen, let alone worn, civvies for over a year. It was quite an intoxicating experience.

Kowloon—sampan

By 11:00 the traders were gone and we went to the troopdeck to make sure that everything was shipshape for the Ship's Master's inspection. After this was completed we cast off and were on our way once more. Part 1 Orders were posted and I was detailed to be a Mess orderly until we reached Singapore. It being almost lunch time, I joined the queue to collect the rations for my Mess table. When the meal was finished and had been cleared up, I went up on deck to find that we were well under way and Hong Kong Island was fast sinking into the sea behind us.

Kowloon washing day

A heavy swell was running, enough to roll the ship around and make us all feel a bit nauseous but it was not as bad as the last time we crossed this stretch of ocean. The nausea eased off after lying down for a while. It was still very muggy on our deck so that it was not unusual to feel sick and uncomfortable. The ventilation really did need to be improved otherwise we would all be choosing to sleep up on deck.

In the tropics again

We had shore leave in both Singapore and Colombo but at both places we were almost bereft of funds. For some perverse reason the Paymaster contrived to pay us the day we left port. As a result I only had eight Straits dollars on me in Singapore and five rupees in Colombo, not enough on either occasion to buy a decent meal anywhere. It was just as well that we only had about three hours ashore in both places, long enough for a good walk on dry land but little else.

In a letter received at Colombo, my mother asked me to try to buy some dried fruit as such things were still scarce in England. She also asked me to get some cheroots for Uncle Reg which he had enjoyed during his time in the RAF in India.

Wandering along a street, we passed several shops selling tobacco. Stopping at one, I asked for cheroots and the shopkeeper brought out quite a selection. We got down to prices but the price asked was far more than I had expected, three times the amount in my pocket in fact. I told the shopkeeper that his price was ridiculous and he lowered it—a little, but it was still much too high so started to walk out of the shop. He immediately reduced the price again but still not enough. He followed me outside into the street and continued lowering the price until it matched exactly the amount I had in my pocket. Since, at no time had I mentioned just how much I had on me, this was most fortunate for Uncle Reg.

Thinking hard for a moment, it became clear that even if I got him to lower his price still further, the amount of money I would have left would be tantamount to nothing, not worth carrying around in fact. I accepted his last price, handed him every last penny I had on me and received a packet of one dozen cheroots to take back to my uncle. The dried fruit for my mother was beyond my means in Colombo, even if I had found some.

We were due to anchor in Aden sometime in the morning and leave in the afternoon and there was doubt whether we would get shore leave there but we did. Today would be the last time when there would be any point writing home. I had about ten shillings (East African Currency Board) with which to buy the dried fruit my mother had asked for—if I could find any. But there was none to be found.

Return to ship Aden harbour

The last leg

After Aden, we would be on the last leg of the journey home. As before, we might stop at Port Said but there was no way we would get shore leave there any more than we had on the way out. The weather throughout the voyage had been pretty good, sunny and warm as was to be expected and with good stiff breezes much of the way from Singapore to keep things comfortable. There was never any of that stifling, sticky, dead calm heat we had on the *Georgic* but there was still time for that.

We still had to traverse the length of the Red Sea. Most nights we had slept up on deck which, although hard, was more comfortable that those hammocks could ever be. Both Brian and I felt pretty fit. I had carefully acquired as much of a tan as my fair skin could ever take but Brian had a very deep tan and been nicknamed 'Wog'.

Suez Canal—Brian with HMS Kenya

In retrospect, living conditions on a genuine British troop ship, the shortness of shore leave at the ports we called at and our straitened financial circumstances after we left Hong Kong conspired to make the voyage home a disappointment. The lack of money, privacy and decent food—it had deteriorated after a few days—the stifling atmosphere at night and a lot of unnecessary 'bullshit' conspired to drive us nuts. It strengthened our desire to get out of uniform, out of the army, back to our homes and families, into civvies, get some decent home cooking inside us and sleep in a comfortable bed with sheets and a pillow again—and with a rainproof roof over our heads at last. Perhaps this was what the conditions on this voyage home were all designed to make us appreciate. It was succeeding in drawing a line very effectively between our time in Korea and whatever lay ahead.

Suez Canal—me with HMS Kenya

The journey through the Suez Canal was uneventful. We passed HMS *Kenya* at anchor on one of the lakes and I saw the huge memorial erected on the eastern side of the canal to Ferdinand de Lesseps, the French architect of the canal. I had not noticed it on the way out.

Of the voyage through the Mediterranean, up the Portuguese coast, across the Bay of Biscay and up the Irish Sea to Liverpool I took very little account. All I noted was that once out of the Mediterranean and sailing north along the coast of Portugal, the weather began to turn cold and we were soon back into our worn out TA battledress uniforms and sleeping below in the hammocks once more.

Epilogue

3rd & 4th December 1952

Two memories remain to mark the end of the journey home. The first occurred at Liverpool where, much to our disgust, we were required to pass through Customs. No allowance had been made for the fact that we were returning home from war. Few of us had much to declare, if anything at all, and even fewer were required to open up their kit bags.

Justice

One chap standing close by was so required. Asked if he had anything to declare, he stated that he had only the permitted allowance of cigarettes. The Customs Officer must have been observing him closely and not inclined to believe him. He asked that he empty his kit bag.

He took all his gear out except something at the very bottom. When asked what it was he said it was his great coat. Asked to remove it, the chap seemed too hesitant so the Officer picked up his kit bag by the bottom and gave it one hefty shake. The rolled up greatcoat shot out onto the floor, unrolled and a dozen or so tins of cigarettes clattered out and rolled in all directions. Everyone turned to see what had happened.

This chap's face turned so red he could have lit one of those cigarettes from it. Then I recognised the baby faced chap who had knocked the pot of beans off the Korean woman's head when we were en route to the docks in Pusan. He looked my way and I grinned at him broadly. He had received his come-uppance with a vengeance. No one felt in the least bit sorry for him.

The second moment came at the end of the train journey from Liverpool to Cardiff where trucks took us from the station to Maindy Barracks. The entrance was through a narrow archway into a parade square enclosed on all sides by barrack rooms. It was a very cold, wet, dark, Welsh night. As the trucks drew to a halt, out of that wet and gloomy darkness came an almost forgotten voice. It rasped out, "Come on laddies, let's be 'aving yew. Fall owt and fall in shahp like." It was no less a person than RSM Visick, 'old bum and tit' as I thought of him. With his stocky build, he had a barrel chest that was always prominent in front and a large behind equally prominent to the rear. He had been the RSM at Sobraon Barracks in Colchester where he had conducted regimental drill parades with a ruthless efficiency, his pacing stick tucked firmly under his arm. RSM Visick had been a man to keep well away from at all times. For whatever reason, probably age, he had not gone to Korea with the 1st battalion and was now here to welcome us back. It was another strange rounding up of things.

Our penultimate piece of official business was to fill out some details on the Certificate of Discharge from Whole-time Military Service. These were collected for the depot commander to complete. After that it was all an anti-climax; one more night in a Welsh barracks on a typical army cot, one more Reveille, one more quick wash and shave and one more army breakfast. We signed our discharge papers, attended our last pay parade, collected our last travel warrant and were on our way. Trucks took us to Cardiff Railway Station. Brian was to serve his TA time with the Hampshire Regiment so it was a parting of the way for us. He had to report to a depot in Winchester, I to one in Dorchester. But we would see each other soon in Bournemouth. And when we did, we would be dressed in the civvies we had bought in Hong Kong.

I phoned home to tell my parents that I was back, that I had one more appointment to keep in Dorchester—reporting in to the office at the Dorsetshire Regimental barracks to start my time in the TA—and then I would be coming home.

My father said he would drive to Dorchester to meet me and take me back home in comfort. That was one thing I had always appreciated about him. While we did not get along too well he was always there for us whenever it was necessary and possible.

The railway journey on branch lines across Somerset and Dorset was soothing, the countryside lush and green in its wintry bareness. At

Dorchester, the last formalities took no time at all. Paid leave was granted to me until 28th December. Before then I would have to find a job.

Walking out through the main entrance of Dorchester Castle, which formed the emblem on the regimental badge of the Dorsetshire Regiment, I saw my father waiting just a little way up the road with the car. There were no hugs, just a huge smile from him in response to my big grin. But with him that meant a lot. Men didn't hug in public in those days, if at all. I was home again and, thank God, as physically intact as when I left. What state the rest of me was in only time would tell.

Acronyms

2i/c	Second In Command
ABC	Australian Broadcasting Commission
AFRS	American Forces Radio Service
BAF	a unit of British army paper currency
BAPO	British Army Post Office
BD	Battledress (standard uniform)
BHQ	Battalion Head Quarters
BKVA	British Korean Veterans Association
BSA	Birmingham Small Arms (manufacturer of weapons, bicycles and motorcycles)
CO	Commanding Officer (of a company or a battalion)
CP	Command Post
CQMS	Company Quarter Master Sergeant
CSM	Company Sergeant Major
CV	Command Vehicle (a mobile CP)
FFI	Free From Infection (a medical inspection)
FMA	Forward Marshalling Area
FOO	Forward Observation Officer (Artillery)
HMT	His/Her Majesty's Troopship
IO	Intelligence Officer
KOSB	King's Own Scottish Borderers
KSLI	King's Shropshire Light Infantry
LDV	Local Defence Volunteers (civilian members of a WW2 organisation)
MO	Medical Officer/ Medical Orderly
NAAFI	Navy, Army & Air Force Institute
NCO	Non-Commissioned Officer (anyone wearing stripes)
OC	Officer commanding—(some operation or other)
O/R	Other Ranks—all non commissioned ranks—Privates to Warrant Officers
PA	Public Address system
PBI	Poor Bloody Infantry
PPCLI	Princess Patricia's Canadian Light Infantry (aka The'Pats')
PTA	Practical Training Area

QM	Quarter Master (an officer)
QMS	Quarter Master's Stores
RAMC	Royal Army Medical Corps
RAOC	Royal Army Ordnance Corps
RAP	Regimental Aid Post (medical)
RAR	Royal Australian Regiment
RASC	Royal Army Service Corps
R&R	Rest & Recuperation—leave (aka Rack & Ruin.)
RHE	Return to Home Establishment (repatriation.)
RIDG	Royal Inniskilling Dragoon Guards (aka 'The Skins')
ROK	Republic Of Korea (South Korea)
RQMS	Regimental Quarter Master Sergeant
RSM	Regimental Sergeant Major
SO	Signals Officer/Office
USAAF	United States Army Air Force
VD	Venereal Disease
	(now STDs—Sexually Transmitted Diseases.)
VE Day	Victory in Europe Day
VJ Day	Victory over Japan Day
WVS	Women's Voluntary Service

VERNACULAR VOCABULARY

Bangers & mash	sausages and creamed potato
Battledress	normal uniform—blouson top, trousers, belt, gaiters and boots
Blanco	a substance applied with water by brush to army equipment (webbing—belts, gaiters etc.) to make it appear clean
Bonce	head, for wearing hats on
Bullshit	nonsense, rubbish, trivial
Bum-boats	port traders who come out in open boats to ships to sell things
Civvies	civilian clothes as opposed to uniforms, aka mufti
Chuffed	delighted, very pleased
Company Orders	disciplinary process for misdemeanors
Cushy	easy, comfortable, lucky
Daps, plimsolls,	rubber soled PT or sports shoes
Demob	demobilisation, discharge from service
Doozy	big, huge, incredible, disastrous, catastrophic
Fieldcraft	the art of moving soldiers across country, adopting defensive positions and/or making attacks on enemy positions
Filch	to pinch or steal
Firefight	a skirmish with an enemy patrol
Fizzer	a charge for some misdemeanour
Flap, in a . . .	in a hurry, panic
Formosa	now known as Taiwan
Gong happy	too eager to win a medal, may lead to rashness
Gook	a Korean porter (not necessarily derogatory)
Jankers	punishment for misdemeanor
Kipping	sleeping
Loo	toilet, bathroom or restroom
Mile	just over 1½ kilometre (1.61 to be exact)
Natter	chat, casual conversation
Niggle, niggly	small irritation, irritating
Nignog	a new recruits, someone being stupid
Nips	Japanese people (indifferent rather than derogatory)
Part 1 Orders	daily posted notice of events
Peckish	hungry
Plates of meat	feet (Cockney rhyming slang)
Pongy	very smelly or stinking

Rocket	a reprimand
Sharp end	the front line of a battle zone
Shirtsleeve order	allowed to remove ties and roll shirt sleeves up in hot weather
Short arm	penis (as opposed to side arm or pistol!)
Skint, broke,	no money or very little
Skive	to avoid, shirk, evade work or duties by any means
Squaddy	British soldier
Square bashing	parade ground drill, marching etc.
Stag	a period on duty, guard or otherwise
Stand to/down	the time at first or last light of the day most suited to attack when all personnel are at their battle stations
Stonk	An artillery barrage
Wog	non-white person, (not necessarily derogatory)
Yank, Yankee	British for US American

NOTE ABOUT BRITISH CURRENCY

Prior to 15th February 1971 British currency was comprised of—
Pound sterling (£), Shilling £1/20 and Penny £1/240 (12 to the shilling)
This is the system referred to in this story.
Today, British currency consists of –
Pound sterling (£), and Penny £1/100 to better cope with exchange rates and the coming of the computer age.

NOTE ABOUT BRITISH IMPERIAL DISTANCES

1 mile = 1,760 yards (= 1.61 kilometres)
1 yard = 3 feet (= 0.9 metres)
1 foot = 12 inches (= 0.3 metres)
(1 inch = 25.4 millimetres)

In 1965 Britain started to adopt the metric system of distance but under protest.

Acknowledgements

M y thanks must go to many people for their encouragement and help with research but first among them is my mother who carefully kept all those letters and thoughtfully returned them to me before she passed on. This has allowed me to revisit and reevaluate experiences that have had a strong influence on my life ever since. I feel that she knew that this might become necessary for me.

Dawn, my wife, who has provided an environment here in New Zealand in which to complete this story. She offered support for me when I struggled to maintain objectivity with the subject.

Brian Langdown, my closest friend during my national service, whose memories provided very useful details for my record of events.

Charles (Al) Haynes, Middlesex branch British Korean Veterans Association, for information and leads concerning the periods spent on The Hook and Hill 355 and about certain events.

Captain Ian Scott, RE, for surprising information concerning Operation Maindy.

2nd Lt. J Bowler who put me in touch with our Intelligence Officer Lt. Salmon who sent me an excellent coloured map covering the positions we were in.

Lawrence Lohan for researches on my behalf at the War Records Office in London.

Martin Duckworth, my oldest school friend & his older brother Jack, for their enthusiasm for my story and encouragement to finish it.

George and Joan Wilby of the Wessex branch of the BKVA for taking my remembrances to the grave of L/Cpl Alec Ahern in the UN cemetery in Pusan, South Korea, and sending me photographs of it and one of Hill 355.

Fred Good of Perth, Western Australia, who gave my writing an initial reading and helpful suggestions.

David Curry of Wanganui, New Zealand, for making a further thorough critical review after I realised that the first edition needed serious revision. This second edition incorporates his suggestions.

The Australian War Memorial, Canberra, for introducing me to *"Australia in the Korean War"* by Robert O'Neill, an excellent, very enlightening, very readable book and a mine of reliable information concerning the attitudes held by our Commonwealth commanders. Also for the record of the story of the taking of Hill 355 in October 1951

Major Jack Gerke, CO C Company 3 RAR who I met in Perth, Western Australia. He personally showed me books and maps covering the role of his company during Operation Commando to take hill 355. This happened three months before I arrived in Korea.

Dave Mullan of ColcomPress, Paihia, who published the first very limited edition.

The Welch Regiment Memorial Chapel in Llandaff Cathedral, South Wales for the Three Feathers emblem on the cover which can be found on the plaque bearing the names of all those men from the battalion who died in Korea. My friend Alex Ahern heads the list.

Regarding the photographs used, these have been either "honestly snapped, scrounged, pinched, purchased or borrowed" and were assembled in the album purchased in Seaforth Camp, Pusan in October 1952. I made no record at the time of exactly where I obtained those that I did not take myself. To anyone recognising photographs that they took, then I thank them for letting me have them all those years ago. If you care to write to me I will gladly acknowledge their true ownership in future editions.

I thank you all.

John F. Hatchard,

Kerikeri,

Northland,

New Zealand,

September 2012

List of Photographs & Maps

Ablutions beneath Hill 355—pg. 222

Mike Churchill, Porchester before going on patrol—pg. 224

Outside D company signals bunker on Hill 355—pg. 228

My 'new' bunker below 355—232

C7s for lunch—pg. 242

Letter from Korean schoolboy to UN soldiers—pg. 247

Northern approach to Pintail Bridge April 1952—pg. 255

"Willow Tree" hill—pg. 256

Korean houses by lagoon—pg. 257

Korean shellfish gatherers near Inchon—pg. 258

A view of B Echelon—pg. 261

View of Imjin from Kansas Line—pg. 262

The regimental mascot's billet—pg. 263

At my signals trailer B Echelon—pg. 265

RQMS Evans and Butch, one of the storemen—pg. 273

En route to Seoul with cultivated paddy fields—pg. 279

Street scene in Pusan—October 1952—pg. 282

UN War Cemetery, 1952, Bill Lansdowne's grave front left—pg. 283

UN cemetery Pusan 2004, Alec Ahern's grave—pg. 284

HMT Empire Pride—pg. 286

Farewell to Pusan and Korea—pg. 287

Hong Kong waterfront from Kowloon in 1952—pg. 290

Empire Pride in Kowloon—pg. 292

Kowloon—sampans—pg. 293

Washing day in Kowloon—pg. 294

Returning from shore leave in Aden—pg. 295

Suez Canal—Brian, aka 'Wog' with HMS Kenya—pg. 296

Suez Canal—me with my best tan ever—pg. 297

Author biography of John Hatchard

Born in Poole, Dorset, England on 12th August 1932, his father was a successful sales manager and champion lawn bowler. His mother, from a seafaring working class background, became a talented paintress at Poole Pottery in the 1920s, a sought after light opera singer and also a champion lawn bowler in later life. She also possessed a deep interest in spiritual matters. Incidentally, his birth name was John Milnthorpe, the reason for the name change is related below.

Immediately after completing his education at Poole Grammar School, John was summoned to complete two years national service in the army. From 1951 and 1952, he experienced service in the front line in Korea with the Welch Regiment. His specialist training as a signaler/wireless operator proved a godsend by keeping him out of harms way but this was still not sufficient to prevent this period from having a profoundly unsettling effect on him.

On returning to civilian life, John worked as a clerk until in 1953 when he was accepted for teacher training at King Alfred's College, Winchester. After completion of the course he taught humanities for eighteen years. Fifteen of these were in high schools in England. On two occasions he taught abroad, six months teaching English as a Foreign Language (EFL) in Zaragoza, Spain and three years teaching EFL for the British Centre in Linköping and Malmö, Sweden. It was in Sweden that he met Hilary his first wife. They married on their return to England, settled south of Bristol and had two children, James and Karin.

Returning once more to high school teaching, John was granted a sabbatical year at Newton Park College, Bath, Somerset specifically on the teaching of English and discovered a small talent for literary research. He produced an extended essay on the mediaeval story—"Sir Gawain and the Green Knight" which was well received. It was at this time that he learned transcendental meditation, an experience that was to connect him with one of his mothers great interests—yoga philosophy.

A year later, wishing to teach in one of the Middle Schools springing up as a result of educational reforms, he taught in a junior school in Hemel Hempstead, north of London, to gain relevant experience. However, with his marriage falling apart, teaching no longer held any interest. With government assistance he attended a course in handmade furniture crafts at Ryecotewood College, Thame, Oxfordshire where he gained City and Guilds qualifications. After a divorce, he had an unsatisfactory job fitting out a canal barge for a company on the Kennet & Avon canal in Wiltshire, left and opened his own business in which he undertook all kinds of work with wood from designing and making furniture, repairs, restoration, fitting out kitchens and general joinery work.

It was around this time that he met, fell in love with and proposed to a woman he met at a yoga class. When she replied that she did not wish to be known as the second Mrs Milnthorpe he replied, "That is no problem. I have no great love for the name either. I have always felt like a Hatchard (mothers maiden name) so I will change to it." A visit to the magistrate's court in Bath, a chat with the Clerk, a sworn statement before magistrates later and he walked out as John Hatchard. He never did marry that woman and his only brother disowned him!

Building on the early influence of his mother who had talked to him about yogic philosophy during his late childhood, his interest in meditation eventually took him to India. He travelled there extensively for six months between 1952-53 and his journal notes of meetings with other travelers, professors, swamis and even a saint eventually filled six notebooks. This journey proved as meaningful for John as the time spent in Korea but in a very different way.

Returning to England, he attended a course on Inner Light Consciousness and met the Rev. Paul Solomon who invited him to the USA to study at the Fellowship of The Inner Light (FIL), a transfaith community in Virginia. Here, to his surprise, he became ordained as a minister in the Fellowship and met Maranatha from New Zealand, a fellow minister. In 1985, after six months in the USA, he returned to live near Oxford, England. A few weeks later, Maranatha joined him and together they set up an organization named ReQuella to manage the logistics for teachers and alternative therapists visiting from overseas. He also worked as the project manager of an Oxfordshire community scheme that provided work for unemployed youth and managed several building sites around the county.

Maranatha suffered a virus infection in 1986 and needed major heart surgery for the second time in her life. After she had recovered sufficiently they married but, a few British winters later, she needed a more comfortable climate and they moved to Western Australia. For a couple of years John worked for TV Channel 7 as cabinet maker to the engineering department. Maranatha took a course in classical homoeopathy. She became the administrator of the school she was studying in and, after graduating became its Principal.

In 1990 Channel 7 hit hard times and John was made redundant. While on unemployment benefit he took a computer literacy course but arthritis problems inhibited his employment prospects and he was granted an invalid pension. This, in effect, left him free to work with Maranatha as deputy administrator of the school and her clinic. He had already developed a keen interest in Homoeopathic history and philosophy and could now research it and write the first semester course in these subjects which he delivered for the next six years.

The School was finally registered as the Oceanic Institute of Homoeopathy, Perth, W.A., and the four year course gained accreditation with the State Government of Western Australia. This was successful enough to qualify for placement on the National Training Register in Canberra, the first such course to achieve this. It sent shock waves through the profession and led to a national standards committee for the training and practice of homoeopathy in Australia being set up. John represented Western Australian interests. Looking back on those years with the Institute he remembers working harder and longer hours than in any previous job—and unpaid.

After six years delivering his course, bureaucratic nonsense decided John was no longer sufficiently qualified to teach in a tertiary institution, not even the course he had researched and written. Believing this was just a revenue raising stunt, he ceased all work for the Institute. Now in need of something to do, he found the letters he had written home from Korea and began work on his memoirs.

Maranatha became ill again and once more in need of major heart surgery. Knowing she would need to give all her time and energy to her recovery, they parted, lived separately and eventually divorced. Their married life had begun with a heart operation and twenty years later ended with another.

Now fully retired and living on his pension, John took up lawn bowls and worked voluntarily for a group called Computer Angels. They 'rescued' unwanted computers, refurbished them and gave them to those who needed but could not afford one—school children, the elderly and the disabled. He learned enough about computers to be able to build and repair them for himself.

However, life in Australia had now lost all meaning. With no family there, no wife and only a handful of good friends, he began to question what he was doing there. He could go anywhere he wanted—to the USA to see his son, to India to follow his interest in yoga and meditation, or to New Zealand, a country he had come to like after several visits over the previous twenty years. Taking a chance with a computer dating agency he met Dawn who lived in the Bay of Islands, New Zealand. Once married to a Methodist minister, after many years they had divorced. The meeting of minds, interests and senses of humour was sufficient to persuade John to take the plunge, book a flight to New Zealand and start a new life there with her. Packing up and disposing of items not wanted on the voyage took John the best part of four months. Finally, on May 2nd 2004, after twenty-two years in arid Western Australia, he arrived at Auckland Airport with Dawn and beautiful wet weather there to welcome him.

They returned to Paihia in the Bay of Islands of the Far North of North Island, New Zealand. Waitangi, the birthplace of modern New Zealand was nearby and Russell, once known as "The Hellhole of the Pacific' lay across the Bay. A beautiful place with a subtropical climate and for this reason also known as "Paradise"

Dawn had a counseling practice in Paihia and in Whangarei, forty-five minutes drive south from Paihia. She was also an organist at the local Uniting Church in Paihia where the congregation quickly accepted John as one of their own. His interest in spirituality and meditation, plus his ordination, led to an invitation to join the worship team. Once every six weeks he lead a worship service in which, drawing on his experience as a teacher, traveller and lecturer, in the 'sermon' slot he did his best to share ideas about life and spirituality that had come to him over the years. Preparing and delivering these services was something he much enjoyed.

During this time he also worked very seriously on his Korean memoirs having been told that a neighbour published small book runs for people, doing the binding and trimming himself. Finally, a run of twenty-one copies of "A Squaddy's Tale; Memories of the Forgotten War" was produced to give to family members and friends.

Two years later, chancing to reread his personal copy, John was mortified by the many poorly constructed sentences and other clumsiness's that had escaped his attention. He undertook a thorough reedit of the book for a second edition. He also decided on another project, to extract a series of tales from the quarter of a million words he had written about his Indian travels.

When the political side of church life became unacceptable he left. Dawn followed shortly after and they enjoyed a peaceful life in a spacious home overlooking the mangroves beside the Te Haumi River and the lovely view over the bay to Russell. However, health issues have meant a move to a more convenient home in Kerikeri.

Much of his time is now spent at the computer with his writing and correspondence. Awaiting attention are the Indian stories, an allegory about Climbing and the lectures on homoeopathic history and philosophy which need editing.

His interest in travel is now maintained vicariously through books, principally on India but also on spiritual and philosophical matters. His love of classical music is deep, especially for singing which he learned to appreciate listening to his mother while growing up. She was a very accomplished and well loved soloist. John has sung with many choirs, a memorable time being in a performance of Verdi's Requiem in Great Malvern, Worcestershire.

He is interested in current affairs and, with sober reflection on events and the state of the world, he has become sympathetic to the ideas of conspiracy theorists but always with a pot of salt nearby! Very recently, watching a DVD about the Mayan calendar proved a complete eye opener and quickly altered the way in which he now regards global events. He enjoys gardening but since the ground beneath the Paihia house was pure clay and on a seventy degree slope this was restricted to several big planters on the deck. In the new home he is enjoying much more success. He still enjoys working with wood but finds less time for this than before. His other big interest is in photography and experimenting on photographs with the computer programmes now available for manipulating them.

Lightning Source UK Ltd.
Milton Keynes UK
UKOW04f1057081117
312367UK00001B/76/P